The German Political System

The German Political System

Guido Goldman
Harvard University

Foreword by **Samuel H. Beer**

Reprinted from *Patterns of Government,* Third Edition

Random House, New York

First Paperback Edition

987654321

This book is a modified version of Part 4 of *Patterns of Government: The Major Political Systems of Europe,* Third Edition, edited by Samuel H. Beer and Adam B. Ulam, Random House, 1973. All inquiries should be addressed to Random House, Inc., 201 East 50th Street, New York, N.Y. 10022. Published in the United States by Random House, Inc., and simultaneously in Canada by Random House of Canada Limited, Toronto.

Library of Congress Cataloging in Publication Data

Goldman, Guido G
The German political system.

Bibliography: p.
1. Germany (Federal Republic, 1949–)—Politics and government. I. Title.
JN3971.A5G64 320.9'43'087 74–535
ISBN 0–394–31820–X

Manufactured in the United States of America

For Alex Möller, statesman and friend

Foreword

This volume is a paperbound edition of Part 4 of the third edition of *Patterns of Government: The Major Political Systems of Europe*. The larger work includes sections on Britain, France, Germany, and Soviet Russia and an introductory part on modern political development—all now available as separate paperbacks.

The five parts of *Patterns of Government* are integrated by the common theme of modernization. But each country account is also written so as to be suitable for study either separately or in conjunction with other countries not considered in *Patterns*. In the latter connection one attractive possibility would be a combination that would include the United States; for in each of the country accounts of *Patterns* a comparison with America, seen as a typical modern polity, is never far in the background of the analysis. Whatever one's preference, the present publication of the introduction and the country accounts as separate books provides the necessary flexibility.

A word about the general approach of *Patterns:* After a brief eclipse, history is making a strong comeback in political science, largely under such headings as "modernization" and "development." A period of neglect was healthy, since it obliged political scientists to decide what use they really wanted to make of history. In the third as in the previous editions of *Patterns*, a leading characteristic of the methodology is the use of both theory and history in the study of contemporary politics. The authors hold that patterns of political behavior in the present can be best explained if we have an understanding of how they originated and what traits they displayed in the past. In taking this view, the authors follow the example of some of the leading figures in modern political science, from Montesquieu to Weber, who used history to enlarge the body of empirical political theory and then used that theory to analyze and explain the historical process as it flows from the past through the present into the future.

Each country is examined as an example of a highly developed modern polity. This approach has two implications. First, it means emphasizing certain features the countries have in common. Second, it means treating these common features as the issue of a course of historical development moved by similar forces, passing through similar phases, and culminating in similar problems. But the stress on the common features of modernity does not lead the authors to overlook the crucial differences that distinguish the four systems. Quite the contrary. To show what is common helps them to bring out the differences more sharply. As a specialist in the country he is writing about, each author is accordingly concerned not only with its common modernity, but also with the traits and tensions that are unique to it.

Harvard University Samuel H. Beer

Contents

The German Political System

One

Tradition Against Modernity in Germany

The development of Germany, as compared with that of other European states, has been unusual in a number of significant ways. No other European polity has had as unstable a past, characterized by as many different political systems or such constantly shifting and impermanent boundaries. No other nation has been as uncertain about its nationhood or confronted by as many geopolitical dilemmas that have led so often to conflict in its external affairs. Nowhere else has modernization raised as many internal problems or resulted in a phenomenon resembling the "German Question." That question has been posed in countless different ways, but always with emphasis on some deeply flawed and unique aspect of German development that might explain the pathology of German history.

Yet, not only as measured against its own past, but also when compared with other Western democracies, the Federal Republic of Germany today appears to be a highly successful modern polity. In terms of the stability of its political institutions and party system, its social composition, economic growth, and political style, the Federal Republic seems to be functioning well as a liberal, constitutional, democratic, modern system. It is broadly similar to Britain and France and in some ways may, in fact, be working better. How can we account for this current success and for the striking failures of the German past? What is it that has changed, and to what degree is this change fundamental and likely to endure? These are vital questions that must be answered, and they require first some consideration of the historical context from which the Federal Republic emerged.

Nowhere is the study of history more relevant or fascinating than in the case of Germany. The Federal Republic is barely two decades old and not fully sovereign at that. It is a sizable fragment of the larger Germany that once existed and faces a second state, the German Democratic Republic, which contests its claims to legitimacy. The Federal Republic was formed under conditions of total defeat and occupation, as one of the few "post-totalitarian" societies that the world has known. Perforce it traces its heritage to several different antecedent regimes. Permanence is not a characteristic of the German experience.

The most distinctive feature of the problem of Germany's statehood is the prolonged fragmentation of the German people. This fragmentation, originally the consequence of the Thirty Years' War and the Treaty of Westphalia, coincided with the onset of political modernization. Therefore, while sovereignty and bureaucracy emerged in Germany at about the same time as they did in France, Germany lacked a comparable central authority and state structure. This was critical, for it meant that to prevent external domination an inherently weak multitude of several hundred states would require strong military force. In part this accounts for the abnormal predominance of military men in the period of early modernization, especially in Prussia, the largest and most powerful of the north German states.

The primacy of security was not solely a consequence of the division of Germany into so many small units. It derived as well from Germany's strategic location in the center of Europe and from the potential size of its population. It is no surprise that the study of geopolitics is of German origin. Geographically, Germany was confronted by a double dilemma. Divided and weak, it could easily be threatened by aggression from all directions. Consolidated and strong, on the other hand, and especially as a unitary state, Germany could—and in later periods would—dominate and overrun those contiguous areas, primarily in the east, which were weak and fragmented themselves. A powerful, aggressive Germany could compel its neighbors to act in collusion. The risk of *Einkreisung* ("encirclement") created special strategic problems for Germany and reinforced the grip of its military element.

In this context the process of German unification could have highly destabilizing consequences for the European state system. These could be even further exacerbated if German aspirations for national integration ranged too far into eastern Europe, where there were few natural or clear ethnic boundaries. German settlements were scattered along the entire eastern Baltic, throughout the Polish territories, and south into the Balkans to the Black Sea. Furthermore, it remained possible that a unified Germany might embrace Austria and the German portions of the Hapsburg Empire. Thus, a nation-state of all German-speaking peoples in central and eastern Europe would create the demographic basis for German preponderance in Europe—which is exactly what happened under the Third Reich.

But instead of becoming preponderant and strong, the German states long remained divided and weak, dominated in the north by Prussia and in the south by Austria. It was not until the early nineteenth century that the movement toward national unification began to gain force. This was a gradual process that lasted through the first seven decades of the century, the result in large part of Prussian-led military campaigns.

The way in which unification came about is significant in several ways. First, because it was associated with war against the French, beginning with the defeat of Napoleon and culminating with the Franco-Prussian War of 1870, the movement toward unification easily became identified with the rejection of the Napoleonic concepts of freedom, democracy, and republicanism. Nationalism in Germany tended to turn in an anti-Western direction. England and France were to be envied but not emulated. And many of the values that accompanied modernization in these two countries failed to find acceptance in a Germany that lacked confidence in its own unity and, therefore, substituted this as a goal in place of political reform.

Prussia was the only military power that could lead a successful series of campaigns to achieve German unity. Unification was, in the words of A. J. P. Taylor, "the conquest of Germany by Prussia." Austria, the sole potential countervailing pole, was left out. The result was that the highly efficient but emphatically conservative military and bureaucratic machine that ran the Prussian government and protected feudal interests would initially dominate a unified Germany as well.

The strength of Prussian conservative and authoritarian forces goes far toward explaining the failure of liberalism to emerge as a powerful force in nineteenth-century Germany as it did in Britain and France. The three prime components of the Prussian conservative state were the monarch, the military, and the bureaucracy, of which the last was perhaps the most distinctive. It was the Prussian bureaucracy that had in the early part of the century carried through a governmental "revolution from above" that more than anything else forestalled social and political revolution in Germany. The administrative reforms of Stein and Hardenberg streamlined the prevailing system of political absolutism and modified its most abusive features. The result was a talented and efficient, if still privileged and oligarchic, civil service, the mandarin core of the much-heralded Beamtenstaat, and the civilian compeer of its military establishment.

Both the civil service and the military were class-dominated, the special domain of the landed aristocracy. Titles abounded throughout the higher echelons of the bureaucracy and the officer corps. In the Second Reich ambassadors and state secretaries were still political fiefs of the large landowners and as late as 1914 all but three of the two dozen generals commanding army corps were noblemen. This reflects the tenacious grip of the small, aristocratic Junker class on the political system of Prussia and, thereby, on the Second Reich. It was a critical but also a curious phenomenon. That a preindustrial aristocratic elite could retain so much power during the period of intense industrialization and rapid modernization experienced by Germany after 1850 requires explanation.

One reason was the strategic placement of the Junkers. Concentrated in eastern Prussia and owning vast estates, they had used their wealth and cohesion to dominate the military and the bureaucracy in Prussia, and they employed these bodies as instruments to limit the prerogatives of royal absolutism. Grain growing largely bypassed the towns, which remained weak and did not develop an elaborate form of commercial agriculture. This meant that in Prussia the landed aristocrats themselves laid the foundations for the political system. They did not, as in England, have the substantial assistance of a mercantile class. This is not surprising. What is unusual is that the Junkers were then able to preserve their position. The reasons for this are twofold. First, Germany at the outset of industrialization was still fragmented; and second, the middle class, which had remained weak, strove to do too much and was then, because of the intense impact of rapid industrialization, confronted with too many problems at once. The failure of the German bourgeoisie to effect meaningful political reforms that would have challenged the position of the Junkers was most responsible for the defeat of liberalism in nineteenth-century Germany.

That the German middle class was relatively weak at mid-century was primarily due to the fact that industrialization came late to Germany. Industrialization did not really begin to take hold on a significant scale in Germany until the 1840s and 1850s. This meant that in 1848, when the German political system was first challenged by liberal forces, the bourgeoisie lacked numbers and financial strength. But while they were not yet strong, the liberals sought to achieve a great deal. They hoped to establish a constitutional system to safeguard individual rights against authoritarianism and, at the same time, to press on toward national consolidation. The continued fragmentation of Germany was a critical deterrent to the liberals' aspirations. In order to overcome it, they would require the cooperation of the monarchs, who opposed their political liberalizing aims. Confronted with a choice between a liberal political system and national integration, the bourgeois forces opted for the latter, which was of much greater economic importance. Unity was substituted for freedom as a goal, which led, as Leonard Krieger has shown, to the fateful divorce of the ideals of liberty and self-government in Germany. Nationalism survived where liberalism did not. Basically, the bourgeoisie allowed Prussia to erect the Second Reich on the ruins of freedom, but with the support of those forces which in England and France were the foremost advocates of freedom. As Engels foresaw in 1851, the German middle class proved to be too weak to overcome the division of Germany and still remain politically effective. It became reconciled under Bismarck to the old ruling order; and herein lies the essential reason why that ruling order, Junker-dominated and authoritarian as it was, persisted largely intact in the period of rapid industrialization, without the liberalizing transformations that occurred in both England and France.

Industrialization

This reconciliation of German liberalism with an authoritarian state and conservative social order was intensified in the years after unification by the effects of rapid industrialization. Because industrialization and national integration coincided, the middle class had considerable incentive to support a powerful and expanding state, which seemed to be the instrument and guarantor of the unity so vital for sustained economic growth. The commercial rewards of Prussian hegemony were enormous for the middle class. Not only did it achieve an enlarged national market, but the state intervened in countless ways to further national economic growth.

In part this was the consequence of the German concept of backwardness in the latter part of the nineteenth century. A vigorous desire to "catch-up," to narrow the gap and eventually overtake English and French industrial output, infused German thinking. A tremendous sense of national economic purpose, reflected in the search for new markets and colonies, in tariff protection and government subsidies, and in the direct role of the state as an entrepreneur and consumer of industrial products, characterized German industrialization.

What this meant is that a state still dominated by preindustrial men of a narrow, landed, aristocratic caste and that adapted itself to industrial purposes was able to escape the liberal pressures for fundamental reform, which typified the English and French experience. In a sense the advantages of backwardness, which Veblen first identified, accrued not only to the economic sector, where late industrialization meant direct access to already refined machinery and methods of production. They also enabled Germany to modernize industrially without undergoing an equivalent social transformation, such as that which created the conditions for an industrial age in Britain. In England the middle class sought to weaken and control the state, but in Germany the impact of rapid industrialization created a very different pattern. There the middle class needed a strong state for its protection, both economic and political.

This need was intensified by the speed of economic growth. Nowhere else during the nineteenth century did industrialization result in the enormous increase in output that occurred in Germany during the four decades following 1870. The indexes of this industrial growth are extraordinary. In less than half a century, Germany became a leading industrial power. Its iron and steel production doubled each decade and by 1910 exceeded that of England. Coke output increased fivefold during the quarter of a century before World War I. In chemical production, electrical-equipment production, railroad construction, machine-goods manufacture, and shipbuilding, Germany grew faster than had any other country in history.

But such growth also caused enormous dislocations. Companies grew too swiftly, became too large, and were, as a result, often poorly financed and prone to overproduce in years of economic recession. Amalgamations, trade associations, and cartels sprang up, each seeking to reduce the risks of a free marketplace. Tariff protection, achieved through the alliance of a vulnerable young iron industry and an inefficient farming system, created artificial defenses against foreign competition. Then, when the domestic market became saturated with German steel or German rye, the government bought or subsidized. These were the concessions that the government was prepared to make to industry, and they were accepted instead of meaningful political reform, especially by the small band of captains of industry who controlled the largest firms. It seemed as though the state could forestall the success of liberal politics by offering economic prosperity in lieu of political concessions. But if profits mollified an otherwise reform-minded middle class, rapid economic growth also created social and political conditions that led that class to fear any radical move against the government.

One of the salient destabilizing features of intensified industrialization in Germany was the sudden sharp expansion of the urban proletariat, whose own efforts to organize politically threatened the position of much of the bourgeoisie. In 1871, at the founding of the Reich, only one in three Germans lived in a town of more than two thousand inhabitants. Forty years later some 60 percent of a rapidly growing population was urban, and the concentration of population in large industrial cities was striking. The population of Berlin almost tripled, and those of the Ruhr and Saxon cities, where industry was most developed, grew even faster. The number of industrial workers doubled during the quarter of a century before World War I, many of them employed in the giant firms that typified German capitalism.

The swelling ranks of urban labor were a source of great unrest in the rigid German political system and led many of the middle groups to rethink their political attitudes toward the state. Germany had missed the middle-class liberal revolution; now it was confronted with the prospect that once the status quo was undermined, labor, and not the bourgeoisie, might be the prime beneficiary of change. Fear of this created a greater propensity for conservative attitudes on the part of the middle class as industrialization advanced. It also fed middle-class determination to assure economic prosperity—no matter what the political cost—so that labor, too, might be compensated through economic rewards for the political concessions that were withheld.

Herein lay the roots of a benevolent social-welfare policy, the so-called

Sozialpolitik of the Second Reich, which was implemented through state action, with the wide-ranging support of the industrial and commercial segments of the middle class. It was to be the counterpart for labor of the protection offered to German industry, and it resulted in some of the most far-reaching labor and welfare legislation of the nineteenth century. Junker-dominated, conservative Germany inaugurated health and old-age insurance, introduced labor courts and social security, and sought to remedy the worst abuses of factory and shop. Social paternalism in the Second Reich seemed to be an enlightened and progressive policy. In fact, it was motivated by the same consideration that had prompted bureaucratic reorganization earlier in the century: that it would be better to reform from above than to risk revolution from below. This was a strategy designed to maintain the grip of an astute feudal class on the machinery of state power.

For the working class, conditions were comparatively good. Despite frequent recessions and an ever-increasing labor supply, unemployment rarely rose above 2 percent. Real wages rose more rapidly in Germany than elsewhere, while the cost of living was effectively held down. The trade-union movement, long proscribed and still politically docile, was nevertheless highly centralized and well led. It began to flourish around 1900, seeking and often obtaining substantial economic and social gains within a system that appeared to be increasingly prosperous, if politically backward.

But if the indexes of growth were impressive and the benefits to the participants substantial, this was still an unbalanced and structurally unsound economic system. Industrialization had wrought a curious pattern in Germany, quite different from the economic pattern in England or France. Companies were larger, the role of the great entrepreneurs more powerful. Yet even the most successful and sizable industries lacked self-confidence, for they had grown large and rich under highly artificial conditions of state intervention and protection. They doubted their own capacity to thrive without special favors from the state. Furthermore, industrialization had failed to eradicate the power of landed interests or to curb the practice of bestowing high offices in the civil service and the military on members of the aristocracy. Raymond Aron has questioned whether this was capitalism at all. Certainly it was a system that was not congenial to the development of a self-assured bourgeoisie that could assert itself and press for political reforms. Rather, it served to strengthen an authoritarian state structure and to produce what Ralf Dahrendorf has termed a "faulted nation." Industrialization failed to move Germany toward modernization, but rather produced what he has defined as "an industrial feudal society with an authoritarian welfare state."[1]

[1]Ralf Dahrendorf, *Society and Democracy in Germany* (London, 1967), p. 64.

The Faulted Nation

This "faulted" quality was vividly reflected in the political institutions of the Second Reich. The federal parliament, the Reichstag, remained a weak and ineffective institution. Although members were elected by universal suffrage, they remained unsalaried until 1906, and they had little power in controlling state action. Constituencies were arbitrarily drawn, the largest containing twenty-five times more members than the smallest. There was no federal cabinet as in England or France. Instead, the Reich was ruled by the Chancellor, who also headed the Prussian government, and by the senior civil service and the authority of the crown. The Chancellor was not a member of the Reichstag, nor was he dependent upon a stable majority within it. There was, in fact, no real sense of government and opposition, and the political parties, of which there were many, remained badly splintered, reflecting the various social and regional cleavages that prevailed in a state so recently united and undergoing such rapid economic change.

Perhaps the most important of these cleavages was the one separating Protestant and Catholic, which resulted in the organization of a separate Catholic party. This development not only further exacerbated the fragmentation of party politics; it also contributed to the complexity of establishing coalitions, since the Center, the party which consistently commanded one-fourth of the vote, lacked a homogeneous base, except with reference to cultural and religious issues. The Center was one of the two parties to achieve a mass constituency in Germany. The other was the Social Democratic party, which, although persecuted by Bismarck, was able by 1912 to gain the largest vote in the Reichstag elections.

Aside from these two, conservative and liberal parties were splintered and narrowly based, dominated by agrarian, industrial, and commercial forces. In a system where parliament meant so little, these parties were unable to promote broad issues, to develop strong personalities, or to produce real leadership. Special interests prevailed, sometimes operating through the parties, but often circumventing parliament and the party system altogether. Instead, a direct process of influencing government action through the representations of lobbyists or national associations or through the personal contacts of business, industrial, or agrarian leaders determined the nature of politics.

But worst of all, this system was extensively dominated by Prussia. In the words of Arthur Rosenberg, an outstanding historian of the period, "Prussia ruled the Empire." The Prussian system of government was in fact a travesty of the modern state. Its electoral system was so weighted that wealthy, and especially landed, interests could control the state parliament and reinforce their grip upon its government. This was of great significance because Prussia comprised two-thirds of the territory and three-fifths of the population of the Reich. In Prussia were located the most industrialized parts of Germany, many of its largest cities, and its capital, with all the intellectual and cultural ferment concentrated there. Here were the most modern parts of Germany, and yet these were saddled with the most conservative political system. Although Prussia became the stronghold of Social Democracy, this was not reflected in its political institutions.

Here was a frozen and rigid system. It was built upon repression and privilege, meeting special needs and protecting vested interests. Economically the system seemed to work, but socially and politically it did not. It had no capacity to adapt and to allocate power and responsibility to the new forces created by rapid economic change. It was as though Germany had experienced only half a revolution, the industrial half. As a result, too many preindustrial preserves remained at the helm. And as time passed, those who ruled without mass support became aware of their own precarious position. The reforms that had been introduced gradually in England and France and that were overdue in Germany would have swiftly led to the displacement of the German ruling class.

This situation was further distorted by Bismarck, who as Chancellor for almost two decades forged the political foundations of the German Empire. A brilliant strategist, skillful manipulator, and forceful personality, he was able to integrate highly heterogeneous forces without making any fundamental or irreversible concessions to them. Thus, despite his apparent achievements, Bismarck practiced a kind of politics of postponement. Social and political cleavages were never reconciled, but rather played off against each other. It was an extraordinary holding operation, a delicate balancing of complex and conflicting forces during a period in which national gains had been achieved that did not yet excessively threaten the other European powers. Bismarck, therefore, was able to utilize the successes of foreign policy for domestic effect. This was a dangerous precedent to set for the future. Dangerous also was the deceptive notion of the strong man in German history, exemplified first by Bismarck and again later by Ludendorff, Hindenburg, and Hitler.

All this posed formidable and eventually insuperable problems for Bismarck's successors. It is not enough to say that only a strong, cunning, and competent Chancellor like Bismarck could operate this system, for it is likely that given the enormity of Germany's problems, no other man, not even a second Bismarck, would have succeeded later on. But in fact, Germany was governed extremely poorly in the years after Bismarck. This was due less to the ineptitude of the several Chancellors than to the exceptional incompetence and capriciousness of Kaiser Wilhelm II—"the irresponsible maniac on the throne."[2]

---

[2]Alexander Gerschenkron, *Bread and Democracy in Germany* (New York, 1966), p. 88.

The system that had seemed to work well under Bismarck soon began to show serious strains. Overproduction in heavy industry and the dire predicament of a chronically depressed and highly inefficient agricultural system led the government to remedies that threatened to undermine the precarious stability of Europe. Tariffs protecting rye and iron were not enough. Immense armament development and naval shipbuilding to absorb surplus steel and an aggrandizing colonial and Eastern policy to assuage the thwarted frustrations of a failing landed aristocracy were poor substitutes for long overdue structural reforms.

These measures were complemented by an increasingly jingoistic, romantic nationalism, which sought through the propagation of grandiose imperial notions to align a divided nation behind its hapless leaders. When Bismarck had effectively atomized domestic opponents, he had given them all something valuable, namely a united Germany. But subsequently, German leaders could not safely continue to utilize nationalism and foreign policy as an outlet for domestic pressures and a unifying ideology for conflicting groups. Germany after 1871 could afford neither a great victory nor a great defeat in foreign policy. The former would fatally upset the balance of Europe; the latter would bring the anachronistic German government tumbling down.

Yet this was not adequately understood by the Imperial government. It sought instead to "divert the pressures created by special interest groups to the outside in the sense of a 'social imperialism' designed and used to substitute expansionism for domestic democratization."[3] Social imperialism seemed the only alternative to social reform. The power of irrational, racist, pseudopopulist rhetoric served to mobilize patriotic and often bellicose sentiments. Curiously antimodern and anti-Western concepts of German nationhood and national destiny gained in force as a reaction against purportedly Western capitalism. *Uberfremdung,* the idea of excessive foreign influence, was a strange but useful concept with which both to repudiate these painful processes as not authentically German and to further the autarkic ambitions of the Junkers and the great industrialists. It helped to identify a foreign source for the dislocations that ailed Germany, much as the Jews would be castigated later as alien internal pariahs. Feelings of domestic anxiety and external inferiority combined to feed the shrill nationalism of the Pan-Germans, who sought that "special mission" for Germany which Johann Fichte, the eighteenth-century German philosopher, had first proclaimed.

Industrialization could not alone resolve the problems afflicting Germany. It had created the economic benefits that enabled the old order to defend its position and to deflect the middle class from its rightful political

[3]Karl Dietrich Bracher, *The German Dictatorship* (New York, 1970), p. 19.

purposes. As a result, parts of the bourgeoisie became feudalized, accepting the values of the landed aristocracy rather than defeating its social and political prerogatives. Without concomitant political and social reforms, industrialization produced deeply antimodern currents in Germany; and the greater the tension between economic change and political and social rigidity, the more this reactionary, nationalistic, and antimodern way of thought came to the fore. The vigor and velocity of economic change collided with the continued social stagnation and political inertia. A country that risked only half a revolution could not become modern. As Ralf Dahrendorf has said so well, "What is remarkable about Imperial Germany is that throughout the industrial revolution it managed to miss the road to modernity."[4] It took another road instead, and that, unfortunately, was one that led to war.

War

For Germany, as for Austria and Russia, World War I was fought largely for domestic reasons: to defend an outdated political system and a petrified social structure. Consolidation of the old order might have been achieved had the war been swiftly won, as was anticipated by those who began it. But a prolonged and finally total war was destined to have just the opposite effect, to hasten the crumbling of that old order. Thus World War I served radically to transform the political and social system of Germany in a way that few had foreseen.

Germany, like all the other participants, was ill-prepared for the war. But it had at once to confront two special problems: conflict on several fronts and the impact of a naval blockade. This meant that a larger percentage of the population was inducted into military service, reducing the manpower available for domestic production at a moment when conditions of extensive self-sufficiency were forced upon the system. Before the war, about one-third of Germany's food and much of its raw materials had been imported. Faced with sudden autarky, the government had to impose wide-ranging economic controls. This meant that the impact of the war on civilian life was more extensive in Germany than elsewhere, a situation that was to have profound effects upon the pre-World War I system.

The first consequence of the war for Germany was a transformation of the army. Mass mobilization and early battlefield losses diluted the Junker predominance in the military services. Military effectiveness replaced social origin as the prime determinant of promotion. A new kind of army emerged, determined to extend its control over the entire country and to

[4] Dahrendorf, *op. cit.*, p. 64.

achieve maximum war production, if necessary by dictatorial means blended with social and economic concessions. In the Reich the army had never reported directly to the Chancellor, but rather to the Kaiser himself. During the war its supremacy became total. By 1916, the Chancellor was its mouthpiece, the Kaiser but a figurehead. Field Marshall Hindenburg took over military command, and General Ludendorff, his brilliant chief of staff, assumed effective control of the country. It has been said that "this day marked the downfall of the Bismarckian Empire and the beginning of the German Revolution."[5] While the war brought Lloyd George into office in England and Clemenceau in France, in Germany it produced a military dictatorship.

But it was a dictatorship supported by industry and organized labor, each of which secured from it important gains. For industry there was mass production, scant control of profits, and the promise of postwar annexations. And for the unions, the war brought de facto recognition and substantial labor reforms that laid the foundations for the right to collective bargaining and the right to strike that would be granted in the postwar period. Under Ludendorff "the army became an agent of revolution from above in order to prevent revolution from below, an agent linking the old order and the new."[6] The decrees of 1916 imposed a kind of wartime socialism. Controls were placed on all civilian labor. Workers were trained for defense industries and could not freely change their place of employment. Unutilized machinery was seized for military production, and strict rationing was extended throughout the country. In war, even more than in peace, the German state gained powers that far exceeded those of other governments at the time.

The ethos motivating these innovations was not to make Germany more modern, but rather to heighten wartime efficiency. They were accompanied by no meaningful political reforms. The old ruling order, now beyond rescue or renovation, had been replaced by a military government, which made no effort to broaden its base, to share its power with parliament, or to secure popular support. The Reichstag, increasingly disturbed by the means and ends of the military, was unable to assert its will. There was no outlet for the rising political discontent. As a result, German society became radicalized.

The agent of this radicalization was the war itself. As it continued, it imposed enormous hardship on the civilian population. Average caloric consumption fell to 1,000 calories per day, and almost half a million people died of starvation. Despite controls, the price of food and clothing

---

[5] Arthur Rosenberg, *Imperial Germany* (Boston, 1964), p. 123.

[6] Gerald D. Feldman, *Army, Industry, and Labor in Germany 1914–1918* (Princeton, 1966), p. 38.

rose sharply in the absence of adequate supplies, and real wages fell. Financed through inadequate loans rather than tax increases, the war eroded the convertibility of the mark and fed an inflation that impoverished important sectors of the lower middle class. While peasants were uprooted through military service and thereby subjected to new political influences, the trade unions began to lose their grip on the industrial working class. Through induction more than 60 percent of the 2.5 million members of the free trade unions were removed from the labor force. In their place, women, adolescents, the handicapped, and others not previously employed worked long and hard hours in German factories. As labor dissatisfaction mounted, the unions, which had won de facto recognition from the army and the bureaucracy, began to lose the control of their own constituencies. By 1917, strikes, officially proscribed by the union leadership, began to surface, first in the vital munitions industry and soon elsewhere.

This specter posed inordinate problems for the military regime. In the absence of victory there was no turning back to the old system. Domestic suffering required that there be some sizable and visible gains to justify the costs of the war. The prospect of German annexations and a punitive peace, which was given a boost by the terms of settlement by which Russia left the war, seemed the only way in which the military and industrial order in Germany could survive the war. So all efforts to seek a compromise peace, such as that sought by a majority of the Reichstag in the summer of 1917, were rejected by the generals and the leading industrialists. The war of annexation was continued, and with it, in the absence of victory, the certainty that the rulers of a postwar Germany would no longer be the same.

Defeat came in the late summer of 1918. As the final western offensive in France collapsed, the generals at last registered what others had known before—that victory was unobtainable. Now, as their own forces threatened to mutiny, they panicked. The Kaiser, so long the instrument of military will, was pressed to sue for peace and to attempt yet another revolution from above to preempt a domestic uprising that could overthrow the entire political order of Germany.

Revolution

The events of October were momentous. Ludendorff was replaced, and the Reichstag began to assert itself, suddenly aware of the vast power available to it in the vacuum created by the military collapse. Sweeping constitutional reforms were passed with desperate speed, the most significant of which made the Chancellor responsible to parliament. Prince Max of Baden, a south-German liberal, was installed as Chancellor, and soon after the Kaiser abdicated, largely on the expectation that this would bring better peace terms from the victorious democracies.

In the same month the leaders of industry negotiated a far-reaching agreement with labor, seeking through expedient concessions to consolidate the vested interest of the unions in preventing a revolutionary overturning of the entire system. This agreement brought great gains for organized labor, including full recognition by a previously hostile industry of both the right to collective bargaining and the eight-hour work day. In defeat the industrialists jettisoned their traditional alliance with agriculture and the authoritarian state, hoping to forestall a workers' revolution through emergency concessions to labor. This strategy was shrewd and proved efficacious. For the union leadership, itself fearful of insurrection, the benefits of a partnership with industry were substantial and more than fulfilled their prewar aspirations. Gerald Feldman, the foremost scholar of these events, has written that "the political and social equality of the working class was tentatively won in war and was finally sanctified in defeat, and therein lay one of the great tragedies of German democracy."[7] For the moment of defeat was fleeting, and the concessions to labor that industry voluntarily sanctified were all too easily reversed as political conditions changed in the years ahead.

The events of October, which established collective bargaining and parliamentarism in Germany, were followed by more revolutionary developments. It was too late for an experiment in constitutional monarchy. The tide of revolutionary fervor was swelling in almost all urban areas and among the restive and embittered armed forces. Guided in part by the Russian experience, workers and soldiers formed councils throughout Germany, and in Munich the municipal government was overthrown and a revolutionary republic established. As the flames of revolution spread, so did the apprehensions of the Social Democratic leadership, which believed in an evolutionary course based on the October constitutional reforms. Forced into action by the swift pace of these events, the Social Democrats resolved to contain the revolution by placing themselves at its helm. On November 9 Friedrich Ebert, a former saddle maker and now chairman of the party, proclaimed the founding of the German Republic. The old government system of Imperial Germany was thereby overthrown, but popular pressure for a more fundamental social and economic revolution was brought under control and soon to a halt.

In order to understand the abortive revolution of 1918, two phenomena must be understood. One is the nature of the Social Democratic party (S.P.D.); the other is the complex of critical problems confronting any regime, revolutionary or otherwise, in the wake of sudden military defeat

[7] *Ibid.*, p. 7.

and which faced the German government at the approach of winter in 1918. After years of persecution under Bismarck Social Democracy had emerged as a formidable force in German politics by the turn of the century. As a party, the S.P.D. had been rent by deep ideological divisions and serious tactical disputes. Gradually its more revolutionary prescriptions had been subordinated to a revisionist and evolutionary program that envisaged piecemeal progress toward a majoritarian and constitutional socialist system. While the dilemmas of democratic socialism in a nondemocratic state had been great indeed, this kind of moderate socialism had made important strides in the last decade before the war. By 1912, with 110 seats in Parliament, the S.P.D. had become the largest party in the Reichstag, commanding about 34 percent of the vote in the national elections of that year.

These gains were matched by an impressive growth in the strength of the trade unions, which occupied a critical role within the party. The unions had done well in terms of securing substantial wage and social security benefits for their members, and they tended on the whole to oppose radical political action, such as the use of the strike for noneconomic ends. Both the party and the unions had developed elaborate and powerful bureaucracies, each of which had a stake in securing further piecemeal concessions within the system and in quelling the more radical and rancorous of their own constituents. Although neither shared in the prewar ruling system, both the party and union leadership had surprising respect for state authority. They had the ingrained German reverence for the law and for that unquestioned ascendency of the state known in German as *Obrigkeit.* Despite the gulf that separated the state and society from the party and the unions, each replicated the authoritarianism endemic in prewar Germany, personified in figures such as Karl Legien, who led the free trade unions for thirty years, or August Bebel, or Friedrich Ebert, whom Carl Schorske has aptly named "the Stalin of German Social Democracy." This leadership was deeply compromised by the war, for which the party had unanimously voted credits in 1914 and during which the unions had collaborated so extensively with the military and industrial establishment.

But the war had exacerbated the old tensions within the party. While only fourteen of its Reichstag members had voted in caucus in 1914 against the war credits, the prolongation of hostilities and the domestic impact of war controls strengthened the radical elements within the S.P.D., who bolted from the majority two years later to form their own party, the so-called Independent Socialists (U.S.P.D.). This faction, though small in number, contained some of the foremost theorists and personalities within the Socialist camp, among them the well-known revisionist Eduard Bernstein and his former adversary, the aging Karl Kautsky. The Independent Socialists were in turn outflanked by new groups on the Left, the most important of which, the Spartakus League, claimed the brilliant leadership of Rosa Luxemburg and Karl Liebknecht.

The radical activity of 1918 was disconcerting for the S.P.D., which was fearful lest the events of the Bolshevik revolution of the previous year by reproduced in Germany. As is so often the case among long-time opposition parties, the S.P.D. was perhaps most conscious of the dangers posed for its aspirations by its own radical secessionists. The turmoil unleashed by the sudden defeat of 1918, for which the German public was entirely unprepared, raised the specter of a violent urban insurrection. This was a prospect that the S.P.D. could not but oppose, in view of its past course and present situation. A party that had rejected revolution so fundamentally in the past could not in 1918 lead a revolution. It could only deflect it, seeking to channel the momentum for change into a transformation of the political system, which would, with the passage of time, provide the electoral support for a gradual restructuring of the social and economic foundations of Germany. For a party that had gained more than one-third of the vote in the last prewar election, this concept of democratic socialism made reasonable sense.

Aside from the fear of popular revolution, the Socialist leaders faced very critical practical problems once they established themselves as the government. Germany, under its military tutelage, had fought the war until it could fight no more. Not only were the armies broken, but civilian supplies were largely exhausted. Shortages were particularly critical in clothing, fuel, and food. The ceasefire was called in October, and the armistice signed a month later. Without sufficient supplies of coal and food, civilian deaths in the postwar winter of 1918 could well have exceeded half a million, the total number that succumbed to starvation during the four years of conflict. More than 6 million soldiers were to be demobilized and the vast war industries shut down, each adding to the million men already jobless. With so much of the population exhausted and undernourished, the new government gave special priority to the kind of economic measures that might provide immediate relief, rather than to those that would reallocate the ownership of German economic resources.

But the Socialists were not well equipped to pursue this course. As an outcast in the old system, the S.P.D. had never effectively shared in the responsibility of government and was entirely untrained for the task that now lay before it. This led to a rather unusual accommodation between the leaders of the new government and the personnel of the old, typified by the continued tenure in office of members of the established bureaucracy and judiciary. Lacking a reservoir of trained talent and imbued with an excessive awe of the professional expertise required to discharge government functions, the S.P.D. leaders appealed to all civil servants to remain in their posts. This move was based on the false assumption that they would remain nonpolitical experts, serving the republic as loyally as they had the monarchy. Fewer than 11 percent of the Prussian civil servants holding high posts were removed from office in 1918. No attempt was made to democratize the bureaucracy until the abortive counterrevolutionary events of the spring of 1920 punctured the naïve illusion of the S.P.D. leaders. It was their failure to purge the old imperial civil service that Hugo Preuss, the prime architect of the Weimar constitution, later saw as the essential flaw of the Weimar system.

This reconciliation of the Socialists with the incumbent bureaucracy was matched by their accord with the military. On November 10, just one day after proclaiming the republic, Ebert, chairman of the newly constituted Council of People's Delegates, secured the support of the army. As Hindenburg reported to his staff colleagues, it was a pact ostensibly designed "to prevent the spread of terrorist Bolshevism in Germany."[8] This effort to ensure against leftist agitation was to result in the brutal suppression of the Spartakist rebellion two months later and in the assassination of the two most intellectually gifted German revolutionaries, Luxemburg and Liebknecht.

For Ebert and his associates the politics of the street offered no solutions for the problems facing Germany. In their view an uprising of the militants could only divide the forces of the Left and stir a right-wing reaction. The six-man Council of People's Delegates, which initially included three Independent Socialists, saw itself as a provisional government preparing the way for a popularly elected Constituent Assembly that would draft and ratify a new constitution. Germany would gain a new political order, based on a democratic parliamentary system. Such a National Assembly was elected in January 1919; and until it could begin its deliberations in the town of Weimar, free from the turmoil of Berlin, the council set about dealing with the economic and political emergency confronting Germany. It attempted to cope with the looming economic breakdown, to prevent the dismemberment of the Reich, and to deal with the victorious allies, whose terms for a peace settlement were not yet known.

This meant that structural reforms were to be postponed until some stability had been restored to the economy, the immediate crisis had passed, and the National Assembly had set up the political and constitutional framework for more far-reaching economic and social measures. But it also meant delaying action and thereby losing a great deal of the momentum for change available in the winter of 1918. With a preliminary agreement between the unions and industry in their pocket, the Socialist leaders felt they could wait for more quiet times before attempting the rigorous task of reallocating the ownership of assets through nationalization and land reform. As a leading Socialist and future Chancellor, Hermann Müller,

[8]Golo Mann, *The History of Germany Since 1789* (New York, 1968), p. 333.

put it: "One can only socialize when there is something to socialize."[9]

But this disregarded the massive support for nationalization that existed in the ranks of labor and among the workers' and soldiers' councils that winter. The Socialist leaders rather naïvely assumed that such seizure of industrial assets would be possible in the years ahead. For them reconstruction was to precede the redistribution of resources. This view was based on the assumption that the elections would produce a majority to support such basic economic reforms. But the elections never did. Socialism never gained a majority in Germany, although it did win 46 percent of the vote in January 1919. The exigencies of that first republican winter and the temporizing of the S.P.D. gave German industry and agriculture a reprieve from the expropriations that they expected and that the Social Democratic party program had promised. This was one of the most ominous and costly miscalculations of the S.P.D. when first it came to power, and one which would in time permit the restoration of the key components of the old order: the Junkers, the army, and industry.

Once again Germany experienced only a partial revolution. This time it was really an unfinished enterprise, for the Socialists had meant to change a great deal more than they were actually able to change. With so much of its prewar social and economic foundations left intact, Germany was once again to miss the path to modernity.

[9]Hermann Müller, *Die November Revolution—Erinnerungen* (Berlin, 1928), p. 198.

Two

The Nazi Conquest of the Weimar Republic

Given the arrested revolutionary events of 1918, everything hinged on the success of the political institutions of the new republic in which the Socialists placed their initial hopes. But these institutions, unfortunately, were also deeply flawed at the outset.

The Weimar Republic

The Weimar Republic was an improvised system. Conditions of military defeat and domestic upheaval were hardly conducive to the creation of a complex and fragile system of parliamentary democracy. The Weimar constitution was a highly complicated instrument, reflecting in part the many compromises struck by the contending political forces represented in the National Assembly, where the Socialists did not command a majority. The fifty-six articles governing civil liberties were too extensive for a population as heterogeneous as that of Germany, and in the subsequent years of crisis these liberties were all too often abused. And the constitution was far too easily amendable. Two-thirds of a quorum of two-thirds of the Reichstag could ratify an amendment, which theoretically permitted fewer than half of the elected members to alter the constitutional foundations of the system. Like so much else that happened at the birth of the republic, this did not suggest a strong sense of permanence.

The federal structure of the state was retained, with Prussia still paramount. The old restrictive and weighted Prussian electoral law was swept aside, which was a decisive change, for it assured Socialist control of this pivotal state. However, the electoral system of the republic was poorly designed. Absolute proportional representation combined with huge districts, each with some fourteen or fifteen representatives, proved corrosive of party stability and coalition government. It meant that all minorities, even those not regionally concentrated, could find representation, which accounts for the profusion of parties in Weimar Germany. There was no incentive for interests to gather or for groups to coalesce. The constant threat of secession made the larger parties subject to the dictates of their most willful members. This served to strengthen the influence of the interest groups, whose power was further enhanced by the frequency of costly elections, which they alone could finance. The political prerogatives of business, agriculture, and labor grew powerful within these parties, because their leaders were able to secure safe parliamentary seats through their high placement on the party-determined election lists.

Control of these lists in the huge districts reinforced the ascendency of party bureaucracies and diminished the opportunities for strong leaders to emerge, a factor that helps explain the importance of mayors, controlling their own large urban constituencies, in Weimar politics.

A pattern developed of self-serving parties unable to identify themselves with the national interest. It reflected and accentuated the divisions in German society. *Parteipolitik* gained a disreputable image, while those forces or institutions which seemed to stand above parties grew more attractive. Parliament and cabinet government were not among these.

The men who made the Weimar constitution, long frustrated in their parliamentary aspirations in the Kaiserreich, sought to make the Reichstag supreme. The Chancellor and his cabinet ministers were dependent upon its confidence. But the fragmentation of political interests reflected in the proliferation of parties and the stark decline of those willing to share in a majority government made it increasingly difficult for such confidence to be obtained. As a result, the republic was governed for ten of its fourteen years by minority cabinets, and even these proved stronger than the majority coalitions, which had to satisfy too many divergent interests to rule effectively. In the seven elections to the Reichstag, only once did the incumbent parties actually gain in votes. For example, before 1924 the S.P.D. as a government party always lost votes, some of which it then recouped during the next four years, when it remained out of office. It is always destructive of stable parliamentary government when electoral opportunities consistently reward the opposition.

What dominated all the regimes in the republic was not so much parliament itself as the party factions within it. They alone made and reshuffled most of the coalitions. Of the eighteen Weimar cabinets, only three fell because the Reichstag formally voted nonconfidence. Far more often collapse came because one party deserted the coalition, often at the behest of a major interest group. Basically, from 1920 there was what has sometimes been called "a second government in the Reichstag." It was not sufficient for the cabinet to decide on a specific piece of legislation; it then had the far more complex task of obtaining the consent of a legislative majority. Not infrequently a party actually represented in the cabinet reversed itself on the floor, a practice which found its absurd extreme when Chancellor Müller subjected himself to his party's parliamentary preference and voted against a law introduced by his own government.

It was the leaders of the parliamentary party groups more than the Chancellor who determined who would serve in the cabinet. Bargaining, often in moments of crisis, could be intricate and prolonged. The result was that the cabinet rarely had a strong parliamentary mandate. Agreement was usually reached only on several initial issues; and as new problems arose, these coalitions were quickly undone. Six of them lasted less than half a year, and none survived for more than twenty months. Even in those of longer duration, the ministers held too much personal power vis-à-vis the Chancellor. Frequently specific ministers would remain in office as Chancellors came and went. These ministers, figures such as Gustav Stresemann of the Foreign Office, Otto Gessler of Defense, or Heinrich Brauns, the Minister of Labor, possessed more distinct and independent influence within the cabinet. This was matched by the importance of the Finance Minister, who was given extensive budgetary powers that further circumscribed the authority of the Chancellor. In short, there were so many constraints and channels of dissention that it proved extremely difficult for a Chancellor to assert himself and to assume effective leadership of his own regime.

This development had not been foreseen by those who forged the new parliamentary system in 1919. At the time broad consensus had been achieved by the three major parties, the S.P.D., the Center, and the newly formed Democrats, who together comprised the so-called Weimar coalition that had won more than three-fourths of the seats in the National Assembly. But these three parties, the intended pillars of the young republic, secured less than 44 percent of the vote in the very first Reichstag election, in June 1920, and the coalition never again commanded a majority in the chamber. The demise of the parliamentarism that was to be the foundation of the Weimar system was registered early. Oswald Spengler, the German philosopher so widely hailed for his prophetic wisdom, predicted with cynical self-assurance that "parliamentarism would always remain alien to Germany."[1] While it was the Right that was most responsible for undermining parliament, the system itself proved so un-

[1]Oswald Spengler, *Preussentum und Sozialismus* (Munich, 1924), p. 64.

workable that conservative observers gained acceptance for their notion that Germans had no natural propensity for a parliamentary regime.

This reflected the early polarization of politics that beset the Weimar Republic. Antisystem parties were soon to score stunning electoral successes, culminating in the extraordinary victory of July 1932, in which the National Socialists and Communists together secured an absolute majority in the Reichstag. But the German parliament had long since abdicated its constitutional grip on power and authority, and the President and the bureaucracy, aided by the renascent officer corps, emerged as the actual rulers of the republic. These forces were to prove themselves dependable instruments for the defense and restoration of the old order long before Hitler seized control.

The office of the presidency had been much debated in the Constituent Assembly. It was modeled very much on the French presidency, but was designed to be immune from the institutional weakness of its Gallic counterpart. Partially as the result of the insistent prodding of Max Weber, who saw the need for a strong and charismatic, integrating national figure to offset the pluralism represented in parliament, the President was to be directly elected, either by a majority on the first ballot or by a plurality thereafter, for seven years, a comparatively long term. He was to be the strong man, standing above the parties in the new political system. This was a somewhat naïve notion, for his powers were in fact immense and, with the demise of parliament, came to be used in extremely partisan ways.

The President appointed the Chancellor and, upon his recommendation, the cabinet ministers, each of whom had to resign if the Reichstag withdrew its confidence. In such a case the President had the power to dissolve parliament and to call new elections. In the Weimar Republic the Reichstag never sat for its full four-year term. Each election but the first was the result of a dissolution. Indeed, the electorate could be asked to vote far too easily and too often. The President had the power to refer any legislation passed by the Reichstag to a national referendum. He could do so as well in the case of legislation on which the Reichstag and the Reichsrat, the weaker, second chamber, in which state governments were represented, failed to find agreement. Conversely, a popular referendum was required whenever at least 10 percent of the voters desired it. In 1919 Eduard David, the veteran Socialist leader, had proclaimed this "the most democratic democracy in the world." But the constant plebiscitary implications of these provisions served to undermine the legitimacy of parliament and to strengthen instead the autocratic powers of the President.

These powers, especially under conditions of declared emergency, were awesome indeed. Article 48 of the constitution provided that where public safety and order required it, the President could, with the countersignature of the cabinet, suspend fundamental rights and decree emergency measures without parliamentary approval. Given the frequent paralysis of parliament and the recurring crisis that confronted the republic, this article was used more than 250 times. Initially, under President Ebert, it was invoked to suppress insurrection and to cope with the acute economic problems at the height of the inflation in 1923. In later years it was often employed to defend the republic against its domestic extremist enemies.

As the incapacitation of the Reichstag increased, so did government by presidential order. Between March 1931 and May 1932 the Reichstag was in session for only six days. It produced two statutes during those fifteen months, while more than sixty measures were decreed under Article 48. But the complexion of the cabinet and of the presidency had changed. The cabinet was now populated by undemocratic men and dominated once again by the Junkers. The tragedy of this vital constitutional provision, as Clinton Rossiter has written, is that thereby "Article 48 became the possession of men who despised the whole idea of Weimar democracy. The Rock of the Republic was converted by Hindenburg and Papen into a bridge leading to despotism, and over this bridge marched Adolf Hitler to his evil power."[2]

Economic Dilemmas

Perhaps even more than all these institutional failings, the economic crises afflicting the republic undermined its foundations and made possible the return to power of the Junkers and the industrialists. From its inception, the Weimar Republic faced dire problems. The peace settlement signed at Versailles contained harsh terms. Germany lost 10 percent of its prewar population, 15 percent of its arable land, all of its colonies and foreign investments, and most of its fleet and railroad stock. It was saddled with a heavy, indeed, a hopeless, reparations burden. Its losses, together with the unsound financing of the war, led to a hyperinflation that had disastrous domestic consequences. At the beginning of the war the mark had stood at 4.2 to the dollar; by January 1919 it had fallen to 9; and then four years later, when the French occupied the Ruhr, it tumbled to 18,000. By the end of 1923 the mark was in fact worthless.

Inflation wiped out the savings of the middle class and pauperized those on fixed incomes. This was critical, because it was the middle class that was growing most rapidly and which therefore could have provided the votes needed by the liberal parties to assure a majority for the democratic Weimar coalition. In 1913, the last prewar year, 43 percent of all German taxpayers had personal assets of less than 50,000 goldmarks. By 1923 this

---

[2]Clinton Rossiter, *Constitutional Dictatorship* (New York, 1963), p. 60.

figure had almost doubled to 83 percent. For a frugal, expanding middle class in a precarious social position, the loss of its savings was a traumatic experience that sharply eroded its confidence in the republic.

However, the inflation benefited the landowners and heavy industry. Indeed, it rewarded anyone who held real assets, and especially those who held such assets on credit. The enormous loss of the value of the mark eradicated much of the farmers' debt on their land, which shrank from more than 17 to less than 3 billion goldmarks. Even more striking were the gains for the iron industry, which used its postwar government indemnity to buy back the mines it had lost in Lorraine and which expanded its holdings throughout Germany by means of the loans that were easily available to industry at that time. Thus, the two economic groups that had cared least about the republic initially found their power substantially augmented, especially in the absence of effective profit controls.

Ironically, the problems for each mounted during the period of stabilization and rationalization that followed the inflation. Agriculture started to slip into what was to become chronic depression. As cheap grain imports from eastern Europe and the United States flooded the German market, prices fell, which produced pressure for government subsidies and protection. From 1925 on, more than half of the farms in Germany operated at a loss, a situation that fed the exodus from the countryside to the cities. The urban population of Germany grew by almost 30 percent during the Weimar Republic, a development which gravely exacerbated the impact of the mass unemployment brought on by the Depression in the early thirties.

The hardships of agriculture tempered any pressure for wide-scale land reform. The Socialists had not pressed for a breakup of the giant Junker estates in 1919, in part because they lacked a developed agrarian program, but also because their more orthodox theorists believed large-scale management to be more efficient and progressive. By the late twenties, the agrarian interests were again sufficiently entrenched within the system to cull special favors from the government. Although some state-initiated resettlement began, the key components of government policy were protection and subsidy rather than the basic restructuring and reduction of agricultural production that was long overdue.

Industry, too, was able to obtain special concessions. Plans for even a partial nationalization of its assets had died an early death. Instead, the Socialists and left-wing Catholics of the Center party sought in the first years of the republic to extend government regulation and taxation. However, the redistributive impact of the government's measures, imaginative though they were, were vitiated by the effects of inflation.

The inflation, which lasted through 1923, had two unusual consequences for industry. Because of the way in which it occurred, the inflation served both as a financial stimulus for the domestic consumer market and as a substitute for a tariff against imported goods. When these two artificial forces disappeared, German industry suddenly found itself with inordinate excess capacity. The result was a further concentration of ownership, with many firms combining to maximize efficiency, and a pattern of increased cartelization to ensure a more stable and less competitive demand. By 1925 one out of ten workers was employed in a giant firm employing more than 1,000 people. In heavy industry, this pattern was much more accentuated. More than 65 percent of all miners and about 55 percent of all ironworkers were on the payrolls of these mammoth companies, the largest of which—the United Steelworks—had well over 200,000 employees. While middle-sized firms suffered, the power of the Ruhr industrialists grew preponderant, and they succeeded in thwarting the attempts of the government to regulate iron and steel production. The Ruhr ironworks were handsomely indemnified for losses sustained during the French occupation of 1923, but the ironworkers, who had suffered more, received no compensation. When firms found themselves in extreme distress due to conditions of excess supply, the state intervened with its so-called cold socialization, rescuing these companies by purchasing them.

Such collusion between government and industry seemed a natural outgrowth of the pattern of extensive state involvement in the economy that had developed since the onset of industrialization. The state served as banker, regulator, customer, and, where necessary, entrepreneur of industrial production. An attitude and policy that sought the maximization of output blended well with the effort to increase social welfare and to raise consumption. These were the fundamental, rather apolitical, aspirations of the trade unions. For them the gains scored during the war were augmented by new achievements. The introduction of unemployment insurance in 1927, the provisions for organized government mediation of wage disputes, and the establishment of shop councils in factories were complemented by important consumer benefits. The construction of low-cost housing, the provisions for rent control, the subsidies for bread and for railroad transport, and the rapid enlargement of municipal facilities were all hailed as important achievements. And so they were while the economic boom of the mid and late twenties lasted. Production in the chemical industry increased by one-third in the four years following the stablization of the mark in 1924, a gain outpaced by that of the iron industry. By 1928 real wages had finally regained the level of the last prewar year, while the ranks of unemployed, enlarged by those who had abandoned the land, held below the half-million mark.

But none of these gains were irreversible, nor were they the result of basic structural reforms. They were the benefits of a booming economy; and once that boom abated, it soon became evident how ephemeral the changes were. Economic power had been left in the hands of a resurgent industry and an ailing agriculture. Too many underlying economic patterns had been left intact. When the Depression came crashing down upon Germany, the forces of the old order were still there, seeking to reassert themselves.

In this enterprise they had potent institutional allies. The President was in their camp, and the bureaucracy and the army had not been purged. The expertise and social prestige of the civil service had been its great defense. As cabinet ministers had come and gone—some twelve dozen in the fourteen years of the republic—the senior state secretaries who remained in office had gained in power. So had the army, despite, or perhaps even because of, the allied restriction limiting it to 100,000 men. That limitation had ensured that the nucleus of the old officer corps would be retained and that only the conscripted citizen would be eliminated. Indeed, this much smaller army had a more aristocratic officer corps than before the war; in 1927 twice as many officers as in 1913 were themselves sons of former officers. And many of those who had been forced into early retirement, knowing little other than army life, flocked to the Free Corps and to the other paramilitary units that abounded in Germany. These were the forces of potential counterrevolution. And in the late days of the republic they controlled Field Marshall von Hindenburg, the senile, octogenarian President who symbolized the crippled state of democratic politics in Germany.

With all its faults, and after having suffered so much stress earlier, the Weimar Republic was unable to withstand the effects of the Depression. The crash that began in America in the fall of 1929 struck the German economy with inordinate severity, because much of the boom had been financed from the United States. Furthermore, the entire structure of German credit was unsound. Foreign indebtedness totaled more than 17 billion goldmarks, far higher than elsewhere in Europe, and far too much of it consisted of short-term loans that had been used for long-term investment. This problem was aggravated by the inadequate ratio of their own capital to borrowed capital in the German banks. The dangers of an acute liquidity crisis, with all its multiplying effects, were enormous. Banks began to fail, and businesses contracted severely. In this situation the German government, wary of huge budgetary deficits reminiscent of the earlier inflationary period, began to cut spending and to pursue a deflationary policy. Half of the federal budget of 1930 had originally been earmarked for social costs alone. These were now sharply reduced, especially the recently established unemployment insurance. Thus, at the very moment when every third worker was in danger of losing his wages, funds were withdrawn from support of the jobless.

By 1932, with almost 7 million out of work and civil servants on reduced salaries, the average weekly income of the German family had fallen 60 percent from its level of four years earlier. Industrial production shrank to half its 1929 level, while exports fell by more. In the wake of this economic calamity, many of the major gains of labor in the country that had innovated such broad programs of *Sozialpolitik* were swept away. It was the working man and the middle class that fared the worst.

The industrialists suffered less. Prices of industrial products and raw materials, carefully controlled by cartel agreement and protected through tariffs, fell less within Germany than they did abroad. And for agriculture, whose depressed condition dated back to the mid-twenties, special emergency relief measures were pressed through by presidential order to save the estates of Hindenburg's Junker neighbors.

As banks faltered and firms closed down, the level of discontent and mass agitation mounted. The chief beneficiaries were the extremist, antisystem National Socialist and Communist parties, which together scored spectacular electoral gains. The revolutionary potential of the ferment that gripped Germany raised a frightening specter for the conservative leaders of the old order, who hoped still, through the army, the bureaucracy, and the President, to exploit the crisis in order to restore some form of the *ancien régime*. But von Papen, the shameless agent of these forces, could not restore a conservative system. The social panic that Theodore Geiger first diagnosed had spread too far among the middle class. And so it was that the conservative leaders, who still controlled vital instruments of state power, made their fateful alliance with National Socialism, a movement that they thought would serve to protect them from a fearful social upheaval.

Collapse into Fascism

The reactionary hope expressed by the alliance of the conservatives with the National Socialists was evidence of how far Germany had strayed from the path to modernity. The industrial process, without the tempering influence of basic social change, had led the old order to embrace a fascist solution in a last attempt to thwart the social revolution now so long overdue.

In this attempt the conservatives badly misjudged Nazism. For Hitler's movement, despite all its promises and wooing of the old order, was emphatically not conservative. To be sure, the movement was an effective force for preventing a violent revolt of the working classes. Its xenophobic nationalism and pseudosocialist rhetoric could serve as a surrogate for the social revolution sought in a mood of growing despair by the lower urban strata. National Socialism could deflect mass discontent from the social revolution so feared by the old order. But in doing so, it would also destroy the underpinnings of that order.

This was a radical and revolutionary movement. It was revolutionary not so much because of its theoretical prescriptions, which were carefully honed to appeal to many different dissident groups. Rather it was the Nazis' quest for total power, their inability to treat any group as inviolate, their need for social self-justification, and their willingness to use new techniques of terror, manipulation, and control that were to provide the revolutionary impulses of their regime. Von Papen and the generals, Hugenberg and the business leaders of the Harzburg Front, and the indomitable Junkers, who had made Hindenburg their spokesman, helped Hitler to gain control of the state, a step of incalculable significance and profoundly revolutionary consequence. Their fear, archaic privilege, and petty self-interest helped pave the way for the revolution. The conservatives were its unwitting handmaidens. Not only did they help to undermine the republic, but it was they who enabled Hitler to come to power legally.

This route to power was a great asset for the Nazis. The image of legality permitted them to use the powers of the existing system for its own destruction. Given the legalism and respect for officials and authority in Germany, this made a great difference. Once Hitler was installed as Chancellor, he was able through swift and skillful manipulation to wrest awesome dictatorial powers from a Reichstag that no longer believed in its own capacity to govern. With these powers applied from above and the terror produced by the Nazi organizations from below, the National Socialists rapidly liquidated or restructured virtually all the institutions of the Weimar Republic.

All parties but the N.S.D.A.P. were eliminated by the summer of 1933, thereby reducing the Reichstag to a fiction and elections to a sham. The Reichsrat was abolished and the separate states, or *Länder,* brought under rigid central control, a move designed to prevent regional resistance to the authority of the new national government. Upon Hindenburg's death the offices of President and Chancellor were merged. The bureaucracy and judiciary were pruned of their more democratic elements. Similarly, the universities were swiftly purged of those faculty members who dared voice opposition to Nazi rule.

In fact there was very little opposition. This was due to several reasons. On the extreme Left, the Communists adhered to Moscow's fatal misreading of National Socialism, which saw in Nazi rule a hastening of the collapse of capitalism in Germany. As for the middle class and the farmers, the Nazis offered them extravagant promises of radical concessions. And the unions and the Social Democrats were paralyzed by fear, by inner divisions, and by preoccupation with the overwhelming economic and social consequences of the Depression. It was the unions and the Social Democrats whose failure to act was most grievous. Both recognized the Nazis for what they were. In many respects the S.P.D. and union leaders were as petty and self-interested as their conservative adversaries. This was manifest in the way in which they withdrew from the last Grand Coalition in March 1930, which felled the government of Hermann Müller, the last Social Democratic Chancellor for almost forty years. It was even more apparent in their failure to react to the arbitrary removal by Chancellor von Papen of the Prussian Social Democratic government in July 1932. With 6 million unemployed, the unions had ruled out a general strike; and the Socialist incumbents refused to defend themselves, although the entire Prussian police force would doubtless have acted loyally on their behalf. By 1933, aside from their courageous vote in the Reichstag against the Enabling Act, the Social Democrats, abetted by the political conservatism of the union leaders, were no longer able to mount an effective counter-offensive. They could only hope to survive Nazi rule by going underground, by emigrating, or by ceasing all political activity.

Nazi rule was to last much longer than most of those who failed to resist its early acts had expected. Its consolidation was extraordinarily swift and its capacity to atomize opposition unusually effective. Within a year the only remaining source of potential opposition was the army. But the army, as well as industry, did well under the new regime. Although the army's autonomy of action was circumscribed, Hitler initiated a program of vast rearmament and reintroduced mass conscription, acts which drew the support of the generals. Furthermore, the purge in 1934 of the more radical elements within the N.S.D.A.P., of its socialistic cohorts and militant revolutionaries, assuaged the army's early anxieties about the scope of the Nazi program. In this early move Hitler favored the generals against his own paramilitary S.A. leaders. It was only later that the S.S. gained supremacy over the army, or rather, within it, but by then Germany was already embarked on the road to total war.

The consolidation of Nazi rule was aided by the fact that the German economy had reached its lowest point by mid-1932 and was now on the upswing. Industrial production rose more than 20 percent in the second half of that year. This reversal in the downward trend was bound to benefit the Nazis, who, in the following year, could take credit for the recovery. The fact that recovery had begun well before the Nazis came to power was quickly forgotten. Unemployment, which had peaked in 1932, fell sharply after 1933, thereby bringing the new regime important labor support.

This improvement was also the result of Nazi economic policy. Its three foremost goals were job creation, the extension of state control, and rearmament. Unwittingly, the government practiced a kind of Keynesianism, but for reasons that had little to do with economic theory. Rather, the Nazis realized that in the absence of any socializing program labor could be placated through the creation of new jobs, an aim which served as a natural complement to the rearmament that was planned for Germany. This in turn offered major benefits to industry, which began to reachieve full production levels by 1937. Indeed, industry fared particularly well during the first four years of the Third Reich. Not only had the Nazis prevented a left-wing revolution, but they produced the conditions for increased output without confiscating any industrial assets.

Instead, the state enlarged its control over the economy. State control had always been sizable in Germany and had increased during the Depression years, when many firms and virtually the entire banking system had been rescued through state takeover. The Nazis continued this trend, however, not so much through nationalization as through stringent regulation. Planning was introduced with the aim of maximizing output and minimizing dependence on foreign trade, which had heretofore played a major role in the German economy. The results were prodigious but costly. Production increased enormously, but so did the dislocations and imbalances within the economy. Germany in the late thirties seemed to be replicating its experience in World War I, when it found itself suddenly cut off from foreign markets and sources of supply. However, this time the barriers were self-imposed, a consequence of the autarky that was sought as an inevitable part of the preparation for war.

Production doubled in the first five years of the Third Reich, primarily in the industrial sector, where massive investment and state contracts were concentrated. Consumer output, by contrast, lagged far behind. By 1938 it had risen only 16 percent above the level of ten years before, while the population had increased by almost 8 percent. The severe restrictions on imported goods meant continuing shortages of basic consumer produce, especially textiles and certain foodstuffs. While consumption suffered, so did wages. Real wages in 1938 barely exceeded the rates of a decade before, and this despite the fact that there was no unemployment but rather a labor shortage. And the stunning display successes that were ostensibly meant to benefit the working class—such as the Volkswagen and the Autobahn—were not really available to the working population at all.

In short, Nazi economic policy did not substantially raise the standard of living above the peak levels achieved in the Weimar Republic. The eminent German economist Gustav Stolper has estimated that in 1937 gross per capita income was below that of 1928. It was only by comparison with the acute depression of the early thirties that the consumer and laborer did well, but the vivid memory of that deprivation created a lower horizon of expectation and diminished pressure for a greater consumer orientation. This was a basic advantage that the Third Reich had over its predecessor, the Weimer Republic.

The emphasis on full employment, autarky, and rearmament led to inflationary developments, which brought the imposition of stringent wage-and-price controls by 1938. The methods of financing of the recovery and of the war was in no sense adequate to the task. Only through strict rationing and ceilings, and even more through the artificial segregation of the German economy from world markets, was the inflationary impact of the Nazi financial policies disguised and withheld from the German population. Without an effective market mechanism, the scarcity of labor and of raw materials in the late thirties was never efficiently resolved. There was a ruthless intraindustry competition for each, which was further exacerbated as the German armies swelled, depleting the domestic labor force.

In no sense was this a sound economy. But it was one that had come to believe in its own myths, primarily that without a successful war Germany could not prosper. In part this myth was reflected in the primitive Nazi notions about *Lebensraum* and in the romantic and irrational cult of colonial aspirations. It was institutionalized during the war, through Germany's systematic plunder of the resources of occupied territories and through its ruthless exploitation of millions of slave laborers. These were morally outrageous, stopgap measures to contend with some of the gross inefficiencies of a partially mismanaged economy. These measures were compounded by the endless rivalry among the many agencies of the state and between party and police power, all of which had important economic prerogatives.

Indeed, economic policies were always subordinate to some other, primarily political purpose in the Third Reich. For a system seeking self-sufficiency, what could be more costly than the extermination of its Jewish intelligentsia and commercial leaders? An efficient system of state labor deployment was not introduced until 1939, and the kind of tough, central planning required for the war effort was not imposed until Albert Speer, partially by accident, was charged with planning responsibility in 1942. The very success of his effort, which was startling and is often cited to refute the efficacy of the allied strategic bombing, demonstrates how poor performance in many sectors had been before.

The Nazis aspired to build an invincible war machine. They succeeded in large part because their enemies abroad failed to do anything meaningful at all until it was very late. But there was no coherent economic vision that extended beyond recovery and rearmament. As Tim Mason has put it, "the needs of the economy were determined by political decisions, principally by decisions in foreign policy, and the satisfaction of these needs was provided for by military victories."[3] Without war the economic policies of the Third Reich lacked a rationale, and without victory the Reich had no hope of any enduring success. Under these conditions the German economic recovery of the thirties was but a great sacrifice on the path to ultimate self-destruction.

The primacy of politics also prevailed in the social sector. Here Nazi efforts proved much more radical and far ranging. Social policy was based on three basic motives: First, there was the need to pulverize traditional group loyalties in order to thwart any pluralistic competition for the monopoly of power sought by the N.S.D.A.P. Second, social policies had to be designed to reintegrate atomized groups and individuals and thereby to secure their compliance, maximize output, and build solidarity for the

---

[3]T. W. Mason, "The Primacy of Politics—Politics and Economics in National Socialist Germany," in S. J. Woolf, ed., *The Nature of Fascism* (New York, 1968), p. 189.

imminent war effort. Third—and perhaps most important—it was necessary to reorganize society in such a way as to justify the position of the new elite, which was composed largely of déclassé, marginal men.

What resulted was an ambiguous complex of programs and a bizarre mixture of old and new. A comprehensive effort was initiated to level society, to break traditional ties and to replace these with new loyalties to party, state, and the Führer. The instrument of this policy was *Gleichschaltung,* or "coordination." In theory this meant that each member of society would lose his social status, regional affiliations, and religious allegiance and become equal in kind, if not in rank, with all others in the Reich. This policy was pursued not to achieve some greater egalitarian equity, but to ensure that the entire population might yield to the supreme purposes of the state and its leader. To this end an ideology of racial nationalism proved efficacious, for it excluded relatively few and yet provided sufficient pariah groups, primarily Jews and aliens, to create a sense of social differentiation between the full-fledged members of the new Reich and the outcasts.

Countless new organizations were established to replace the many that had been proscribed. Labor, women, youth, farmers, shopkeepers, indeed, virtually every segment of society was meant to be restructured. Even the most basic units of social life—the family, the church, and the school—were subjected to the sweep of radical reform. But the proliferation of new organizations and the verbiage of social transformation were deceptive. Several groups were relatively immune from this process. Businessmen, except Jews; the landed aristocracy; the civil service; and the senior army officers were not compelled to change very much so long as they allied themselves with Nazi purposes. Resistance was not tolerated, but neither was change required of all groups. The burdens of Nazi social policy were distributed very unequally. Thus, it is fair to conclude as Franz Neumann did, that National Socialism still preserved many of the features of a class society and that, in fact, the traditional, conservative classes fared a great deal better than did the others.

This was partly the result of the fact that Hitler never developed a very consistent economic and social theory. It was also the consequence of the fact that the Third Reich only lasted for twelve years and for half of this period was totally preoccupied with waging war. Indeed, contrasted with the comparatively slower pace of events in the Soviet Union or Italy, its social policies took hold with remarkable speed. But as Karl Dietrich Bracher, an outstanding scholar of National Socialism, has shown, the result was that "traditional and revolutionary elements continued to exist partly fused and partly as rivals."[4] These rivalries in turn multiplied as the new agencies established in the Reich began to compete with each other.

---

[4]Bracher, *op. cit.,* p. 235.

Foremost among them was the N.S.D.A.P. Here was a radical party composed predominately of middle and marginal strata within society and which had to justify its position as a new elite. Much of the social policy that was implemented, or at least enunciated, was intended to buttress the position of the new groups that came to power through the party. Many of these groups were composed of members from lower-middle-class backgrounds and from outlying regions within the Reich or beyond its boundaries. They were outsiders, alienated men, whose sudden success represented, as Neumann first put it, the spectacular rise of the plebian. And they were young. In 1934 65 percent of the N.S.D.A.P. members were under forty, which was the median age in the first Nazi cabinet. Hitler in 1933 was younger than John Kennedy had been at the start of his presidency.

This social group needed to justify its claims to rule the Reich. It was this purpose more than any other that defined its social policy. Basically this was a negative motivation. There was no way to explain why this particular petty bourgeois constellation of men should hold the exclusive right to rule. Unable to devise a class doctrine, it sought to identify with the largest category, the ethnic nation, and to designate society as a classless entity. The result of all this was that the Third Reich achieved what David Schoenbaum has termed "a dual structure of society." Individuals and groups moved both in their traditional worlds and in the new world forged by the Nazis. It was not so much that a new class was produced but that old ones were weakened.

Ralf Dahrendorf has argued that "National Socialism was not an historical episode but the German revolution."[5] If so, it was only a revolution in the negative sense of destroying. It was, as Hermann Rauschning has called it, "a revolution of nihilism." In the course of German history, and particularly with respect to the politics of the Federal Republic, this was a critical phenomenon. For what Hitler did was to remove many of the illiberal forces that had stood in the way of modernization and democracy in Germany.

This was at best only half a revolution. National Socialism itself was not primarily a modern movement. It retained far too many irrational, romantic, and explicitly antiindustrial themes and aims. Basic conflicts, such as the one between its agrarian ideals and its industrial performance, were never resolved. Its incredible racial policies and practices were a throwback to the most primitive level of mankind. And even if Dahrendorf is right, that "Hitler needed modernity, little as he liked it,"[6] it remains true that only through defeat, occupation, and a gradual reconstruction of

[5]Dahrendorf, *op. cit.*, p. 416.

[6]*Ibid.*, p. 404.

German political life, could modernization lead to a liberal, democratic, and pluralistic political system. If National Socialism weakened the underpinnings of the old order and hastened the process of modernization, it installed in its place a despotism that could only be removed by massive foreign intervention. It was the events after 1945 that laid the basis for a new political and social order. Through their policies and by their defeat, the Nazis, at a horrendous cost, had pulled down the foundations of authoritarianism in Germany. In a way their defeat in 1945 wiped the slate clean as the defeat of 1918 never had. For the first time since industrialization had come to Germany, there could be a new beginning.

Three

The Allied Interregnum

The new beginning in German politics occurred under conditions of extreme deprivation and adversity. The devastation wrought by the war and by the despicable racial and political practices of the Nazi regime was on a scale unprecedented in modern European history. The German extermination camps had annihilated millions of Jews and other peoples. The regime's fierce totalitarianism had forced thousands into exile, had decimated the German intelligentsia, and had destroyed the foundations of civilized life for most of its population. These twelve years of domestic holocaust and the havoc produced by a total war fought to its futile and utter end had, by 1945, consumed all the resources of the German nation and left monumental wreckage in its wake. Although the Poles and the Russians and certainly the Jews had suffered more, Germany was now the desperate victim, a broken country at its "zero hour."

Almost 4 million German soldiers had been killed in action, and perhaps half that number of their civilian compatriots had perished in the concentration camps, as victims of Allied bombing, or from want of food and medical care. Some 5 million homes had been either partially or totally destroyed, and 20 million Germans were homeless. Twelve million German soldiers were prisoners of war, and a like number of civilians were destitute and adrift—belonging to a new postwar category of "displaced persons." Germany's transportation system was virtually ruined. Five thousand railroad and motorcar bridges had been destroyed, 90 percent of German harbors were inoperative, and some 50 thousand tons of wreckage were strewn in the Rhine.

In 1946, when figures on the ravages of war were first tabulated, economic production stood at one-third the level of ten years before. Indeed, it has been estimated that no less than one-third of all the assets of Germany were consumed or destroyed during the war. And this was before Germany had even begun to bear the cost of the reparations that were to be imposed by the victors in their vain attempt to gain some indemnity for the prohibitive cost of the war. The losses in German property rights abroad totaled at least $1 billion, and the value of the goods surrendered to the Allies at the war's end (such as the remains of the German commercial fleet) or sequestered by them immediately after the war, exceeded this amount.

Human suffering was extreme. Food was in particularly short supply and was to remain so for the first two postwar years. The coalmines were barely operating and fuel was scarce. Virtually nothing remained of normal life. There were no theaters, no newspapers, and few schools or hospitals. And amid this material deprivation, those who survived suddenly experienced the frightful shock produced by the allied liberation of the concentration and death camps. The pointlessness of the war, the burden of having fought it for so long, the sudden self-elimination of the Führer and many of his cohorts, and the vengeful brutality of the invading Russian armies (whose own losses had greatly exceeded those of the Germans), combined to create a mood of abject pathos, of guilt mixed with fear, as Germany was confronted with the evident depravity of its past and the despair of its uncertain future.

This postwar situation was unlike any other in German history. The stark contrast with the events that had followed World War I was manifested in many ways, and the substantial difference between these two postwar experiences is important in explaining the subsequent fate of the political systems that emerged from them. Each system was deeply affected by the conditions prevailing at its birth, and after World War II these were to be much more fortuitous for the growth of a stable, modern, and democratic entity—at least in part of Germany.

What were these differences? First, as we have seen, the domestic devastation experienced in the second defeat far exceeded the suffering in 1918. This time the Allied victory was clearly visible. Peace had come not through surrender, but through total physical exhaustion. This meant that the impact of the last stages of the war was far greater for the civilian population, but it also precluded the acceptance of any notion of a "stab in the back," such as had grown popular in the Weimar Republic as a slogan of the Right against those who had sued for peace or signed the Treaty of Versailles at the end of World War I.

This time most Germans shared a sense of their own responsibility for the events that had brought their country the debacle of total defeat. This perception was strengthened by the sudden demise of the Nazi leadership by suicide, escape, or Allied incarceration. Not only was there no nostalgia for the old regime, but that regime itself vanished. Despite the millions who had been members of the N.S.D.A.P., hardly anyone in June 1945, believed in a continuation of Nazi rule. In 1918 many had opposed the removal of the Kaiser and subsequently had yearned for a restoration of the imperial government. But after World War II there was no comparable movement or sentiment. The Nazi experience had been too horrendous, and its restoration was too unthinkable. The fact that there was no turning back created a mood that was much more amenable to a fundamental transformation of the political system as well as an inclination to endure very substantial social and economic changes in order to ensure a new beginning.

The posttotalitarian situation was unique. Essentially, the slate had been wiped clean. The Nazi rulers had gone and had left a political vacuum at the helm. And with the removal of Admiral Doenitz and his regime by the Allies, Germany was left with no successor government. Initially, there were few indigenous claimants for the right to constitute a national regime. Nor had the many émigrés who now returned to Germany formed a government in exile. Instead, it was the Allied military commanders who now organized the new administration of Germany. The responsibility for decision making in these difficult years was to be shared with the victors. This meant that at its weakest hour, when the opportunities for any successful national political action were so severely circumscribed, no German party had alone to carry the burden of negotiating with the victorious enemy, as the Weimar coalition had been compelled to do—at great cost to its domestic image and support—in the period following 1918.

Indeed, the occupation of Germany may have been the most salient difference between the two postwar experiences. In 1945 Germany was divided into four zones of occupation. It lost substantial territory in the east, and temporarily in the west, without being asked, as it had been at Versailles, to acquiesce formally to such postwar punitive measures. In fact, it was never asked to sign a formal peace treaty; the matter was postponed time and again by Allied disagreement. This meant that the initial losses of sovereignty and terrain could to some degree be disguised as provisional, thus incurring far less outspoken German protest at the time of the losses.

The Occupation also raised the specter of the fragmentation of Germany. From the beginning each of the four powers pursued somewhat different policies in its zone and discouraged interzonal German political activity. This meant that local politics, namely the governance of the towns, the municipalities, and the states, or *Länder,* into which each zone was subdivided, became the first arena for postwar German politics. Prussia was eliminated as an entity, subdivided among several zones and shorn of its easternmost provinces, which were either ceded to the Soviet Union or transferred by unilateral Soviet action to Polish jurisdiction. If Germany was to reemerge as a national unit, the benevolent support of the occupying authorities was essential. The new German political leaders would have to cooperate with the victors and temper any nationalistic impulses, which could only inhibit Allied acquiescence to national integration. In each zone, therefore, the new local leadership sought to adapt its policies to those of the occupying power. There was no forum for a national protest movement such as characterized early Weimar politics.

The conflicts that soon emerged among the Allies created new opportunities for German political action. In contrast to 1918, there was no enduring, monolithic solidarity on the part of Germany's wartime enemies. As the Cold War developed and new international divisions superseded the wartime antagonism, German politicians were able to identify positively with the Allied power ruling their zone, thus removing themselves more rapidly from the pariah status of a vanquished enemy. Only for a year or two did all Germans share a common enmity toward all the Allies. By 1947 the division of Germany into two camps, one Soviet, the other Western, created a new belligerence that removed the immediacy of the one that had accompanied and then followed the war. Both camps became the exposed forward lines of confrontation in the Cold War, and in that context each found itself the object of new Allied priorities in which each government sought to consolidate that part of Germany in its domain, rather than to weaken and punish it further. The primacy of anticommunism in the West and of preventing further Soviet encroachment in Europe created the conditions for the emergence of a West German entity that would soon find itself embraced as an ally by the very powers that occupied it. If the Occupation served as a kind of catharsis, the Cold War brought the opportunity for swift reacceptance by the Western Allies of their German charges.

The process was facilitated by the rather enlightened policies pursued by the Western occupying powers. The brunt of the Allied denazification proceedings and reparation measures was borne immediately after the war. Germany was spared the continuous and prolonged negotiation with the Allies over its reparations debt that had so deeply undermined the capacity of the Weimar regimes to construct a credible foreign or financial policy. The bulk of its payment agreements, including the unprecedented commitment to render restitution and indemnification to its Jewish and other civilian victims, were promulgated after the German economy had begun to recover its strength in the 1950s. Further jurisdiction for denazification was passed on to German authorities by the Allies in the late forties, although here, perhaps, the resulting postponement and somewhat dilatory prosecution were less commendable.

But even in the first years after the war, when harsh measures were imposed by the Allies, they were the dictates of an occupying authority, responsibility for which did not have to be shared by an indigenous government. It was far better to press hard in the beginning, when German perceptions of their own responsibility for the evils of the war and the Nazi system were still fresh and when the Germans' desire to repudiate their own past was still strong, than to adhere to a sustained policy of punishment and retribution over a long period. And by imposing severe measures at the outset, the Allies facilitated a restructuring of German political life, which was vital for the success of the political system that developed in the years that followed.

The Cold War

Originally, there was broad agreement among the Allies on the nature and purposes of postwar policy in Germany. The wartime terms were quite unsparing. At Casablanca, Roosevelt enunciated the Allied aim of seeking an unconditional German surrender. Several months later, at Quebec, he secured Churchill's reluctant acceptance of the punitive measures envisaged in the Morgenthau Plan (named for the United States Secretary of the Treasury), which did not, it should be said, have the support of the foremost German experts in the Roosevelt administration. Under this plan German industry would have been substantially dismantled and the country would have reverted to an agricultural economy, the hope being that economic impotence would ensure its future political docility. This rigid anti-German sentiment found expression in the initial decrees of the American military command, especially in the basic document of the early Occupation, Joint Chiefs-of-Staff Directive (J.C.S.) 1067. The British never fully shared this view, although the concept of a Europe free of German industrial competition was not unattractive to them. Soviet policy sought to combine three aims: to obtain maximum territorial and industrial reparations, to keep Germany permanently weak, and to further pro-Soviet and Communist forces within Germany as a whole. Except for the last of these, the French position did not differ substantially from that of the Soviet Union when, in 1945, France was finally invited to join the tripartite European Advisory Commission that was to make policy for postwar Germany.

Each of the Allies obtained a separate zone of occupation. After the territorial losses in the east, the placing of the Saar under French administration, and the separation of Austria, what remained of Germany was divided four ways. The French zone, which was belatedly carved out of the territory earmarked for United States occupation, was far smaller than the others but directly contiguous and, therefore, more vital, to France. Each Allied military command was supreme within its own zone, but initially, mainly at Soviet insistence, some effort was made to promote a central administration. This was to be overseen by the Allied Control Commission, which was to deal with problems affecting Germany as a whole and with the administration of Berlin, which was itself subdivided into four Allied sectors.

But it was soon clear that no central political authority was to govern Germany. Once the war ended, the Allies quickly lost their common approach to the problem of Germany. The French held out from the start against any unitary regime that might hasten the rebuilding of a powerful Germany and jeopardize as well the eventual absorption by France of the Saar region. A series of unilateral Soviet actions in Germany and Eastern Europe led the United States to a swift departure from the spirit of Yalta. At the Yalta Conference, the Soviet Union had been assured of sweeping territorial gains in Eastern Europe. But even before the war ended, in April 1945, the Russians announced a unilateral pact with the newly imposed Polish Communist regime, ceding to it the administration of the territory to the east of the western Neisse River, which contained some 26,000 square miles and a German population of over 3 million. This act, which remained a subject of controversy for years, was vigorously protested by the Western Allies. It was a harbinger of the discord and distrust that was soon to come.

By the time of the Potsdam Conference, in the summer of 1945, disagreement among the Allies was already manifest. Although the four Allies still agreed to pursue a common policy, each adopted its own priorities in its zone of occupation. The Soviets moved swiftly to institute wide-ranging economic reforms, to extract maximum reparations, and to structure the reemergence of local German politics in their zone in such a way as to favor the pro-Communist forces. These events, combined with the pattern of Soviet policies elsewhere in Eastern Europe, quickly caused the United States to alter its approach in Germany. The views of the men in the field —of General Lucius Clay and his advisers Robert Murphy, Lewis Douglas, William Draper and others—began to prevail over those of the Washington officials who had devised the first plans for the Occupation. Two factors fed the revision of American policy. First, there was the mounting concern about Soviet actions and intentions. Second, there was the dire economic and financial condition of Germany. The notion that Europe might again become strong while Germany, at its heart but at the same time the exposed flank of the western camp facing a Soviet-dominated East, remained weak did not seem realistic. Thus it was not long before the severe tone of American policy toward Germany was tempered. Within the first year of the Occupation, concern for the economic rehabilitation of Germany, or at least its western zones, began to replace the punitive and debilitating spirit of the first postwar plans. General Clay lost little time in suspending the delivery of reparations from the American zone to the Soviets. And his administration undertook effective steps to create the conditions for a more stable development in the western zones.

This change of policy was matched, as much as it was provoked, by Soviet actions in its zone of occupation. The Soviets pressed on with basic land reform and nationalization of industry and with a harsh program of industrial disarmament. Some 1400 factories were dismantled and their equipment shipped east to the U.S.S.R. Within three years of the end of the war less than 40 percent of the means of production in the Soviet zone were left in private hands. This course was unacceptable, for both ideological and political reasons, to the Western Allies. So was the Soviet-dictated subjugation of the non-Communist political parties in the eastern zone. The events in Hungary, Poland, and, subsequently, Czechoslovakia, were ample evidence of Soviet unwillingness to tolerate the evolution of free democratic political movements in Soviet-occupied Europe. This pattern, above all, convinced the Western Allies to change course in their German policy: to rebuild and defend their zones, thereby forestalling the further expansion of Soviet influence and potential control into Western Europe.

The conflict that was developing among the Allies was reflected in the growing disagreement at the several conferences on Germany that convened during 1947. The meeting of foreign ministers in Moscow in March of that year registered the hopelessness of achieving any economic unity among the four zones, let alone political cooperation. By December, when the ministers met again in Moscow, the division of Germany into two camps seemed imminent. And, indeed, it was. Within three months the Soviet representatives had left the Allied Control Commission. With the introduction of a single currency in the three western zones in June 1948, the rupture was irreparable. The Soviets responded with the blockade of Berlin, which was located without adequate access agreements deep within the Soviet zone, and began to lay the foundations for a separate state, the German Democratic Republic, which was proclaimed a year later.

These developments strengthened the determination of the Western Allies to establish a single entity comprising their three zones. Initially, the French were reluctant to adopt this course of action, fearful of any central German authority that might again become a power on the European continent. It was only when the French fear of the Soviet threat became greater than its fear of Germany that Paris acceded to the Anglo-American plans to press on with a coordinated policy encompassing each of the three western zones. By 1948 this process had gained powerful momentum.

Reemergence of German Politics

The reconstruction of German politics had begun at the local level. Local authorities were established in 1945 in the towns and municipalities and at the county and district level. But the key entities for German political administration became the states, or *Länder,* into which each of the zones of occupation was divided. Their boundaries, except in the cases of Bavaria in the south and the city-states of Hamburg and Bremen in the north, had little historical or cultural continuity with the past. On the whole they were rather artificial creations, but they soon gained a vested and enduring stake in their own continuance. There were four *Länder* under American occupation, three in the south (Bavaria, Württemberg-Baden, and Hesse) and one, the port city of Bremen, in the north. Together they contained some 17 million people, which was also the population of the Soviet zone in the east. The British zone was larger and potentially more wealthy. To promote inter-Allied harmony and as a concession for British acceptance of the Morgenthau Plan at Quebec, the Americans had reluctantly allocated the more populous and industrial northern zone, including the Ruhr, to England. Here, too, there were to be four *Länder,* descending from the agricultural border area of Schleswig-Holstein in the north, through Lower Saxony and the city-state of Hamburg, to the giant industrial *Land* of North Rhine-Westphalia in the south. These areas had a combined population of some 22 million Germans.

The French zone, carved out at a later date during the war, was smaller than these, containing far less territory and a population of only 6 million. Here the *Land* boundaries separating Rhineland-Palatinate, South Baden, and Württemberg-Hohenzollern were highly arbitrary and artificial. Indeed, the entire southeastern subdivision of the old states of Baden and Württemberg made relatively little sense and was to be a source of some difficulty and of subsequent revision in the years ahead. But perhaps most significant for the French was the hope of absorbing the Saar, with its vast coal resources, into France. The administration of the Saar had been a subject of prolonged and bitter dispute between France and Germany after World War I. This time the French were encouraged to believe that the permanent economic union of the Saar with France would be a safe final solution to this thorny but vital problem. In fact, the population of the Saar initially, in 1947, voted to favor such economic union, a move that helped to forestall punitive industrial measures by the French occupying forces. But this was to be only a provisional arrangement. In time the Saar became subject to the international agreements relating to coal and steel production in western Europe; and by the mid-fifties it was returned to West Germany, in accord with the changed preference of its people and with the benevolent acquiescence of the French.

German *Länder* governments were quickly organized in 1945 and 1946 in the western zones of occupation. The Minister-Presidents, or governors, who were at first appointed and then elected in the *Länder,* played an important role in the reorganization of German politics in the postwar period. Figures such as Fritz Schäffer and Hans Ehard in Bavaria, Rheinhold Maier in Baden, Wilhelm Kaisen in Bremen, Hinrich Kopf in Lower Saxony, and Karl Arnold in the largest *Land,* North Rhine-Westphalia, had a significant and lasting impact on the shape of political life and the definition of the political system that emerged in the West. The Americans and British pressed on in 1946 to establish the first zonal German authorities, the *Länderrat* in Stuttgart in the United States zone and the *Zonenbeirat* in Hamburg for the British occupied areas. By the end of that year, in view of the worsening economic situation in Germany, the first interzonal authority was created, the so-called Bizonia, whose jurisdiction extended over all the British- and American-occupied territories, except for Berlin.

The Bizonia, or United Economic Region, as it was officially called, was soon to serve as a kind of German quasi-government, with several institutions of its own, including, by 1948, an Economic Council, an indirectly elected *Länderrat,* a High Court and a Central Bank. At first its jurisdiction was to be limited to social, economic, and financial issues, and its legislation, like all laws promulgated in occupied Germany, was binding only upon Allied approval. Although the French still opposed the establishment of authentic, indigenous zonal authorities—let alone interzonal ones—the Bizonia was in fact the real predecessor of the Federal Republic, which was proclaimed, with French agreement, in the summer of 1949.

The Allied powers also encouraged the development of nonfascist German political parties. With the collapse of the Third Reich, the S.P.D., many of whose leaders had been in exile or imprisoned in the Nazi camps, at once reestablished itself. So did the Communists, the K.P.D., whose leadership returned from Moscow and began to organize throughout Germany, but with greatest effect in the Soviet zone. Fragments of the old Center party, which had been strong in Catholic areas before 1933, became active and began to combine with other liberal and conservative forces to launch a new party, the Christian Democratic Union, or C.D.U., whose structure remained highly centrifugal and federal, varying in composition and policy from *Land* to *Land* and from zone to zone. In Bavaria, the first of the *Länder* to organize a government and the *Land* with the strongest sense of its own past, the party took a different name, the Christian Social Union, or C.S.U., and a separate organization, a distinction that has continued to this day. Christian Democracy, with its stress on social concerns, was a novel product of World War II, which created such great human suffering in Germany and elsewhere that a concept of social reconstruction in place of individualistic priorities held wide appeal. Indeed, Christianity was one of the few credos to survive totalitarianism and war in Germany, and the early debates within the C.D.U. suggest how far toward a collectivist ethic thinking in Germany had moved.

For the future of these parties and the many smaller ones that emerged, the growing division in occupied Germany and the constraints imposed by the Soviet Union on democratic processes in its zone were of great significance. Following the Communist electoral setbacks in Hungary and Austria in 1945, the Soviets forced an amalgamation of the S.P.D. and the K.P.D., doubtless fearing that the popularity of the former would totally overshadow and outdistance the appeal of communism in Germany. In the October 1946 Berlin elections, the last to be carried out on a city-wide basis, the new, merged Socialist Unity Party (S.E.D.), which was Communist-dominated, secured less than one-fifth of the vote. Even in the old Communist stronghold of Wedding, where the K.P.D. had gained 60 percent of the vote in 1932, the new S.E.D. obtained less than 30 percent in 1946. This only strengthened the Soviet intention to suspend the free electoral process. And although the noncommunist parties continued to be officially sanctioned in the Soviet zone, the occupying government made certain that no party would be in a position to challenge the primacy of the S.E.D. in that zone.

This meant not only that free elections and a democratic political process would be barred from the Soviet zone. It also meant that the postwar S.P.D. was to lose a very large part of its former constituency, for its strength before 1933 had been concentrated in many areas that were now under Soviet rule. Prussia, for example, had been predominately Protestant, and a stronghold of socialism. For the new Christian Democratic movement the divison would also be significant. Many of its most liberal and progressive figures, such as Jakob Kaiser and Ernst Lemmer, had their base in the eastern zone, which was lost to them after 1947. The result was that more pro-Western, traditional, and socially conservative forces within the C.D.U., perhaps best personified by the remarkable Konrad Adenauer, were able to firm their grip on the party and found themselves the beneficiaries of the partitioning of Germany. The removal of the Soviet zone meant that the political arena for the C.D.U. in what remained of western Germany would contain a substantially higher percentage of Catholics than had any single German state since unification. Also, the partition that grew from the Cold War was bound to reward those political leaders who espoused a more outspokenly pro-Western policy. No figure was to conform better to Western needs and aspirations than Adenauer himself, as did the party that he forged so much in his own image.

By 1948 the Western powers had resolved to establish a West German state. From February to June of that year representatives of the three Western Allies and the three Benelux countries met in London despite vigorous Soviet protests. The six-power conference initially planned to improve Bizonia and to seek effective French cooperation with it. But in view of the worsening East-West relations, the conference went much further. In the end it recommended measures to further European economic integration and to found a West German state. In addition, it called for an International Control Authority for the Ruhr and for stringent military controls to minimize the fears of the French and the Benelux countries regarding the potential resurgence of German power.

The west German Minister-Presidents and the mayors of Bremen and Hamburg were called upon to convene a Constituent Assembly to draft a constitution for the new state. Initially they were somewhat reluctant to do this, fearing that such action would perpetuate the divison of Germany. A compromise formula was struck. The German body was termed a Parliamentary Council, with its purpose defined as that of drafting a Basic Law, which sounded less permanent than a constitution. Like so much else that characterized the birth of the new state, such gestures to its ostensibly provisional nature were intended to assuage the opposition of those who still hoped that Germany might remain undivided.

The membership of the Parliamentary Council comprised sixty-five delegates from the eleven *Länder,* each elected indirectly by the several *Landtage* or *Bürgerschaften,* which were the supreme legislative and electoral organs in each *Land.* Berlin, whose status was to remain special, was entitled to send five observers. It was in this body that the first parliamentary parties were formed. The S.P.D., which was more effectively organized on an interzonal basis, and the C.D.U.-C.S.U., which remained more federal in structure, each had twenty-seven delegates. The liberals were represented by five members, and three smaller parties, including the Communists, had two apiece. At the first meeting of the Parliamentary Council, on September 1, 1948, Adenauer, the chairman of the C.D.U., was elected president of the council.

The deliberations of the Parliamentary Council, which met in Bonn for many months, were long and often heated. The terms of the Basic Law that it drafted with Allied counsel and approval laid the foundations for the new state that was soon to be proclaimed. On the whole, the document and the process that produced it were remarkably successful. In contrast to the proceedings in 1919, the legal framework for the new republic was laid with greater deliberation and under far less disruptive domestic conditions. To be sure, there were forces within Germany that remained disappointed with the structure devised for the new state. Indeed, for substantially different reasons, two *Länder,* Bavaria and Lower Saxony, initially did not want to ratify the document. But once their protest had been registered, they, too, acquiesced, for this was the path toward the regaining of German sovereignty. Here was a basic difference from the constitutional process of the Weimar Republic. In 1949 there was little scope for a nationalist outcry against the constitutional movement toward a new republic. National self-assertion for Germany meant one of two choices:

Either it would respond positively to the opportunity to participate in the establishment of a new West German state, no matter how limited its sovereignty or how unsatisfactory its structure; or it could seek a political framework for Germany as a whole. The latter meant cooperation with the Soviets. And in the wake of all that had happened in the Soviet zone and in Eastern Europe and in the aftermath of the Berlin blockade, this course was not readily available to West German politicians, however much some might have preferred it. West Germany would either remake itself in the image of, and under the continued tutelage of, the Western powers, or it would remain weak and without an effective voice in its own future.

And so it was that sovereignty began to flow back to Germany—but to a Germany that was to remain divided. The Basic Law was promulgated in May 1949. Elections for the first parliament were held that summer, and a cabinet was established, headed by Konrad Adenauer, in mid-September. With the formal establishment of this government, Allied military administration of West Germany formally came to an end. To be sure, the Western powers reserved for themselves very extensive rights with regard to essential German affairs. It would take years before the new republic could manage its own foreign policy, and even then, only under major constraints that remained as consequences of its curious birth. But the conditions at the time of the establishment of the new regime were auspicious in at least one respect. The Allies, who had been the bitter wartime enemies of Germany, stood prepared to embrace this new political entity. This was an advantage that had not been available to the Weimar Republic in its early years, much to its subsequent detriment.

The establishment of the Federal Republic came at a timely moment in history. The Cold War had divided Europe, but brought its Western components closer together. European integration and the muting of national antagonisms provided Germany with a great opportunity. So did the task of domestic reconstruction. The worst years of German economic and social upheaval had passed. They had been endured under occupation. Conditions within Germany at the time the new regime assumed power were still dismal and onerous; the point of departure by which its success would be measured stood at a very depressed level. Thus the strength of Germany's recovery would seem all the greater compared with the abject misery of the postwar years, years in which there was no national German government to share the responsibility for the harsh conditions within the country. The Allies had carried the burden during these difficult years. After four years of Allied rule, 1949 was a fortuitous year for the Germans once again to begin to manage their own national affairs.

What happened in West Germany was replicated in the Soviet zone. Here, too, a provisional constitution was drafted. Controlled elections were held and a separate state, the German Democratic Republic, was proclaimed in the summer of 1949. But this was a highly artificial construction, far more the product of Soviet will than of any authentic indigenous political process.

The division of Germany was a consequence of Hitlerism and a lost war as well as a reflection of the starkly transformed political and military situation in Europe. Although this division was untoward, it facilitated the task for the West German leadership of regaining acceptance abroad. A divided Germany was weaker than a unified nation and, therefore, the source of less fear and resentment on the part of its western neighbors. The existence of the German Democratic Republic was also to serve a useful purpose, for it was to become the prime target of the animosity of the Western powers. If the G.D.R. represented the "bad" Germany, then the government in Bonn could far more easily find acceptance as the "good" Germany, a role which became all the more available to it as the Cold War intensified.

All this created unusual opportunities for Adenauer. This extraordinary and venerable figure, who had first been a contender for the German chancellorship in 1921, saw and seized these opportunities and thereby greatly expedited both the acceptance of the Federal Republic by the Western Allies and their relinquishing to it of many of the powers that they still retained in 1949. Although Adenauer stood as a singular symbol of the continuity of the new Germany with elements of the past, his tenure did not signify a restoration of the old groups. For much had changed in West Germany, especially during the Occupation. The social bases of politics and the ideological setting in which the political system evolved had been basically transformed. The years of defeat and the Allied interregnum had furthered the social revolution in Germany. The many obstacles that had stood in the way of social modernization had receded as a result of Germany's experiences during these years. What had begun during Hitler's pernicious rule had been substantially extended during the Occupation. Germany, at the launching of the Federal Republic, at last had the opportunity to emerge as a modern nation.

At first the Allies, and particularly the Americans, had sought a radical transformation of the socioeconomic bases of German society. This was in part the ethos and purpose of the Morgenthau Plan and J.C.S. 1067. Denazification, demilitarization, and industrial decentralization were to be the instruments through which the German elite was purged from its powerfully entrenched position. In the first two postwar years these policies were widely applied. By the end of 1946 almost 1 million individual denazification cases had been processed in the United States and British zones. All military installations, machinery, and appliances and even some civilian aircraft facilities were systematically dismantled. Most industries linked with war production were banned. The production of ocean-going ships, airplanes, heavy machine tools, synthetic rubber, aluminum and magnesium, and many other goods that had potential military application was prohibited. The level of output in many other industries was severely restricted. According to the Level of Industry Plan introduced in 1946, which represented a softening of J.C.S. 1067 in the United States zone, steel and basic chemical production was to be limited to less than one-third the output of 1938. The volume of trade was to be reduced to three-fifths of the level achieved ten years before. Many of the giant firms that still remained were broken up. The twelve largest coal and steel producers were divided into twenty-eight firms, and I.G. Farben, the mammoth chemical company, was parcelled into four separate units. Likewise, the huge banks and industrial cartels were carved up, although many of these would soon recombine.

These measures, which were invoked with stringent severity at first, were soon tempered by the unforeseen gravity of economic conditions in Germany in 1947 at a time when Soviet intentions began to be viewed with greater alarm by the Western powers. While many Socialist and anti-Nazi figures in Germany called for more basic economic reforms, including the nationalization of industry and fundamental land reform, the occupying authorities recoiled from such sweeping and ideologically unpalatable policies. As Lewis Edinger has observed, "the Western occupation powers rejected the price of such drastic changes when they resolved that economic recovery had to take precedence over 'political reconstruction'."[1]

But it was not such pragmatic considerations alone that motivated Allied moderation in the economic sphere. Ideological predilections accounted for the American vetoing of the socialization clause in the Hessian state constitution. Similarly, the American Occupation authorities blocked measures requiring labor codetermination in industrial management, even though they were supported by both the C.D.U. and the S.P.D. Ostensibly, the Americans argued, such procedures would strengthen Communist representation in German factories and would excessively hamper management. In fact, they smacked too much of socialism for the Americans to accept. It was only in the British zone, which was, to be sure, the industrial heartland of western Germany, that such social and industrial innovations made some headway, securing the benevolent, if limited, support of the Labour government in England.

The Western powers sought to break the power of the old groups, but not to institutionalize socialist experiments. They rejected any extensive redistribution of property in their zones. Land reform was never seriously attempted. This was not so critical in the West, because the large estates were located primarily in the Soviet zone or east of the Oder-Neisse boundary, under Polish or Soviet rule. The division of Germany and the

[1]Lewis J. Edinger, "Post-Totalitarian Leadership: Elites in the German Federal Republic," *American Political Science Review,* 54, 1, 1960, p. 77.

radical land reform instituted in 1945 by the Russians had eliminated the Junkers as a force in German politics. But even under Hitler they had hardly played a role. The day of landed feudal politics had already passed in Germany.

While economic reforms fell far short of a basic transformation of the system in western Germany, social change in the years of occupation ranged quite far. This was partly the result of a deliberate Allied policy to reconstitute a democratic, posttotalitarian elite. This was a kind of "artificial revolution," an exercise in controlled revolutionary change. Its impact was most substantial among the political elite. The entire higher echelon of German government, first at the *Land* level and later at the federal level, was totally restructured. The new government and party leadership was partially recruited from among figures who had entered politics in the Weimar Republic only to withdraw or emigrate after 1933. But most of its members had entered political life for the first time in the postwar period. Only 6 percent of the members of the first Bundestag, the lower federal house elected in 1949, had sat in the Reichstag before 1933, whereas well over 40 percent had served in the Bizonia economic council or in the Parliamentary Council that drafted the Basic Law.

The recruitment of a new political elite was matched by the new leadership, part of which returned from exile, in the trade unions and in the higher tiers of the postwar civil service. For much of the bureaurcracy this restructuring meant only a temporary occupational displacement, but even so, the regaining of old positions often required a frank repudiation of any previous antidemocratic sentiments. As Wolfgang Zapf, an eminent German sociologist, has shown, the general turnover in the West German elite structure was far greater during the 1945–1949 period than in either 1919 or 1933. To be sure, there were sectors that had relative immunity. One was the church leadership, which had remained rather apolitical; another, curiously, was the very highest level of big business, where, despite the prosecution of Krupp and Flick at Nuremberg, substantial continuity of ownership was maintained, reflecting the American predilection for private property and the priority attached to economic recovery, which complicated any commitment to reallocate industrial resources.

But the overall pattern was highly significant. Hitler and the Occupation together eradicated the grip of the old, preindustrial groups on German society and politics. The experience of Fascist dictatorship and war had made right-wing, antidemocratic politics an unattractive, indeed, a hopeless, option in postwar Germany. Totalitarianism followed by defeat had largely leveled society. The Occupation removed many among the remaining elite. Gradually, as German politics reemerged, great opportunities became available for those who sought to enter politics. The sudden rise of political newcomers was facilitated by the policies of the Allied interregnum. Through the effect of Allied policies Germans really were "forced to be free," as John Montgomery, the American political scientist, has shown. In many ways this phenomenon was a byproduct of other aims. John Gimbel has argued "that the politics of the American occupation were governed largely by a range of interests rather than by the attempt to democratize Germany."[2] These interests included anticommunism, the effort to reduce Occupation costs, cooperation with the French, the defense of free enterprise, and containment of the Soviet Union.

But nonetheless, the Western Allies did lay the foundations for a democratic political process. They did this in part by assuming responsibility for the governance of Germany in its worst and weakest hour and then by gradually nurturing the rebirth of German political life and the structuring of stable institutions conducive to a democratic process. Their economic measures were half-hearted and often inconsistent, their social revolution artificial, but sweeping in its impact. Without the Occupation the development of a new national government would have been far more painful and contentious. Despite the many mistakes and missed opportunities of this period, Germany was given a chance to refind itself after the horrors of Hitlerism and the war. Psychologically, it had been shaken by the Fascist experience from its propensity to substitute authoritarianism for individual freedom; economically, it had been leveled by defeat; and socially, it had been substantially reshaped during the Occupation. The four years of Allied rule were critical for the new beginning which found its constitutional expression and institutional form in the Basic Law and the establishment of a federal government in 1949, thirty tumultuous years after republicanism and revolution had first been attempted in Germany.

[2]John Gimbel, *The American Occupation of Germany* (Stanford, 1968), p. 249.

Four

The Constitutional Order

The political institutions of the Federal Republic appear to have functioned remarkably well over the past two decades. In part this was the result of the fact that the most difficult decisions were all made before the republic was established. As Alfred Grosser has suggested, "when the new state was born, the period of dramatic changes was already over."[1] This was in sharp contrast to the experience of the Weimar Republic, which had to confront the most painful choices during its very first years and which emerged from this process weak and divided. Indeed, the example of Weimar and of the bitter disputes that accompanied its birth helped to shape a much more stable and balanced system in 1949.

The drafting of the Basic Law and the founding of the new state were highly deliberate and relatively harmonious processes. Several factors were conducive to promoting a broad consensus in place of the debilitating discord that prevailed in 1919. First, the constitutional process promised to restore substantial sovereignty to German institutions. This served as a powerful incentive for consensus among the competing aspirants and groups in the German political arena after 1945. For the restoration of sovereignty required Allied acquiescence, which, in turn, depended upon some fundamental agreement among those German representatives who participated in the drafting and ratification of the Basic Law.

[1]Alfred Grosser, *Germany in Our Time* (New York, 1971), p. 77.

Many Germans may have felt reluctant to participate in a process that would restore limited sovereignty to only a part of postwar Germany, leaving it permanently truncated and divided. To minimize this possibility, the constitutional vocabulary emphasized the provisional nature of the document. Its preamble clearly stated that the Basic Law was "to give a new order to political life for a transitional period" and further stipulated that the Parliamentary Council had "also acted on behalf of those Germans to whom participation was denied," namely, those in the Soviet zone.

In addition, through the Occupation Statute, which came into effect simultaneously with the Basic Law, the three Western Allies reserved for themselves extensive rights and responsibilities. This meant, on the one hand, that the prospect of reunification could be kept alive, while on the other hand, important incentives were maintained for the new German government to continue to seek cooperation with the West in order to regain the many residual powers that the Allies retained. All this helped to broaden support for the new constitutional order.

Curiously, the legitimacy of the new regime was never substantially challenged. The Parliamentary Council had only been indirectly elected. Authority had devolved on the new German government more from above, that is, from the Allied Occupation, than from a clear electoral mandate. But this had its advantages, for it meant that many of the basic issues that defined the nature of the new system could be removed in the beginning from the potentially contentious arena of electoral politics. And because an agreement with the Soviet-controlled eastern zone was regarded as an unappealing and unrealistic alternative by most West Germans in 1949, the course of cooperation with the Western Allies seemed natural and desirable, and, therefore, more legitimate. When it was challenged in subsequent years by some of the S.P.D. opposition, the German government was always able to point to its further gains in authority and jurisdiction, which the Allies swiftly increased in the period after 1949. It proved difficult and unrewarding to rouse electoral sentiment against a process that continued to restore vital powers to the West German state. The early nationalism of the Left, which sought reunification in place of the Western alliance, was thus undermined by the growing national power of the German government that it opposed. This meant that, in contrast to the situation in 1919, it was not possible to foment national aspirations in an anti-Western direction and thereby question the legitimacy of the new regime.

Other factors helped firm the legitimacy of the new state. This time there was no nostalgia for an old order. This meant that the new system, no matter what its faults, was not subject to attack from quarters, primarily on the Right, that sought the restoration of an *ancien régime*. Second, although many of the figures who shared in the launching of the Federal

Republic were relatively new to political life, most of them were imbued with a vivid sense of the institutional weakness of the constitution that had been drafted thirty years before. It was as though "the specter of Weimar stood at the cradle of the Bonn Basic Law."[2] So did that of the Third Reich. Thus there was a very explicit effort to forge institutions that would be free from the failings of the Weimar system and to codify individual rights that would prevent the abuses of a dictatorial regime. There was little outright euphoria over democracy or republicanism as such, but rather a prudent awareness of their potential deficiencies. This cautiousness created a much more sober and enlightened atmosphere for the drafting of the Basic Law and served to scale down expectations, which, in turn, meant less disappointment of the sort that could be channeled into antisystem opposition.

The Basic Law

The greatest shortcoming of the Weimar institutions was their vulnerability to breakdown under conditions of stress and internal discord. Rather than building consensus and ensuring stable government, the Weimar constitution extended ostensibly democratic prerogatives that actually undermined effective parliamentary government. The Basic Law sought to remedy this defect.[3] It strengthened the role of parliament, especially in its capacity to produce government-sustaining majorities, and it substantially enhanced the authority of the Chancellor and his cabinet. The broad powers of the presidency and of the mass plebiscites that afflicted the later years of the first republic were sharply reduced. Essentially, the practice of continuous, direct democracy, which had been enshrined in so many ways in the 1919 constitution, was now blunted. In the Federal Republic the national electorate would, barring unusual circumstances, go to the polls only once every four years and then only to elect its parliamentary representatives. All other elections, either for Chancellor or President, would be indirect. And given the considerable difficulty and, therefore, unlikelihood of midsession parliamentary dissolutions, the elimination of frequent referenda, and the absence of by-elections, the voter would not again be asked to express his direct preference within the four-year interval, except at the local and *Land* levels—and the effect of those elections on national politics would remain somewhat muted.

While the direct expression of the voter was thus reduced by the Basic Law, the individual rights of the citizen were enumerated with great care.

[2]Friedrich Karl Fromme, *Von der Weimarer Verfassung zum Bonner Grundgesetz* (Tübingen, 1960), p. 210.

[3]For a text of the Basic Law see Appendix C.

Here the relevant historical experience was that of the Third Reich, with its oppressive flaunting of all human liberties. The first nineteen articles of the Basic Law precisely state the fundamental and inalienable rights of the German citizen. Many of them enunciate rights that were grossly abused by the Nazis. Any form of national, religious, racial, or sexual discrimination is proscribed (Articles 3 and 4). The extradition of German citizens to foreign countries is prohibited, and the withdrawal of citizenship is ruled out when such loss would result in a German's becoming stateless (Article 16). Freedom of speech, movement, assembly, and association are guaranteed, except where they might be abused "in order to attack the free democratic order." In such a case their suspension requires an affirmative ruling of the Federal Constitutional Court (Article 18).

The Basic Law has undergone frequent and substantial revision since 1949. It can be, and has been, amended by a two-thirds majority of both houses of the federal parliament. However, the fundamental principles relating to the dignity of man and the democratic constitutional order guaranteed in Articles 1 and 20 may not be amended. These provisions, drafted with a memory of the iniquitous abuses of the Third Reich, are designed to reinforce the right of the individual to live in a free and democratic political system. Indeed, Article 20 provides that "all Germans shall have the right to resist any person or persons seeking to abolish that constitutional order, should no other remedy be possible."

The articles of the Weimar constitution relating to religious freedom are included as an appendix to the Basic Law. These guarantee freedom of association to form religious bodies and protection against discrimination for reasons of creed, and they prohibit a state church. Article 102 of the Basic Law has also abolished capital punishment. Article 4 specifically affirms the right of conscientious objection to military service. The document is, in fact, a very explicit and liberal statement, extending generous civil rights to every West German citizen.

Citizenship itself is defined in terms which take into account the special political problems of the Federal Republic. According to Article 116, the right of citizenship applies to any person "who has been admitted to the territory of the German Reich within the frontiers of 31 December 1937 as a refugee or expellee of German stock . . . or as the spouse or descendant of such person." Also, those who were deprived of their citizenship during the Third Reich are automatically deemed citizens if they reside in the Federal Republic, or they may apply to become such if they reside abroad. This has made it possible for the large stream of refugees and expellees who entered the Federal Republic since 1945 to become citizens without delay. It also holds open this right to the population of the German Democratic Republic (G.D.R.). In fact, the people of East Germany are given an explicit right to affirm a more permanent constitution. The very last article of the Basic Law decrees that its jurisidiction will cease "on the day on which a constitution adopted by a free decision of the German people comes into force." However, developments since 1949, when this clause was drafted, suggest that such a day is unlikely to come and that the Basic Law is to remain the enduring constitution of the Federal Republic.

The Judicial and Legal System

The Federal Constitutional Court is a major new innovation of the Federal Republic. It serves as the guardian of citizens' rights, as the arbiter of the federal system, and as the ultimate judge of the constitutionality of parliamentary legislation and acts of government and of the democratic legality of German political parties. No similar institution exists in Britain or in France, nor did the Weimar Republic have an equivalent body. Its Federal Constitutional Tribunal remained weak, intended primarily to adjudicate disputes among the *Länder* or between a *Land* government and the national regime. Yet it was precisely the conservative predilection and the often antidemocratic bias of the overall Weimar judiciary, most of which had been appointed before 1918, that helped to undermine the democratic ethos of its constitution. Political justice was a dangerous precedent in a country that traditionally ceded such awesome power to the rule and interpretation of law. And so, in 1949 an elaborate machinery was devised to create a supreme judicial body that would protect the individual rights and democratic processes that were codified in the Basic Law.

A special procedure of selection was devised for the Federal Constitutional Court. Article 94 of the Basic Law stipulates that half of the members shall be elected by the Bundestag and half by the Bundesrat, the two houses of the federal parliament. Subsequent legislation in 1951 provided that eligible candidates over forty years of age were to be selected from two lists, one containing all judges with at least three years of prior service who were willing to be nominated, the other including candidates who were proposed by the federal government, by a *Land* ministry of justice, or by one of the party groups in parliament, but restricted to nominees who were suitably trained in law. The eight members of each of the two chambers of the court would be elected from the two lists. Three would be elected from the first list to serve for life; five would be elected from the second to sit on the court for an eight-year term, after which they would remain eligible for reelection. Compared with the arbitrary process of selecting Supreme Court justices in the United States, this carefully balanced and complex procedure provides a more systematic and professional means of recruitment for the highest court.

The scope of the court's mandate for legal interpretation is quite broad. The court has been a very active participant in the shaping of the federal political system. It has made decisions in a great variety of fields. Some of its judgments have been narrow, legalistic, and merely technical. Others have had sweeping political impact, especially its two rulings in the 1950s banning the right-wing Socialist Reich party and the Communist party. It has often intervened in electoral matters when called upon to do so and can, through the rendering of advisory opinions, greatly influence the content and direction of intended legislation or government action. Judicial review in this form was previously unknown in Germany.

In addition, the court can act on constitutional complaints brought to it by German citizens. It is the body that would try the President of the Federal Republic if impeachment proceedings were brought against him by the parliament, and it would also sit in judgment on any member of a federal court accused of an impropriety by a two-thirds vote of the Bundestag. It is the arbiter of all disputes between the various organs of the Federal Republic, including those among the *Länder* or between a *Land* and the federal government.

With such wide powers, it is not surprising that the court has been subject to occasional criticism. For one thing, its operating procedure is governed by directives of parliament and its statutes have been often revised, which has created some confusion and an impression of frequent departure from established practice. Second, it has failed to impress itself on public awareness; few in Germany know the name of its president. The court has also been criticized for being too slow and secretive in its deliberations and for reviewing so few cases. The prospects for a successful hearing on a case brought by a private citizen are very dim. Only some 3.5% of the 1,500 annual complaints are actually heard. Of these, one out of three yields in a ruling in favor of the plaintiff. This is obviously not a very promising mechanism for the redress of a private grievance.

That the court has the power to rule on politically controversial issues is most significant. Given its capacity to render advisory opinions, the court has become an active, if often reluctant, participant in the political process. For example, its decision in June 1973 not to sustain the legal challenge of the state of Bavaria against the Basic Treaty between the Federal Republic and the G.D.R. clearly removed an obstacle to the foreign policy of the federal government. Rather than remain a mere legal referee, the court has assumed on occasion the role of definer of the rules of the game. As such it tends to become an important factor in the calculations of the other actors—parliament, the parties, the federal executive, and the *Länder* governments—in determining the positions that they choose to take. This might provoke controversy reminiscent of the politically biased justice characteristic of the German past, which would diminish the stature of the court as the ultimate arbiter, constitutional voice and protector of individual rights. Yet despite such criticism, the court has been a successful innovation within the federal system, so much so, that Alfred Grosser has termed it "the most noteworthy of the Federal Republic's institutions,"[4] especially when contrasted with the comparable institutions in Britain and France.

The judiciary as a whole plays a much more important role in Germany than in either of these two democracies. The German legal system is more complex and elaborate, the number of judges far greater. There are more than 13,000 professional full-time judges in the Federal Republic (of whom fewer than one thousand are women). Despite its federal structure, Germany has a single, integrated legal system. The application of law is uniform throughout the republic and does not vary among its units, in contrast to the pattern in the United States, with its parallel structures of state and federal courts.

In Germany, however, there is a dual system of a different sort separating the regular and the special courts. The regular court system for trying civil and criminal cases is organized as a single hierarchy ranging from the local and district courts at the lowest level to the Federal High Court (Bundesgerichtshof) in Karlsruhe at the apex. This high court serves as a supreme appeals court in civil and criminal cases and holds the right of original jurisdiction in matters of treason or conspiracy. Its several sections, which contain over one hundred judges, also review decisions throughout Germany in an effort to assure the uniformity of the law throughout the country, a task that the Basic Law originally intended for a special supreme federal court. Such a court has, however, never been established and the constitutional provision for it was deleted in 1968 by an amendment to the Basic Law.

The special courts are a more unusual phenomenon in Germany and derive from an old tradition. Judicial agencies to settle administrative claims against state and local governments have existed since 1872. Most of these were eliminated during the Third Reich but since 1949 have been reconstituted as administrative courts, with the Federal Administrative Court (Bundesverwaltungsgericht) established in Berlin. The special courts for finance and labor were created during the Weimar Republic. The Federal Finance Court (Bundesfinanzhof) was reestablished in 1950 in Munich, together with the Federal Labor Court (Bundesarbeitsgericht) in Kassel and the Federal Social Court (Bundessozialgericht) in Essen, the latter to deal primarily with social security and welfare disputes. Each of these heads a pyramid of lower tribunals that extends downward through the *Länder* to the district level. Judges of these high courts are appointed jointly by the appropriate federal minister and a committee for the selection of judges consisting of the competent *Land* ministers and an equal number of members elected by the Bundestag, the lower house of the

[4]Grosser, *op. cit.,* p. 92.

federal parliament. A joint panel representing these various courts sees to the preservation of uniformity of jurisdiction among them.

This maze of courts has created a host of judges—there are more than eight hundred in West Berlin alone! The procedure for their selection emphasizes special training and examination and early appointment to lifetime employment in the judiciary. This practice differs sharply from that in England and the United States, where many practicing lawyers are elevated to the bench. In Germany, law students nearing the end of their studies may opt for specialized training for the judiciary, which, together with probationary experience, may require an additional seven or eight years of preparation. Movement through the courts, from the lowest level upward, is part of career advancement. There is little room, except in the case of the Federal Constitutional Court and some of the special administrative and financial courts, for those outside the judiciary to make a late entry at a senior level.

This accounts for the special perspective of the German judiciary. In view of their numbers, judges do not find themselves in a particularly exalted position. Because of their training and civil service status, many view themselves primarily as administrators of the law. Great attention is given to technical detail and less to fundamental principles of jurisprudence. In view of the large number of lawyers in the German civil service, it is not surprising that a kind of exacting legalism, with its conservative and noninnovative implications, has characterized a good deal of government administration and judicial review.

In Germany written law has far more weight than in Britain or France. In part this is the consequence of the Germans having experienced so many different systems over the past century. Tradition and precedent may be suitable for the British legal system, but in Germany, each political system has produced legal precedents which might be highly unacceptable today. Furthermore, in view of the extraordinary abuse of legal sanctions under the Third Reich, general proscriptions of the kind found in French law, even if only rarely applied, would not be suitable in Germany's case. These historical factors help explain why German law is so explicit. It is a system in which action tends to be judged by reference to what the lawbooks actually license or forbid, rather than in an informal context of consent and restraint.

The enumeration of individual rights is, therefore, more specific and more elaborate in the German system. The Basic Law is especially precise in defining the social rights of German citizens. In part this derives from the German concept of the social-welfare state, and many of the articles have been taken directly from the Weimar constitution. According to Article 6 of the Basic Law, "marriage and the family shall enjoy the special protection of the state." It is further stated that children born out of wedlock must be provided with equal opportunities—although this clause may have reflected the special problem of postwar fraternization between the occupying armies and the indigenous population! However, it was not until 1969 that specific legislation provided for equal rights for illegitimate children.

Education falls under stringent state regulation, although the Basic Law ceded primary jurisdiction to the *Länder* governments in an effort to take into account the differing denominational concentrations in the various states. Through Article 9, the Social Democrats were able to secure their right to form trade unions and to bargain collectively. But they were less successful in pressing the cause of nationalization of land and industry. Article 14 safeguards the right to private property and severely circumscribes the state's power to expropriate it, reflecting the antisocialist attitudes of the American Occupation authorities and leading commercial and industrial forces within Germany after the war.

In 1969 Article 91a was inserted into the Basic Law in order to extend the jurisdiction of the federal government in the areas of social planning, the expansion of higher education, and the improvement of regional economic development. The Basic Law also contains rather specific obligations on the part of the state to provide indemnification and subsidies for those who are economically or otherwise deprived. In particular, war victims, refugees, and economically backward regions are entitled to government support. The concepts of social responsibility and of the state as an equalizer were injected into the Basic Law in 1949, which is not surprising, given the postwar deprivation at the time.

As a whole, the German bill of rights ranges further than comparable documents in France, England, or the United States. But then none of these countries had a totalitarian past. To be sure, some of the provisions of the Basic Law guaranteeing individual rights have been modified by amendment or by the stipulations of the German penal code. For example, Article 4 originally had banned military service, but conscription was subsequently introduced by amendment in 1956, although with very specific safeguards of citizens' rights and parliamentary control over the armed forces. And while Article 10 specifically provided for the secrecy of the mails and telecommunications, the Allied powers retained rights of censorship and wiretapping until 1968, when these were terminated (or at least transferred to German authorities) with the adoption of special emergency legislation.

The constitutional amendments dealing with a state of emergency *(Notstandsverfassung),* which were passed after some bitter debate in 1968, completed the process whereby the Western Allies surrendered their residual powers to the German government. The only rights and responsibilities retained by the Allies were those dealing with Berlin or "Germany as a whole," which is to say, reunification and a peace settlement. Revisions of the original Occupation Statute of 1949 had come swiftly. In

March 1951, the federal government was given authority to establish its own Ministry of Foreign Affairs. The entire statute was replaced by the Convention of 1955, which came into effect with German ratification of the Paris agreements of the year before and which paved the way for German participation in N.A.T.O. The Allied High Commissions were now replaced by embassies, and relations between the Federal Republic and the former occupying powers were virtually normalized.

However, the Convention of 1955 still ceded to the three powers certain rights of control and intervention, ostensibly to safeguard their armed forces on German soil, in a situation of external threat or domestic subversion. If such an emergency were to develop, the Allies were entitled to reassume many of the sovereign rights that they had yielded to the German government. The legislation of 1968 satisfied the Allies' proviso that this right of intervention should lapse once the Federal Republic had adopted satisfactory emergency measures of its own. It became a sensitive internal issue, because many groups in Germany, especially among the trade unions and the extraparliamentary opposition (which had surfaced in the late sixties), saw such legislation as being dangerously reminiscent of previous emergency provisions in the Weimar constitution, which had been all too easily abused in times of domestic stress. The legislation provided for the suspension of certain processes and rights if one of three threatening situations were to develop. In two of these, a vote of two-thirds of the members of both houses of parliament was required before special emergency measures could be invoked. It was only in the third instance, the so-called internal state of emergency *(innere Notstand),* that no formal finding of parliament was required. Since this emergency condition itself was defined in somewhat ambiguous terms, and in view of the anxiety with which German authorities and the German people tend to respond to unrest and disorder, it was this provision and its potential implications that aroused the most intense controversy. However, the new legislation did provide that even in a state of declared emergency the critical role of the Federal Constitutional Court would not be impaired, and should parliament not be able to assemble for reasons of external attack or internal danger, the role of the two houses would be exercised by a standing Joint Committee composed of eleven members from each body.

An important incentive for the passage of the emergency amendments was the suspension of the continued Allied right of intervention. Once this had occurred, the Western Allies retained for themselves only the special rights and responsibilities relating to Berlin and Germany as a whole, including the unification of Germany and the peace settlement, which had been included as Article 5 of the Convention of 1955. While there has been little movement toward German unification, the status of Berlin has changed substantially over time, emerging as an anomaly in the present-day German system.

Berlin

Fundamentally, the division of Berlin was effected, although not formally recognized by the Allied powers, by the end of 1948. In view of this development, the Parliamentary Council clearly intended to incorporate West Berlin as a full-fledged *Land* into the Federal Republic. Because of the complex problems of access to the city, located deep within the Soviet zone of occupation, the Western Allies were eager to give emphasis to their own continued jurisdiction over the city. For this reason they took steps to discourage or prevent the unqualified inclusion of West Berlin within the new federation. While Article 23 of the Basic Law listed greater Berlin as a *Land,* the Allies vetoed paragraphs 2 and 3 of the first article of the Berlin constitution of 1950, which provided that "Berlin is a Land of the Federal Republic of Germany" and that "the Basic Law and other legislation of the Federal Republic of Germany applies to Berlin."

This meant that federal law could not be applied automatically in West Berlin, but had, in effect, to be adopted by special enactment. Since 1952, according to special legislative procedures approved by the three Allies, federal laws have generally been ratified by the Berlin assembly. However, the special emergency legislation passed in Bonn in 1968 is not applicable to West Berlin. Neither is the provision for military conscription introduced elsewhere in the federation in 1956.

Elections to the lower house of the federal parliament, the Bundestag, have not been held in West Berlin as elsewhere. Instead the city is represented by a delegation indirectly elected by the Berlin assembly, as though this special provision would somehow diminish the formal linkage between the city and the institutions of the Federal Republic. Furthermore, the Allies ruled initially, and again as recently as 1969, that the twenty-two Berlin delegates in the Bundestag could not participate in the election of the Chancellor, although they could cast full and equal votes in the federal convention which elects the President of the Federal Republic.

Yet in virtually all other respects West Berlin is fully integrated into the federal system. Its delegates to both houses of parliament may vote in their committees as full members and cast advisory votes in plenary sessions; these votes are counted separately and are not binding. They also participate in the election of the officers of both chambers and may serve as such. In 1972 a Berlin deputy, Marie Schlei, was discussed as a candidate for the presidency of the Bundestag. And in 1957 Willy Brandt, then mayor of the city, served as president of the Bundesrat and, as such, officially stood in as head of state for the President of the Federal Republic, Theodor Heuss, while he traveled abroad. Four years later and then again in 1965 Mayor Brandt actually campaigned as the designated candidate for the office of Chancellor of his party in the federal elections for the Bundestag.

Not only has West Berlin functioned very much as a *Land* within federal politics, but it has also remained, until recently, the symbolic capital of a future reunified Germany. This image has long been actively promoted by the West German government, and it facilitated the choice of Bonn, rather than Frankfurt, as the initial capital of the Federal Republic, which placed the government center in the Catholic Rhineland rather than in an urban socialist stronghold.

Since 1954, every federal convention for the election of the President has met in Berlin, most recently in 1969, over loud Soviet protest. In October 1957, the new Bundestag formally opened its deliberations in Berlin. Each year until 1970, several of its committees met periodically in the divided city, thereby striving to keep alive the image of the traditional capital in Berlin. The Federal Administrative Court is located there, as are a number of federal agencies, especially those administering the vast social security and insurance programs. As a result, more than 20,000 federal government employees work and live in Berlin, an important economic stimulus for the city. In addition there is the huge federal subsidy that is provided by Bonn from special revenues derived from all the other *Länder* and which in 1971 totaled 4 billion marks. In that year roughly 42 percent of the municipal budget of West Berlin was provided by the federal government.

It is likely that the greatest long-term dilemma of West Berlin will be due to social and economic development rather than to external threat. Since the war there has been a serious population imbalance. More than one-fifth of its inhabitants are over the age of sixty-five. Elsewhere in the Federal Republic the comparable figure is 13 percent. Women constitute more than 56 percent of its population, which slightly exceeds 2 million. And a good proportion of the young are in Berlin because the draft is not.

Despite the reduced level of employable men, job scarcity has occasionally posed problems for West Berlin. Its industry is too concentrated in one sector, that of electrotechnical manufacturing, which employs one-third of all industrial workers in the city. A downturn in this sector, which is heavily export-oriented and therefore vulnerable, could have a severe impact on the urban economy.

There are other structural problems. Less than 1 percent of the goods produced in West Berlin are sold to the contiguous areas of East Germany. More than four-fifths of its production is sent westward over considerable distance to the Federal Republic, and a good portion of this is for further export abroad. This has made the matter of unencumbered civilian access to the West essential not only for the political security of this large municipal enclave, but also for its continued economic viability.

For this reason the Four Power Agreement on Berlin, which came into effect in June 1972, was hailed as a constructive development. The agreement among the four Allies substantially eased the flow of civilian traffic to and from the city. It reinforced Allied respect for the links that tie West

Berlin to the Federal Republic and extended, if somewhat ambiguously, the recognition by the Soviet Union for the right of West German consular authorities to represent West Berliners in eastern Europe. It also once again made possible visits for residents of West Berlin to the surrounding G.D.R. and, especially, to the eastern section of their long-divided city.

This pattern of relationships, with all of its complexity and ambiguity, reflects the special and difficult political, economic, and geographic problems of Berlin. It remains the most vivid symbol and manifestation of the Cold War and the postwar partition of Germany. As a result, no unit of the federation poses greater problems for the central government than does West Berlin. Yet precisely because of these problems the role of the federal government is far more substantial in Berlin than in any other *Land.* Ironically, the very fact that Berlin is not fully represented in parliament, combined with its growing economic dependence on federal support, has made it more subordinate to Bonn than any of the other *Länder.*

Federalism

If the arrangement in Berlin seems anomalous, German federalism as a whole is a rather curious and complex web of relationships. In view of German history, this should come as no surprise. Germany has always been plagued by a federal problem. The Constitution of 1871 gave expression to the centrifugal forces at the root of the newly unified state. But with the predominant position of Prussia assured, German federal experience, at least until 1933, tended to focus on the problem of Prussian supremacy. During the Weimar Republic it was generally thought that Prussia could dominate the rest of Germany. As the Prussian government invariably featured the Social Democrats as its largest party, Catholic opinion outside Prussia viewed any accretion in central authority with marked apprehension. This especially typified the attitude of Bavaria, which, throughout the Weimar years, was partially represented in Berlin by its own political party, the Bavarian People's party. But it also characterized thinking in Catholic portions of Prussia itself, especially in the Rhineland.

The actions of the Third Reich, which virtually did away with the *Länder* and invoked a monolithic centralism, only served to strengthen these Catholic sentiments, which came to play a vital role in determining the role of federalism in the Basic Law. By 1949 the problem of Prussia had been removed by the division and territorial reduction of Germany. But the prospect of a unitary state remained an anathema to the Catholics, and especially to the Bavarians, who again swiftly reestablished their own regional parties. One of these, the Christian Social Union (C.S.U.), stands today as the largest party in Bavaria, although it is directly affiliated with the C.D.U. at the national level.

The Social Democrats in 1949 very much favored a strong central government, for a number of reasons. First, given the enormous scope of the economic reconstruction deemed necessary, the S.P.D. was eager to avoid regional obstacles to national planning. Second, as a unified and centrally directed party itself, the S.P.D. did not want to cede substantial powers to local and *Land* groups. The strength of Social Democratic support was certain to be in the cities and not in the rural areas. Yet it was likely that the latter would gain a substantial grip on several *Land* regimes and thereby find effective representation of their economic interests and more conservative outlook. This is, in fact, what occurred. Besides the three "city-states" of Berlin, Bremen, and Hamburg, the S.P.D. commanded a consistent majority in only one other *Land,* Hesse, during the first fifteen years of the Federal Republic.

In the dispute over the role of federalism in 1949, the Christian Democrats obtained important support from the Allies. The French feared a recrudescence of a strong, centrally governed West German state, and the Americans believed in the virtues of their own federal government, although the pattern in Germany was to emerge quite differently. Furthermore, that each Ally was sovereign within his own zone of occupation meant that each tended to identify with the local, *Land,* and zonal German authorities who had been installed or elected during the four-year Occupation period. Thus, it was to be expected that the Basic Law would recognize the fairly far-reaching powers of the *Länder,* despite the fact that they were so arbitrary in design, unequal in size, and unrepresentative of any historical experience.

Still, the Basic Law prescribed in substantial detail the means whereby a territorial restructuring of the *Länder* might be undertaken. Indeed, Article 29 proclaimed that "the division of the federal territory into *Länder* is to be revised by a federal law with due regard to regional ties, historical and cultural connections, economic expediency and social structure. Such reorganization should create *Länder* which by their size and capacity are able effectively to fulfill the functions incumbent upon them." The Allies were not happy with the broad implications of this article and sought to postpone its implementation until a peace treaty, which might necessitate a restructuring of all Germany, had been signed. But they did support Article 118, which called for a reorganization of three small states in southwestern Germany whose boundaries were particularly artificial and inconvenient, largely because they had been constituted in order to allocate territory for French administration out of the American zone of occupation. In 1951 a restructuring did occur, and a single state, named Baden-Württemberg, took the place of the three that had been formed when the Federal Republic was first established.

This proved to be the only change within the original *Länder* division of the Federal Republic. The only other alteration in the structure of the

Federal Republic occurred in 1956: the reabsorption of the Saar as a *Land* in the federation. Previously, the Saar had been administered by the French, originally with the aim of annexing it to France. But the French proved enlightened and fair in responding to the preference of the indigenous Saar population to amalgamate with West Germany instead. And so, this economically vital, though small, region, which had been a source of so much controversy in the twenties and thirties, was restored to German rule on January 1, 1957, thereby becoming the eleventh *Land* of the federation.[5]

Since then there has been no territorial revision. However, there has been discussion about a fundamental reorganization of the *Länder*. The amendments to Article 29, which were adopted in 1969, spell out the procedure for such a development. It is one of the few cases in the German system calling for a referendum. More recently a special commission of experts recommended in 1972 that, in the interests of a more efficient and balanced structure, the Federal Republic be recast into five or six more equally sized states (in addition to West Berlin).

But such change will be difficult to achieve. Each *Land* has acquired too strong a vested interest in its own survival to countenance happily its own absorption into a new entity. This has meant that West Germany is saddled with a rather unbalanced federal system. The discrepancy between the large states like North Rhine-Westphalia and Bavaria and the very small *Länder,* such as Bremen or the Saarland, is considerable. To some degree, North Rhine-Westphalia has emerged as the new Prussia, with its huge population of 17 million, great industrial resources, and proximity to Bonn. Yet in contrast to Prussia, no strong state identity has developed here. The artificiality of most of the *Länder* boundaries has forestalled the growth of regional loyalties. So has social and territorial mobility and the massive influx of refugees from the East. A much smaller proportion of present-day Germans now live in the *Länder* in which they were born, so that the resulting ties between the local populations and their state governments are much weaker than they were in the past.

The fact that most of the *Länder* trace their origins to the postwar period —that is, to just before the establishment of the federation—has meant that the central government could cede far greater powers to them without risking a serious diminution of its own authority. Perhaps the sole exception to this pattern has been Bavaria, and Bavarian politics have posed special problems of their own. But even there separatist tendencies, reminiscent of the German past, are unlikely to develop. Regional particularism is intersected by too many other interests to remain a formidable factor in German political life.

---

[5]For a list of the *Länder* see Appendix B.

In part this is the result of national party politics, which has discouraged regional priorities. The S.P.D. has traditionally favored a strengthening of central authority. As the opposition at the federal level for the first twenty years of the Federal Republic, it could thus hardly champion local and *Land* grievances. And the C.D.U. has been rather loathe to do this, too, first because it has constituted the federal government for so long and also because a movement in this direction might intensify the centrifugal forces within its own ranks. The easy movement of leading political figures from office at the national level to office at the *Land* level and vice versa has also muted conflict. All too often a state Minister-President (or governor) has moved to a cabinet position, or a leader within the federal opposition has seized an opportunity to further his career and build up a political base by shifting laterally into a key *Land* ministerial post, as Helmut Schmidt did in 1961 when he left parliament to join the cabinet in his native city-state of Hamburg. In fact, the national opposition has at times been led by a regionally-based figure. This was the case for the S.P.D. under Mayor Willy Brandt from 1964 to 1966 and it is true as well for the C.D.U., which elected the governor of Rhineland-Palatinate its chairman in 1973.

This pattern suggests the curious kind of horizontal or functional federalism that exists in the Federal Republic. The states and the federation do not operate in separate spheres. Rather, their prerogatives and practices are interdependent within a single system. This pertains to both legislative and executive functions. As John Ford Golay has put it, "legislative and policy-making power has been concentrated at the center, with the officials of the state governments participating directly in the exercise of that power."[6]

How does this system operate? The Basic Law suggests a compromise between central and regional powers. It distinguishes three types of legislation: exclusive, concurrent, and residual. The federation has exclusive jurisdiction to legislate in matters involving foreign affairs, nationality, passports and immigration, currency, customs, the federal railroads and air traffic, postal and telecommunications services, the legal status of federal employees, copyright, and cooperation between the federation and the *Länder* in criminal matters. Article 71 provides that "on matters within the exclusive legislative powers of the Federation, the *Länder* have authority to legislate only if, and to the extent that, a federal law so authorizes them."

A further twenty-three subjects are enumerated in the Basic Law as falling under the concurrent jurisdiction of both the federation and the *Länder*. This includes civil and criminal law; law of association and assembly; affairs of refugees; public relief; war indemnities; economic law; labor

[6]John Ford Golay, *The Founding of the Federal Republic of Germany* (Chicago, 1958), p. 28.

law; and legislation affecting expropriation of property, ocean and coastal shipping, road traffic, and a number of other items. Article 72 authorizes the *Länder* to legislate on these issues "as long as, and to the extent that, the Federation does not use its legislative power." It stipulates the right of the federation to legislate if the matter cannot be dealt with effectively by the *Länder* or would thereby prejudice the interests of the *Länder* and where "the maintenance of legal or economic unity, especially the maintenance of uniformity of living conditions beyond the territory of a *Land,* necessitates it." This last proviso actually gives the federation a very broad mandate to act on matters listed under the heading of concurrent legislation.

Under the terms of Article 70 all residual powers of legislation, that is, those that are not enumerated in the Basic Law, fall under the jurisdiction of the *Länder.* The primary domain for such state action is in the realm of cultural affairs. It is in matters of education, religion, and cultural life that the *Länder* have the most substantial independent prerogatives for separate legislation. As a result, it is often the Minister of Culture at the *Land* level who is, next to the Minister-President, the most important figure in a German state government. Such certainly was the case in the long incumbency of Alois Hundhammer as Bavarian Minister of Culture. In many ways he was the dominant figure in Bavarian politics throughout the 1950s.

More recently a greater professionalism has characterized *Land* governments, especially in the selection of the state minister of culture, who is responsible for educational policy. Academic figures such as Hans Maier in Bavaria, Peter von Oertzen in Lower Saxony, Ludwig von Friedeburg in Hesse, and Bernhard Vogel in Rhineland-Palatinate play a vital role in the politics of their *Länder.* This reflects the importance of the cultural prerogatives that rest with the states and explains the resistance of the *Länder* governments until recently against any substantial intrusion of federal agencies in this sphere. But the need for coordinated planning as well as the cost of educational expansion have become so great that such resistance has faded in the interest of a nationally cohesive policy.

There has, in fact, been a continuous decline in the importance of the *Länder* in direct lawmaking. Today the division of the legislative function between Bonn and the eleven state parliaments is more symbolic than real. However, this is not seen as a problem. The shift from *Land* to central responsibility in certain areas of legislation has not been met by strong local resistance. The movement toward centralization in Germany, much like the movement toward regionalism in France, is accepted as necessary to offset the exaggerations in the political system. For most German state officials this process has seemed an inevitable consequence of the growing number and complexity of issues that clearly require both a nationwide approach and a national solution.

Also, the *Länder* retain and exercise very far-reaching powers in the implementation of all laws, including federal legislation. By far the larger part of the German bureaucracy is at the state level. State civil servants outnumber their federal counterparts four to one (excluding the separately-administered federal enterprises, the railroads, and the post office). In taxation as well Bonn shares its powers with the *Länder*. In the apportioning of income tax, for example, the federal government and the states share equal amounts of 43 percent of the total receipts, the rest being allocated to the cities and smaller communities.

The *Länder* also have very extensive and diverse means of influencing legislation at the federal level, powers which they use with skill and effectiveness. Each is represented by a special plenipotentiary in the federal capital, which is a useful link for those states located at some distance from Bonn. The long-time Bavarian representative Franz Heubl and the former Berlin emissary Horst Grabert (who subsequently moved to a key position in the Chancellor's Office) were influential figures in federal politics. Finally, it is important to note that the states in West Germany possess substantial powers of legislative authority in the upper house of parliament, the Bundesrat. Indeed, federalism in Germany has developed as a complex process operating on a multitude of different levels, creating a unique web of shared responsibility between the center and the states.

Five

The Federal Government

While the *Länder* have retained important rights, it is really the federal government that has gained preponderant power in West Germany. Its institutions, comprising a diverse and rather balanced mixture, derive both from the experience of the German past and from the inventiveness and sober design on the part of those who drafted the Basic Law.

The Federal Parliament

Like so much else in the Federal Republic, present-day parliamentary institutions have been influenced by a rather extraordinary diversity of historical experience. In part they derive from the national legislatures of prior regimes. The parliamentary provisions of the Basic Law (Articles 38–53) also draw heavily on the experiences of other democracies, especially those of the occupying powers. The resulting amalgam is a unique mixture of indigenous and foreign factors, and it includes several novel arrangements.

Certainly the strongest historical influence on these provisions of the Basic Law was the apparent failure of the parliamentary institutions of the Weimar Republic. As has been seen, the Weimar institutions were both too strong and too weak. The potency of the Reichstag in the fourteen years of the first Republic was best exemplified by its negative powers. It could, and often did, undermine a government even without formally unseating it. The Reichstag was able to prevent the emergence of a strong Chancellor and cabinet who could induce, if not compel, parliamentary support for a legislative program. At the same time parliament remained weak within the overall political system. In the presence of a stalemate, or in the absence of a clear and stable legislative majority, the President was able to assume virtually dictatorial emergency powers. Even in its best years, the Weimar Republic had been characterized by a kind of dualism between government and parliament, and at its worst, it was susceptible to arbitrary rule by the decrees of one man alone.

The Parliamentary Council sought to remedy the major faults of this system. While it strengthened the role of parliament, it also firmed the position of the Chancellor in relation to the legislature. In this it struck a much healthier balance, and on the whole its purposes have been realized. In the Federal Republic, parliament is less dependent on the executive than in Britain or France, though still far more so than in the United States. Parliament has emerged as a more reliable and effective institution than its predecessor under the Weimar constitution, but at the same time it has become more subordinate and responsive to the Chancellor and the government bureaucracy.

In part this is the result of the parliamentary provisions codified in the Basic Law, and as such it reflects the intent of those who drafted them. But the stability and compliance of parliament is also the result of several other factors. To a large degree it is made possible by changes in the party system and electoral law, which have proved far more conducive to stable politics than before. Also, the fourteen-year incumbency of Konrad Adenauer as Chancellor helped to shape an orderly and very workable pattern of relationships between the cabinet and the legislature. Especially in view of the force, skill, and prestige of Adenauer, the Chancellor's Office grew substantially in power. This pattern was reinforced by the increasing complexity of many of the issues that had to be resolved and on which parliament was far less well equipped to act than the executive agencies of the government. Indeed, the decline of parliamentary prerogatives, which can be seen in most advanced political systems, has had a marked impact on the Federal Republic. However, here it has been seen as less of a problem, for two reasons. First, the interlude of sixteen years without free elections and a parliamentary system meant that the decline was less obvious and measurable. Second, the fact that the accretion of executive powers in Germany was identified with political stability and economic prosperity was sufficient to satisfy the majority of the electorate, which could still recall the chaos associated with parliamentary politics under the Weimar regime. Only more recently, as the memory of past failures receded and new problems of leadership developed, has concern begun to grow over the substantial imperfections of the current parliamentary arrangements in the Federal Republic.

The Bundesrat

The Bundesrat, or Federal Council, is the upper chamber of parliament. In its structure and role it very much resembles German institutions of the past. Since unification, the German parliament has always had a strong federal component. This was particularly the case in the Bismarckian system, in which the Bundesrat played a very vital role. The prerogatives of the second chamber, renamed the Reichsrat, were substantially reduced in 1919 in an effort to firm the hand of the national government. As a result, the upper house remained a rather ineffective institution, although the power of the larger *Land* governments, especially those of Prussia and Bavaria, was not effectively curbed.

The framers of the Basic Law sought quite deliberately to strengthen the role of the second chamber for several reasons. First, the *Länder* predated the establishment of federal institutions, and, therefore, the Parliamentary Council, which was entirely composed of *Land* representatives, had an interest in providing the state governments with a strong voice at the federal level. However, the danger that the larger *Länder* would regain predominant influence in parliament was diminished by the elimination of Prussia from Germany and by certain provisions that gave the smaller *Länder* a larger voice in the Bundesrat.

This development was encouraged by the Allied Occupation authorities, who were reluctant to cede too much power to national institutions and who, in any case, sought to counterbalance the accretion of power at the center by a strong involvement of *Länder* representatives in the decision-making process at the federal level. For this purpose the Bundesrat has served very well. It has injected a strong state voice into the federal parliament as well as increasing parliament's expertise on complex issues of legislation.

The four articles of the Basic Law dealing with the Bundesrat are brief and explicit. They provide that each of the *Länder,* now eleven in number, shall be represented by three to five members. Each *Land* is entitled to at least three delegates. Those with a population of more than 2 million have four, while the states with populations above 6 million are entitled to five representatives. This arrangement clearly favors the smaller states. Thus, for example, the three smallest *Länder,* the Saarland, Bremen, and Hamburg, have nine representatives for a combined population of 3.7 million, or one member for every 410,000 inhabitants; whereas the four largest *Länder* have only twenty representatives for a population of 44 million, or one for every 2.2 million people. By contrast, the Reichsrat in the Weimar Republic allocated seats in direct proportion to population, with one seat for every 700,000 citizens, which provided Prussia and Bavaria with great influence.

This overrepresentation of the smaller *Länder* is reinforced by the fact that each *Land* is entitled to equal membership on each of the committees of the Bundesrat. Therefore, since most of the legislative activity is concentrated in the committees, Bremen has as strong a voice as North Rhine-Westphalia. This originally served the purposes of the S.P.D., which was assured a majority in the three smaller *Länder* of Hamburg, Bremen, and Berlin, and thus modified its initial opposition to an arrangement that ceded such important powers to the *Länder* at the federal level.

Article 51 provides that the Bundesrat will consist of members of the *Länder* governments that appoint and recall these members. Alternates may be designated to attend in place of members. But invariably they are also members of their state executive institutions and thus bring substantial expertise to the consideration of federal legislation, which the popularly elected members of the lower house generally do not. In the case of all eleven *Länder,* the head of government, be he a governor or mayor, officially leads his state's Bundesrat delegation. Other members are most often the state minister for federal affairs (who is often the plenipotentiary in Bonn) and the state ministers of finance, interior, or culture, depending on which figures are most powerful in the respective *Land* cabinets. But it is usual for alternates to attend in place of these ministers unless particularly important or controversial legislation is under discussion.

The Basic Law provides that each *Land* delegation must cast its vote in the Bundesrat plenary sessions as a bloc, which means that even where a state government is a coalition of two parties (which is often the case), such partisan division is not reflected in the votes of the Bundesrat as a whole. This can lead to a curious situation. For example, early in 1972 the federal government, composed of a coalition of Social and Free Democrats (S.P.D. and F.D.P.), technically could count a majority of twenty-three out of the forty-one Bundesrat delegates (excluding those from West Berlin) as *Land* ministers who belonged to one of these two parties. Nonetheless, the Christian Democratic (C.D.U.-C.S.U.) national opposition maintained a majority of one vote in the upper house since it governed as the larger party in five of the *Land* governments, which, among them, held twenty-one votes in the chamber.[1] The only way in which this situation could be reversed was through the defeat of the C.D.U. in one of these five states, which demonstrates the importance of state elections for the federal government.

The provision for bloc voting has served to cast the Bundesrat member much more in the role of a representative of his state's interests, substantially cutting across party lines.This arrangement has given the state governments a major voice in federal legislation. It has also facilitated the shifting of senior political figures between federal and *Land* politics. For

[1]The terms Christian Democratic or C.D.U. used in the text generally apply to the Christian Democratic Union and its Bavarian affiliate, the Christian Social Union (C.S.U.).

example, both Willy Brandt and Kurt Georg Kiesinger became the Chancellor candidates of their parties while heading *Land* governments and both had the opportunity to gain greater national prestige through positions taken in the Bundesrat, in which Brandt served a one-year term as President. Although this post is largely ceremonial, it does provide for substantial national exposure. But more than that, the Bundesrat, through its composition, requires the *Länder* governments to take a stand on a great variety of national issues and thus reduces the provincialism that would otherwise characterize *Land* politics. It has also made it even more attractive for national political leaders to move to state office without relinquishing a voice in national legislation. This has occurred on a number of occasions. For example, in 1958 Kurt Georg Kiesinger gave up his seat in the Bundestag to become governor of Baden-Württemberg. Gerhard Stoltenberg did the same in 1971 to head the government of Schleswig-Holstein. Similarly, Klaus Schütz resigned as permanent state secretary in the Foreign Office in 1967 to succeed Heinrich Albertz, who had faltered and resigned as mayor of West Berlin. In each of these cases the move to the leading position in a *Land* government served to enhance the national careers of the political figures. In the case of Kiesinger it led to his subsequent election as Chancellor of the Federal Republic in 1966.

One difficulty with this arrangement is that the composition of the upper house is very much affected by the outcome of the *Land* elections, which occur periodically during the usual four-year term of office of the lower house. Indeed, the majority in the upper house may shift several times within this period, which can pose some problems for a Chancellor and his cabinet. The impact of state elections at the federal level has meant that the state campaigns are waged much more on national issues and that the election results are seen as a kind of approval or rejection of the national government. Such a continuous process of elections can prove somewhat destabilizing for the political system in the long run and has been the subject of substantial critical debate in the Federal Republic.

For example, the Brandt government, elected in November 1972, was to confront the first of a series of critical *Land* elections within sixteen months of coming into office. Usually the period is even shorter. In 1966 Chancellor Erhard faced a major election in North Rhine-Westphalia, the most populous and powerful German state, some eight months after his party's strong showing in the federal elections. The poor showing that it registered in this *Land* election played an important role in the breakdown of his coalition government and his political demise four months later.

It is really more the frequent referenda on national issues implied by this procedure than the possible loss of a supporting majority in the upper house that is most complicating for the federal government. The loss of a majority need not be crippling. It did not occur during the first twenty years of the Federal Republic because the Christian Democrats, who dominated the federal government, always commanded a margin in the Bundesrat. As a result, during this period fewer than two dozen bills were blocked by the upper chamber.

For the Brandt government, which came into office in 1969, the hostile majority in the Bundesrat has posed larger problems. The stunning victory of Brandt's Social Democrats in the 1972 elections did not improve their position in the upper house. While the federal government was able to add a solid 6 percent to its popular vote in these elections, the opposition had gained by an average of 2 percent in the various state Landtag elections during the previous three years, and these elections determine the composition of the Bundesrat. However, demographic factors should favor the S.P.D. in the years ahead. The *Länder* of Hamburg and Hesse, both Social Democratic strongholds, are nearing the population level at which each would be entitled to an additional delegate and vote in the upper chamber.

Controlling the Bundesrat is less important than it might seem because of this chamber's limited mandate on legislation. Its approval is required only on those issues on which the states possess the concurrent right of legislation. Here its veto can be absolute. But on all other issues the Bundesrat stands possessed of only a suspensive veto. This means that its negative vote can be overridden by the lower house. If the Bundesrat rejects legislation by a majority, a simple majority of the lower chamber can override. If the rejection is by two-thirds—which would be a very rare instance—a two-thirds vote in favor is required in the Bundestag.

Most points of conflict between the two chambers of parliament are resolved in the Committee for the Joint Consideration of Bills, composed of eleven members from each house. Here the two chambers are equally represented with the chairmanship alternating every three months between the two. Great emphasis is placed on conciliation. Article 77 of the Basic Law stipulates that the Bundesrat members of this Joint Committee are not bound by instructions from their *Länder*. Usually the Committee is convened at the request of the Bundesrat, but it can also be called together by the Bundestag or by demand of the federal government. During the first twenty years of the Federal Republic only twenty-eight bills considered in the Joint Committee failed to find agreement and subsequent enactment.

The Bundesrat convenes every other week during the annual sessions of parliament. Its greatest asset is the expertise that it brings to bear on legislation. Most of its members are senior civil servants from the *Länder* and, as such, they are well equipped to scrutinize legislation introduced by the federal bureaucracy. Other persons commissioned by the *Länder* may also participate in the committee sessions of the Bundesrat, which have the power to secure the participation of members of the federal government. It is here that legislation is usually first considered and it is in the committees of the Bundesrat that the government bureaucracy often encounters its most substantial examination and challenge, especially where planned legislation affects the interests of the states.

The expertise of its members compensates for the lack of prestige that attaches to service in the Bundesrat. There is no German equivalent to an English lord or an American, or even a French, senator. The sole exception is the office of President of the chamber, to which candidates are elected for a one-year term from among the Minister-Presidents of the eleven *Länder*. The mayor of West Berlin is eligible for this post, even though the Bundesrat delegation from that city has only an advisory vote in the plenary sessions of that body.

The Bundesrat itself rarely introduces legislation. From 1949 to 1969 only seventy-two bills that originated in the upper house were enacted into law. Such bills must be submitted by the federal government with a statement of its views to the lower house within three months after passage in the Bundesrat. Most bills originate with the federal government. They are normally submitted first to the Bundesrat, which is entitled to state its position within six weeks. Bills of exceptional urgency may be submitted by the government to the Bundestag within three weeks of presentation to the upper house. Budgetary bills are submitted to both houses at the same time.

There are several reasons why the Bundesrat is the first to consider proposed government legislation. First, it is a courtesy to the *Länder*. It permits the Bundesrat members to consult their governments for instructions before deliberating in committee on the legislation. Even more important is the expertise available through the Bundesrat. Therefore its initial response is vital to the government and may lead to extensive redrafting of a bill before it is passed on to the Bundestag.

After a bill has been considered and voted on by the lower house, it is presented for a second time to the upper chamber for a so-called second passage. If there is disagreement it is usually at this point that the Joint Committee of Consideration is invoked. Should the Committee substantially alter the content of a bill, it must be resubmitted to both houses. Occasionally this can lead to further changes and a new session of the Joint Committee is required. This occurred less than a dozen times during the first twenty years of parliament, in which well over two thousand bills passed the chamber.

The Bundesrat shares in the ratification of foreign treaties. It also plays a vital role in the provisions relating to a state of declared emergency or defense which were appended to the Basic Law in 1968. Article 53a provides for the establishment of a Joint Committee of parliament in case such an emergency is declared. One-third of this body is composed of members of the Bundesrat and two-thirds is composed of deputies of the Bundestag. Each *Land* is entitled to be represented by a Bundesrat member of its choice who shall not be bound by instructions (whereas the Bundestag members are selected on the basis of party representation). In most instances in which the federal government might contemplate the suspension of constitutional rights and the declaration of a state of national emergency, it could only do so with the approval of the Bundesrat, that is to say, with the agreement of a majority of the *Land* governments. Federalism in Germany thus plays a very substantial role in the parliamentary system, primarily, but not exclusively, through the upper house.

The Bundestag

It was in the drafting of the provisions pertaining to the lower house, renamed the Bundestag, that the framers of the Basic Law gave particular attention to the experience of the Weimar Republic. The negative powers of the Reichstag had been altogether too great and far too often had succeeded in nullifying the program of Weimar Chancellors and their cabinets. Although the Reichstag could prevent action, its position in the political system was not strong because under Article 48 recourse could so easily be had to extraparliamentary rule by decree reinforced by national plebiscites.

The Parliamentary Council sought to remedy these defects. First of all, it sought to increase the constructive powers of the lower house. This was done in a number of ways. The responsibility of the chamber in electing the Chancellor was substantially augmented, and the powers of the federal President in proposing candidates very much circumscribed. While the President still retains the authority to propose an initial nominee to the house, if such a candidate fails to receive a majority the Bundestag can, under the terms of Article 63, elect a Chancellor of its own choosing within fourteen days of the first ballot. If the candidate receiving the largest number of votes does not obtain a majority, the President has the option of either appointing him Chancellor or dissolving the chamber.

These provisions very much reduce the role and influence of the President in the appointment of the Chancellor. In fact, the President is not likely to propose to the Bundestag a candidate who cannot secure a majority if there is another figure who will clearly obtain more than half of the votes in the chamber. The power to select a Chancellor really rests with the Bundestag. But it has been substantially circumscribed by the party and election system. Actually, since 1949 it has been the parties that nominate their candidates and the voters who determine the outcome of the election, although there is some scope for subsequent negotiation among the various party leaders in those situations where federal elections fail to provide any one party with a majority of the seats in the Bundestag. In these instances the President has never played a critical role. When in 1961 President Lübke sought to intervene on behalf of a grand coalition, his efforts were seen as obstructive and proved rather counterproductive.

The Chancellor need not be a member of the Bundestag. Indeed, Kiesinger was not a member of the house at the time of his election, nor was Brandt when he stood as the Chancellor candidate in 1961. This was often the case in the Weimar Republic as well. However, since 1949 a much larger percentage of the cabinet has been composed of members of the lower house, which reflects the strength of the Bundestag in the system. The negotiations for selecting the cabinet often take many weeks and can prove quite complicated. Only once, in 1957, did one party command a majority in the chamber, which means that coalition government has been an almost constant feature of the Federal Republic. There have been a few cabinet members from outside parliament, but this has been the case much less frequently than in the Weimar Republic. For example, all eighteen members of the cabinet that was established in November 1972 were members of the Bundestag. The average number of years of membership in the lower house was nine. However, three members of the cabinet (Bahr, Maihofer, and Vogel) were newly elected to the Bundestag in 1972. Another four (von Dohnanyi, Ehmke, Focke, and Lauritzen) had just completed their first terms. The right to be able to debate in the Bundestag and answer interpellations is important for cabinet ministers, so that it has become unusual for them not to be members of the lower house.

It is difficult to dissolve the Bundestag. As mentioned, one instance would be if the Bundestag failed at the outset to provide a majority for the election of a Chancellor, but this is a fairly unlikely contingency. Article 68 provides that if a motion of the Chancellor for a vote of confidence is not assented to by a majority of the Bundestag, the President can, upon the proposal of the Chancellor, dissolve the chamber within twenty-one days. The Chancellor must place his motion forty-eight hours before a vote is taken. In case of a dissolution, new elections must be held within sixty days. However, the right to dissolve lapses as soon as the Bundestag elects another candidate Chancellor by a majority vote. Therefore, this is not a very reliable instrument for an incumbent Chancellor except with the prior agreement of the opposition, since he may find himself displaced rather than able to compel new elections.

This did occur, in fact, for the first time in September 1972. It was utilized by Chancellor Brandt, whose majority had disappeared through a series of defections to the opposition, but he first secured the agreement of the opposition, which was also seeking a way out of the stalemate that threatened to block all action. On this occasion the 248 members of the opposition (exactly half the house) registered their nonconfidence while the cabinet abstained, which left only the 233 other members of the government coalition parties to vote in favor of the Chancellor's motion. With this planned defeat, the Chancellor immediately demanded, and President Heinemann promptly ordered, a dissolution of the Bundestag, although Article 68 allowed the President three full weeks to comply with the Chancellor's request. However, in this case the government was not eager to defer dissolution lest the opposition had reversed itself and possibly elected a candidate of its own (for which it would have needed one more vote than it seemed to have). Brandt was able to risk using this procedure because he could be certain that Heinemann, a party colleague, would immediately dissolve the chamber. Where the Chancellor and President are not of the same party, Article 68 is less dependable.

These provisions have served to enhance the role of the Bundestag and to create greater stability for government in the Federal Republic. There is no escape to presidential emergency government. Although the Chancellor can wield extraordinary powers in a state of emergency, there are legal safeguards that make it unlikely that such a state would be declared if normal parliamentary procedure produced a protracted stalemate—as so often happened under Weimar. While all of this has served to stabilize the role of parliament, a number of measures were drafted by the Parliamentary Council to firm the position of the Chancellor as against that of the Bundestag.

By far the most important of these is provided by Article 67, which states that the Bundestag can declare its lack of confidence in the Chancellor only by electing a successor by a majority in a secret ballot and then requesting the President to dismiss the incumbent. Under these circumstances the President must comply with this request. In the Weimar Republic it was always a great deal easier to establish a negative majority than a constructive one. But in the Federal Republic, given the strength of the parliamentary parties, it is difficult to envisage the circumstances in which this procedure could be successfully invoked to remove a Chancellor.

A vote of constructive non-confidence was taken on April 27, 1972. The opposition proposed the candidacy of its leader, Rainer Barzel, to the Bundestag. During the preceding eighteen months five deputies had bolted from the ranks of the government coalition in favor of the opposition. This left the government a margin of only one seat more than half the house (exclusive of the Berlin delegates, whose votes are not binding). At least two further defections were expected because of the government's controversial *Ostpolitik* (eastern policy).

However, the opposition motion failed by a margin of two. It is probable that the two votes which Barzel required were denied him by members of his own party, the C.D.U., in the secret ballot. Subsequently it turned out that one of these was cast by a Christian Democratic backbencher, Julius Steiner, who later claimed he had accepted the funds to change his vote. Also, the government parties, being unsure of the loyalty of their entire membership, violated the principle of a secret ballot by asking their members to abstain and, in so doing, to remain seated, so that anyone seeking to bolt the ranks to vote against the government would have been easily identified as he rose to cast his ballot in the urn.

The circumstances surrounding this critical vote unleashed a bitter dispute. The opposition charged that, in effect, the government had stolen the election through the tactics it employed. The leaders of the governing Social and Free Democratic coalition, in turn, repudiated the legitimacy of the actions of the opposition. They disavowed the propriety of a maneuver which could only secure a majority vote by soliciting individual defections from the government parties. Much discussion hinged on the role of the purported principle of an "imperative mandate," which, if honored, did not leave a deputy with the right to desert the government his party supported.

This issue is both complex and ambiguous. On the one hand, Article 38 stipulates that deputies of the Bundestag "shall be representatives of the whole people, not bound by orders and instructions, and shall be subject only to their conscience." This clearly entitles each member of the Bundestag to vote exactly as he pleases, with his party or against it. However, insofar as half of the members are elected by proportionate representation depending on the strength of votes won by their parties, it can be argued that the proper action under such circumstances is to resign from parliament to make way for an alternate deputy on the party's list, which is the normal manner of succession whenever a vacancy occurs. This, in fact, happened in the case of two Free Democrats, who first voted against their party and for Barzel and then quit their seats in favor of the two alternates at the top of the reserve list, who proved loyal to the government.

This debate demonstrates the strength of party discipline, both in theory and in practice, in the German system. It also severely challenges the right of individual deputies to "cross over" from the government ranks to the opposition or vice versa. Such crossing of the aisle had not been common in the Bundestag until 1970. What made it so critical in this period was the very narrow gap between the two sides and the resulting precarious majority of the government. Under these conditions a wavering deputy commands too much power.

Article 67 was not designed with this situation in mind. It is a useful instrument when a fundamental party realignment within a governing coalition takes place, as occurred so frequently in the Weimar Republic. Had the F.D.P., the small coalition partner of the Social Democrats, jettisoned its partnership with the S.P.D., a constructive vote of non-confidence leading to the election of a new Chancellor (conceivably Barzel) with an effective governing majority would have proceeded smoothly and well. In effect, the threat of such action would have led the incumbent to resign, which is what occurred in the fall of 1966 when the Erhard government, led by the C.D.U., collapsed due to the withdrawal of support from it by the Free Democrats.

However, had the motion succeeded on April 27, 1972, the new incumbent, Rainer Barzel, would have had as narrow a governing majority as did the Chancellor he had replaced. This would not have created a stable basis for government nor obviated the need for new elections. Thus, Article 67 does not provide a useful way out of the kind of stalemate that afflicted German federal politics in 1972. Under such conditions even a strong and popular Chancellor can be relatively helpless.

Under more normal conditions, however, with a dependable majority in the lower house, the Chancellor is indeed in a strong position. The parliamentary parties of the government have little incentive to cause difficulties for their own cabinet. Party voting is highly disciplined and, therefore, usually easily predicted. Even the government of Chancellor Brandt during the life of the sixth Bundestag with its ever-diminishing majority suffered only a single legislative defeat before invoking Article 68 in September 1972.

The increasing complexity of the issues on which votes are taken has served to limit the powers of the Bundestag. Most of its members are no match for the bureaucracy, which can deliver expert advice to its parliamentary parties. This places the opposition at a substantial disadvantage, especially as most members of the Bundestag have very limited staffs. This situation has also meant that a great deal of the real work of the Bundestag occurs in committees, where legislation can be amended in time if it appears to be encountering substantial resistance.

Indeed, the average member of the Bundestag is not a very powerful figure. He is poorly compensated, which reflects a German tradition opposing paid professionalism in parliament, even though Article 48 provides that "deputies shall be entitled to a remuneration adequate to ensure their independence." Basic compensation was originally set in 1949 at a meager 7,200 marks annually, the same figure as was paid for a member of the Reichstag in 1932. It has been increased several times. But even though the basic salary rose to some 16,000 marks by the mid-sixties, this amount only barely exceeded the median income of skilled industrial workers. Salaries today are fixed as a modest percentage of ministerial compensation. In addition, deputies receive an average of 50,000 marks annually for travel and office expenses. While these figures do not, in fact, seem adequate to "ensure independence," they are higher than in England, Scandanavia, or the Benelux countries, and are slightly more, after taxes, than what a French deputy receives.

Staff assistance is not adequate for the legislative responsibilities that confront members of parliament. This has meant that most members pursue a second career, often merely to secure a sufficient income. It has also made service in parliament attractive for civil servants. In Germany the professional civil services *(Beamtentum)* comprise a larger category than in many other countries. For example, teachers and university professors, the higher echelons of the railroad administration, managers of radio and television and many other sectors tend to be *Beamten.* Article 137 specifically guarantees the right of civil servants and other public employees, including professional soldiers, to stand for election. In parliament this group is numerous and growing in size. In the seventh Bundestag, elected in 1972, about 34 percent of the deputies were civil servants. Although civil servants must take leave from their posts to enter parliament, they receive the equivalent of their pensions as a supplementary salary while they serve, which eases the economic strain.

Another solution for the underpaid deputy is to take a second salary for working for an interest group: a union, business lobby, or professional association. Some 10 percent of the seventh Bundestag is comprised of trade union leaders. The business community is also strongly represented. Such direct interest group representation is an established tradition in German politics. In the Weimar Republic the Reichstag was populated with major industrialists, labor leaders, bankers, and the like. In addition, a separate economic parliament, the Reichswirtschaftsrat, played an active role at the time. This trend is less accentuated today. But the practice has still enabled German interest groups to exercise a very direct role in influencing legislation.

These factors have contributed to making the position of backbencher in the Bundestag less than attractive. They have led to a high level of absenteeism and have created a two-tiered system in the Bundestag. In the outer circle are the many relatively uninfluential, often poorly informed, and frequently absent members, whose primary involvement tends to be on a few select issues of direct concern to some professional or interest group. Real power is deferred by this group to an inner circle constituting the party parliamentary leadership, which wields a great deal of power. Together with the officers of the Bundestag and its Council of Elders, the latter group constitutes a highly effective elite that runs the Bundestag and largely determines the outcome of legislation.

The party professionals at the helm are clearly favored in this system, and they have a diminished interest in its reform. Together party professionals comprise about 20 percent of the Bundestag membership. It is they who control committee assignments, determine the agenda of the house, and decide on who within the party delegation may speak in plenary debates. In the case of the party or parties supporting the government, its parliamentary leaders play an important role in shaping the legislation that the cabinet presents to parliament.

The parliamentary front benches include most of the opposition leaders who would constitute a cabinet should their party come into office. However, unlike the British system, here there is no shadow cabinet among the opposition ranks, although in 1972 the C.D.U. did attempt to name one. While there are often specific spokesmen on certain issues, the allocation of prospective cabinet posts cannot be made before an election, since it may depend on negotiations with a coalition party that can be conducted only once the election results are known. It would also be difficult to name a shadow cabinet composed only of Bundestag members, since the recruitment of a cabinet may include party figures from outside parliament. In the case of the S.P.D., its national leader in opposition for many years, Willy Brandt, was not a member of the Bundestag. Given the federal structure of government, a party may wish to reach out to one or several of the *Länder* regimes in allocating cabinet posts.

It has proven difficult under these circumstances for an outsider or a young recruit to rise rapidly in parliament. There have been some exceptions, such as Hans Apel, Hans Friderichs, or Manfred Wörner, each of whom experienced a very rapid rise to a position of power after entering the Bundestag in 1965. But most striking—and unusual—was the exceptional career of Karl Carstens. Within six months of having won his first election to the Bundestag in 1972, Professor Carstens was named parliamentary floor leader of the opposition Christian Democrats in the wake of the sudden resignation of Rainer Barzel in May 1973. But Carstens had an extraordinary background. He had served for a decade as an outstanding state secretary in the Foreign Office, the Defense Ministry, and the Chancellor's Office. Still, his meteoric rise in the parliamentary party was astonishing, the more so as his entry into the Bundestag had been marred by a poor showing in his direct constituency in Plön, which had been won by his C.D.U. predecessor quite handily in previous elections. As a result, Carstens entered the Bundestag through a high position on the *Land* list of Schleswig-Holstein.

On the whole, the parliamentary party leadership has not been easy to penetrate. This is often seen as a defect of the Bundestag. It appears private and unspontaneous in its deliberations, very much in the grip of a small, self-recruiting hierarchy of party leaders. In the absence of direct primaries, the party parliamentary leadership cannot easily be challenged from outside, except by the interest groups, whose power within this system, and especially within the parties, is considerable. Indeed, the Bundestag often behaves in a manner that suggests that it sees these groups as its chief clients and constituents, especially in the rather hidden committee deliberations in which the content of most legislation is determined. Throughout, "the sense of public participation in politics through parliament is not well developed."[2]

Indeed, a kind of public apathy has characterized popular attitudes toward politics and, in particular, toward parliament, in the Federal Republic. Until recently there seemed to be poor communication between parliament and the people. However, the crisis of 1972 with its dramatic events captured much public attention and interest. The televising of important plenary sessions, in which deputies are meant to speak extemporaneously,

[2]Gerhard Loewenberg, *Parliament in the German Political System* (Ithaca, 1966), p. 434.

has stimulated public awareness. But, overall, there has been a decline in the importance of plenary debates. Instead, committee sessions are becoming more and more the locus for real parliamentary discussion. This is a result of the increase in the technical complexity of most legislation. As a whole, the Bundestag has never achieved the kind of educative function of the British House of Commons or the U.S. Senate.

But this is also caused by the reluctance of the German public to become involved in politics, which is partially explained by the historical experience of the years before 1945. Several studies have shown that the willingness to become active in community affairs is much lower in the Federal Republic than in either Britain or the United States. In Germany, the public has repeatedly expressed much more confidence in administrators than in legislators. German political culture has cast the parliamentarian into the role of a *Staatsdiener,* or "servant of the state." There is an inherent mistrust of opposition where it might threaten to destabilize politics or undermine a regime. Orderly procedure is greatly preferred in this system to ideological controversy.

All this has served to diminish the role of opposition and to foster a seeming consensus and identity of interest among the several competing parliamentary parties. It helps to explain the absence of extremist or ideological parties in parliament. By the mid-sixties, especially under the grand coalition of the two major parties during 1966–1969 in which the parliamentary opposition was reduced to some 6 percent of the seats in the Bundestag (held by the F.D.P.), it appeared that the real locus for opposing views was moving outside parliament altogether. This gave rise to a marginal radical movement, the so-called extra-parliamentary opposition (*Ausser-parlamentarische* Opposition, or A.P.O.). Within the Bundestag there was a growing sense of stultifying bureaucratization. Those who knew how to operate within the system succeeded, whereas those who sought to challenge and change it found themselves effectively thwarted. The expert and the party professional did well, but the critic or the member who disregarded the established leadership got nowhere. Under these circumstances parliament functioned smoothly, if monotonously, and at a substantial cost.

More recently this trend has been changing. The confrontation of 1972 had an electrifying impact. Suddenly, in the election campaign of that fall, Germany experienced a burst of political mobilization. Alongside organized party activity, numerous and often spontaneous civic action colored the campaign. The resulting turnout in the November elections was record breaking. Almost 92 percent of those entitled to vote made their way to the polling stations. And the results seemed to suggest a greater polarization, or at least differentiation, among the parliamentary parties. Both the conservative right and the radical left claimed to have scored some striking victories. While the more conservative Christian Democratic candidates did well in the south (and especially the C.S.U. in Bavaria), the S.P.D. saw its left wing double in size, increasing the number of its Bundestag seats to about fifty, or more than one-fifth of the party total.

The grip of the party leadership within the Bundestag is reinforced by party control of the electoral process. Only those parties which secure three seats in direct election or 5 percent of the total vote may be represented in the Bundestag. This rule has served to eliminate a great number of the smaller parties that so plagued the Weimar Republic. But it means that an independent candidate not supported by one of the three major parties cannot succeed. Thus, anyone aspiring to a parliamentary career is ineluctably drawn into one of the three parties, and one of these, the F.D.P., is in constant danger of falling below the 5 percent voter-support level. Furthermore, the Bundestag has adopted a rule that only parties that gain twenty-five seats or more may caucus as a parliamentary party *(Fraktion).* Since important prerogatives such as committee representation are allocated on the basis of caucus strength, a minor regional party that gained several direct constituencies could not have an effective role in the lower house. In order to maximize their numerical strength, the C.D.U. and its Bavarian affiliate, the C.S.U., have constituted a single caucus since 1949, which made this the largest parliamentary party in the Bundestag with the right, or at least the votes, to propose the president of the chamber until 1972.

The pivotal control of the nominating procedure by the central party hierarchy makes penetration from outside very difficult indeed. Anyone above the age of twenty-one who has been a citizen for at least a year may run as a candidate for the lower house. Only one-half of the seats in the Bundestag are contested as single-member constituencies. The other half are allocated on the basis of proportional representation to the parties that secure more than 5 percent of the vote, taking into account any disparities that may occur in the direct-constituency elections. For numerical accuracy the d'Hondt system is used.

Each voter casts two ballots. He votes once for the candidate of his choice in his constituency (there are 248 constituencies throughout the Federal Republic). He also casts a second ballot for the party of his choice, on the basis of a list ranking the nominees of the parties within his *Land.*[3] The composition of the *Land* list is critical, for high placement on it is the equivalent of assured victory. Yet the sequence of names on the *Land* list is not decided by means of a popular primary but is controlled by the party leadership. This is exactly as in the Weimar Republic, except that at that time there were no direct constituencies at all. Today there are none in West Berlin. Its twenty-two deputies are indirectly elected by its assembly,

---

[3]It is these second votes that are tabulated and cited below to indicate party performance in the various federal elections.

which does not stand for election at the same time as the Bundestag elections elsewhere in the federal territory.

This procedure means that in Germany, in contrast to the situation in Britain, the national party leadership can allocate a safe seat to any candidate of its choosing. Indeed, the *Land* lists need not be headed by prominent politicians of that particular state, although as a rule they are. For example, in the 1969 Bundestag elections the S.P.D. *Land* list for North Rhine-Westphalia was headed by Willy Brandt, the former mayor of Berlin, and by Karl Schiller of Hamburg, because they were deemed the two best vote-getters in the party and, therefore, particularly valuable at the top of a slate from the most populous of the German *Länder*.

Turnover in the Bundestag has been fairly high. About one-quarter of its membership is new every four years. There were 154 first-term deputies elected to the sixth Bundestag in 1969 and 149 to the seventh in 1972, which means that well over half of the house was replaced within this seven year period. The highest turnover in 1972 was among the Free Democrats, fifty percent of whose deputies entered the Bundestag for the first time in that year. Of the 149 deputies who did not return from the sixth Bundestag into the seventh, 115 chose not to run again. Thus, relatively few incumbents—thirty-four in all, or about 7 percent—were defeated in the 1972 elections.

But while the turnover figures are striking, they are somewhat deceptive because of the high continuity of party leadership within the house. Furthermore, most of those who enter for the first time are substantially in debt to the party leaders or to some interest group, although recently there has been more emphasis on ceding to the constituencies a larger voice in the designation of their candidates and on broadening democratic procedures in selecting nominees. In the seventh Bundestag there were only ten members who had sat in the first Bundestag elected in 1949. Among them were powerful figures such as Chancellor Brandt, the two former Chancellors, Erhard and Kiesinger, Herbert Wehner, and Gerhard Schroeder. Wehner, the powerful S.P.D. parliamentary leader, and Alex Möller, his proficient deputy, were sixty-seven and seventy years old, respectively. Still, the German situation does not approach the seniority system of the U. S. Congress.

The average age of the seventh Bundestag deputy in 1972 was 46.5 years, roughly the same as a member of the American Congress, but higher than the average in the French and Italian parliaments. There is a gradual trend towards rejuvenation. While deputies are becoming younger, they are also better educated. Of the new members elected in 1972, 70 percent had attended a university or other advanced institution of higher education. Eleven percent of the Bundestag is composed of professional academics or teachers. The educational level is highest for the Free Democrats and the C.D.U. It is significantly lower for the S.P.D., reflecting the lower income social strata of much of its constituency and leadership. Only two-thirds of its deputies have completed the gymnasium (the special, humanistic high school which is a prerequisite for university entry).

Women, however, are poorly represented. They constitute less than 6 percent of the seventh Bundestag, which corresponds to their low level of participation in politics. Most female deputies enter the Bundestag through the *Land* lists, which are composed with some sexual, regional, and denominational balance in mind. Only six of the sixty-nine women elected to the seventh Bundestag won direct constituencies. In part to compensate for this imbalance, the S.P.D. decided to elect Annemarie Renger, a long-time deputy (since 1953) and former secretary of Kurt Schumacher, as president of the chamber in 1972. In addition, one of the four vice-presidents, Liselotte Funcke of the F.D.P., is also a woman.

The positions of real power within the Bundestag are narrowly held. They include the party caucus leaders; the Presidium and the Council of Elders of the chamber; and the committee chairmen, some twenty in number. Altogether they comprise a small elite that controls legislation, rules on procedure, and determines advancement within the house. The impression is one of deliberate and careful control. Membership within this elite is usually decided by the party leadership, and once appointed, incumbents tend to remain in their positions for relatively long periods. Eugen Gerstenmaier, for example, served as President of the Bundestag for almost fifteen years. It would be difficult to point to another European parliamentary system with such extended tenures in office.

The Council of Elders *(Ältestenrat)* serves as a kind of steering committee for the house. It consists of the Presidium (composed of the president and four vice-presidents) and twenty-three members of the three parties selected on the basis of their relative representation in the Bundestag. This council determines the agenda for each week and distributes the committee assignments, but with the prior agreement of the party leaders. Committee assignment is a crucial power because of the vital role exercised by the committees. Indeed, the committee system has often been cited as one of the most successful features of the German parliamentary tradition. It even functioned quite well during the Weimar Republic, when everything else in parliament seemed to be faltering.

A peculiar feature of the present system is that committee chairmanships are assigned on the basis of party representation in the Bundestag as a whole. This means that even minority opposition parties, provided they have no less than twenty-five members, are eligible to head one or several of these committees. Even during the period of an absolute majority of the C.D.U./C.S.U., in the legislative period between 1957 and 1961, the opposition S.P.D. controlled nine committee chairmanships.

Because the committees are among the few areas of the Bundestag where staffing is adequate, this control of committee chairmanships is especially crucial. For the opposition lacks access to the ample expertise possessed by the government bureaucracy and available to its parties. Another source of expert information in the committees are the interest-group representatives. This representation is particularly high on the committees that specialize in areas of interest to particular groups. Thus, while only 10 percent of the membership of the Bundestag elected in 1957 represented farming, more than three-fifths of the members of the agriculture committee had farm backgrounds.

Committee sessions can be open or secret. Usually, members of the government bureaucracy participate in them. Article 43 of the Basic Law stipulates that the Bundestag or its committees "may demand the presence of any member of the Federal Government," a power clearly not available in the United States system with its concepts of separation of powers and the executive privilege. From time to time a committee will choose to hold open hearings on pending legislation, but these are not frequent in Germany. Committees of investigation, which are provided for in the Basic Law, are also relatively rare. Article 44 permits one-fourth of the membership of the Bundestag to call for a Committee of Investigation. Where such a committee seeks to uncover government wrongdoing (as in the case of the Steiner affair investigated in 1973), the committee chairman and its majority will be of the government parties, which may mute the vigor of its inquiry. Indeed, the entire control function of parliament, best evidenced by the formal interpellations of cabinet ministers during plenary sessions, has not posed a serious challenge to the government's prerogatives.

In another area, that of military affairs, there has been a real effort to obtain parliamentary supervision. The Basic Law makes special provision for the Committees on Foreign Affairs and Defense. They do not disband with parliament, but continue to serve in the intervals between two legislative terms. Furthermore, early fears about remilitarization also led to several special regulations. Article 45 states that the Committee of Defense "shall also have the rights of a committee of investigation." The Basic law requires the election by secret ballot of a Defense Commissioner *(Wehrbeauftragter)* of the Bundestag. His role is "to safeguard the basic rights and to assist the Bundestag in exercising parliamentary control" in military affairs.

The Basic Law also calls for the establishment of a Standing Committee to protect the rights of the Bundestag as against those of the federal government in the interval between legislative terms. It is one of a number of measures intended to forestall the hegemony of the executive branch reminiscent of the German past. But, in fact, the involvement and preponderance of the executive in parliament is very extensive. Usually assured of majority support, capitalizing on its superior command of information and expertise, and having free access to the committees and the Council of

Elders, the government is in a far stronger position to exert its will than is the opposition. Most legislation is introduced by the government, not by members of parliament. A great deal of it is enacted into law. Since 1949, almost 90 percent of all the legislation introduced by the government has been passed by parliament, whereas less than one-third of those bills proposed by members have made their way into law.

Usually, legislation is first presented to the Bundesrat, after which it is considered in either two or three readings, with intermediate deliberation in committee by the lower house. The most frequent parliamentary intervention is in the area of finance. The German parliament has considerably greater control over spending and the budget than do the British or the French legislatures, though less than does the United States Congress.

On the whole, there are few surprises and rarely any reverses for a government in parliament. In the absence of free votes on important legislation and given the grip of the party leadership, the outcome of most votes can be safely forecast. Indeed, during its first two years, the S.P.D./F.D.P. coalition established in 1969, with a majority that shrank to only six, did not lose a single major vote. This is strong evidence of the power of the government vis-à-vis parliament in the German system. It is a situation in which legislative opposition has consistently become weaker and less effective. Given a strong and stable party system, the Chancellor and his cabinet have been the main beneficiaries of this development. It is really more the contending pressures within their own party or coalition than the formal opposition in parliament that poses constraints that may force the hand of a Chancellor or his cabinet colleagues. To be sure, in the period from 1970 to 1972 there was a serious problem of the erosion of a government majority through the defection of a number of its original parliamentary supporters. However, the success or failure of a government usually depends to a greater degree on the capacity of its leaders to prevail within their own camp. It was primarily in instances where the leaders failed to do so that a government was enfeebled and began to falter. Thus in the German system it is not so much parliamentary as intraparty dissidence that will most often set the real limits on legislation and policy. Keeping a cabinet or a coalition satisfied may prove much more difficult than securing a Bundestag mandate for government legislation.

The Chancellor and the Cabinet

Without question the chancellorship has emerged as a very powerful position in the Federal Republic. This is largely a realization of the intent of the Parliamentary Council. The Basic Law is relatively brief in the eight articles (62 through 69) that deal with this office, but they confer great powers upon the Chancellor. Once a Chancellor is elected by the Bundestag, it is exceedingly difficult for that body to remove him. As has been seen, the Basic Law provides for the removal of the Chancellor by the lower house in only one of two ways. Article 67 stipulates that the Bundestag must first elect another candidate by a majority vote of all its members before it can displace an incumbent Chancellor, as it sought but failed to do in April 1972. A similar provision in the constitution of North Rhine-Westphalia has twice been invoked successfully.

The other provision for the removal of a Chancellor, which is included in Article 68, applies only after the Chancellor has called for and lost a vote of confidence. Should the Bundestag then elect a new candidate by an absolute majority vote, the Chancellor is replaced. However, if the Bundestag cannot do this—and again the party system makes it unlikely—the Chancellor may ask the President to dissolve the chamber and call for new elections, as occurred in September 1972. This article is a very balanced instrument because it places certain constraints on both the Chancellor and the Bundestag.

While these provisions insulate the Chancellor from an easy erosion of his parliamentary majority, the strength of his position depends to a large degree on his control and influence within his own party or coalition. In each of the two cases when a Chancellor resigned while in office, it was due to internal party pressures. Konrad Adenauer made way for Ludwig Erhard in 1963 largely at the behest of his own party, which, for various reasons, was eager to induce the retirement of a figure who had stood at the helm for fourteen years. When Erhard then faltered three years later, it was the defection of the Free Democrats from the governing coalition and the substantial criticism from within the ranks of his own C.D.U. that left the Chancellor little choice but to resign.

Both of these examples show how much it is party control and personal qualifications of leadership that determine the strength and effectiveness of a Chancellor. Where an incumbent has a firm grip on his party, a strong working agreement with its coalition partners, and the capacity for effective leadership, the Chancellor's office provides wide-ranging powers and prerogatives. These have grown very considerably over time for a number of reasons.

First, there is the fact that the first Chancellor of the Federal Republic, Konrad Adenauer, was a particularly forceful figure who remained in office for fourteen years, during which time his party, the C.D.U./C.S.U., won four successive elections. Second, Adenauer knew well how to use foreign policy to strengthen his position, and he successfully wrested important concessions from the Allies, which lent greater prestige and popularity to his position. In a country whose sovereignty was once so restricted, that remains divided, and that stands as a point of confrontation between East and West in Europe, it is not surprising that issues of foreign and national policy play an important role in shaping public support for a Chancellor.

Much the same holds true for Willy Brandt, who first became Chancellor in 1969.

Third, the power of the Chancellor within the cabinet is strongly defined in Germany. Federal ministers are appointed and dismissed by the President at the request of the Chancellor, and Article 65 states that the Chancellor determines, and assumes responsibility for, general policy. While individual cabinet ministers can exert powerful influence on policy, it is the Chancellor who retains ultimate control, provided his position within his party and his popularity among the electorate remains strong. The position of Vice-Chancellor, often allocated to the leader of the smaller party joining a coalition, carries some prestige but relatively little formal power. Certain of the traditional ministries, especially those dealing with foreign affairs, defense, the interior, economics, and finance, carry special weight. Overall, the German cabinet system is less collegial than Britain's, although again much depends on the respective power of the Chancellor and his ministers within their parties. The Federal Republic has had the greatest continuity and stability of cabinet membership of any European parliamentary system. In its first twenty years there were only eighty-two figures who served in the cabinet. In one case, that of Gerhard Schroeder, cabinet membership extended over sixteen of these twenty years without interruption. This was, of course, in part the consequence of the fact that one party, the C.D.U., dominated the government for these first twenty years. The situation has changed since 1969, when for the first time an incumbent government was removed due to the results of a federal election.

Cabinets have occasionally become large and unwieldy. This is a result of the fact that the Federal Republic has always been governed by a coalition of two or more parties. A recent innovation has been the naming of ministers without portfolio. Two such appointments were made in 1972. The cabinet that was assembled in December of that year was relatively young and professional. The average age of its eighteen members was fifty, and fully half the cabinet was composed of men in their forties.

Five of the eighteen were members of the F.D.P., the junior coalition partner. Five were new to the cabinet, and three of these also entered the Bundestag for the first time in 1972. There was but one woman in the cabinet, Katharina Focke, who was only the fourth woman to have served at cabinet level since the establishment of the Federal Republic.

The cabinet was well-educated. Seven of its eighteen members held doctoral degrees and, of these, two were professors. Two cabinet members were trade union leaders, one a former bricklayer, the other once a miner. Regional factors played a secondary role. Only two cabinet ministers entered directly from positions in *Land* or municipal governments, but many had had previous experience at the state or city level. But doubtless none could match the record of Lauritz Lauritzen, the federal Transport Minister, truly a man from all regions. Since 1951, he served in the governments of West Berlin, Schleswig-Holstein, Lower Saxony, and Hesse, and as mayor of Kassel, as well as at the senior level in three federal ministries. This is a tribute to the flexible career patterns offered by the German federal system, which permits such extensive movement and rewards it with advancement.

Within the cabinet the role of the Chancellor has grown measurably. It very much suited Adenauer's personality and style to retain as much power for his own office within the cabinet as possible. The key chancellery position of state secretary is one of the most powerful in Germany. Under Chancellor Brandt the post was for a while upgraded to ministerial rank, and Horst Ehmke, a leading political figure within the S.P.D. who had been a member of the previous cabinet, was placed in this post. Under his direction the *Bundeskanzleramt* (Chancellor's Office) sought to make a more systematic effort to plan policy and coordinate efforts among the ministries, a task which seems more urgent in view of the growing complexity of government today.

A second innovation, introduced in the late sixties and adapted in part from British practice, has been the appointment of parliamentary state secretaries, who play the role of junior ministers and maintain close liaison with the Bundestag. But the pivotal position within the ministries often is still that of the permanent state secretaries, who stand at the head of the federal bureaucracy. It is they who, to a large degree, command the fundamental loyalty and respect of the vast ministerial bureaucracy. Often they, too, are members of the major political parties, although it is generally assumed, though not always the case, that the civil service will act in a nonpartisan manner. But the distinction between the senior political and purely administrative bureaucracy is somewhat blurred in Germany, certainly more so than in Britain.

This has posed some serious problems for the S.P.D., which first entered a cabinet in 1966 and did not head one until three years later. It found that twenty years of C.D.U. domination of government had affected the political outlook and party preferences of some of the senior administrative personnel. This was particularly important because the German minister is more closely surrounded by bureaucrats than are ministers in Britain or France. Often, the prestige of a senior civil servant may exceed that of his minister. Furthermore, there is a general reverence for administration and mistrust of partisan criteria for selecting or promoting administrative personnel. Thus, the S.P.D. was hard put to remove or reassign many civil servants. The decision of the new F.D.P. foreign minister Walter Scheel to retire twenty-six senior diplomats was attacked as unwarranted political patronage by the C.D.U. opposition. The removal of twelve of the state secretaries who had served C.D.U. ministers raised a shrill political outcry. Yet it would seem that these moves were unavoidable if the new cabinet was to have fundamental confidence in its bureaucratic and diplomatic personnel.

Still, there is relatively little place in the German system for widespread bureaucratic patronage. First of all, most senior civil servants have tenure. They can be transferred laterally or retired (which is costly), but not dismissed without cause. Furthermore, there is a real need to achieve geographic, rather than party, balance. Article 36 of the Basic Law specifies that "civil servants employed in the highest federal authorities shall be drawn from all the *Länder* in appropriate proportion."

The power of the German civil service is often criticized as a weakness of the government system. Its prestige derives from a period that predates the unification of Germany. In many respects it has more continuity with the past than any other institution in the land. Although its administrative competence is high, it has remained somewhat castelike, with access to its higher echelons very restricted. Recruitment for the top ranks has been closely geared to the educational system, which itself has retained certain class features. The higher service has a vast preponderance of law graduates, and entry is dependent on passing examinations that generally require substantial legal expertise.

Administrative service in the Federal Republic still offers considerable status and security. The official has assured tenure until he reaches retirement age and very generous pension rights. The bureaucracy itself remains subdivided into several tiers, and membership in its highest rank brings special prerogatives and exclusive access to the key positions in government. All this has provided the senior bureaucrat with a special sense of esprit de corps, of membership in a privileged group. It has provided the government with a powerful and effective administrative machine, but one whose ingrained preference is to keep things as they are and that often remains resistant to extensive change, especially of the sort that seems to derive from a partisan motivation.

This can, of course, pose problems for a Chancellor and his government. It set a particular challenge for the new regime, an S.P.D./F.D.P. coalition, that came into office in 1969. For the first time in forty years, a Social Democrat, Willy Brandt, assumed the chancellorship. His government had to contend with some popular mistrust of its programmatic intentions and with some administrative resistance. Yet its capacity to govern was facilitated by several factors. First, it had already shared in the cabinet under Chancellor Kiesinger. It was also able to draw upon some administrative personnel from those *Länder* regimes that had been under its control. This aspect of the federal system proved a real asset for the opposition when it came into power. The Chancellor himself had gained substantial government experience from his many years as mayor of West Berlin.

The key factor in government remains the Chancellor himself. Increasingly, distinctions among the parties have become muted. As ideology has faded and as telecommunications have improved, the image projected by the contender for the chancellorship has become a powerful factor. For a popular Chancellor, the frequency of state elections may be a useful means of demonstrating his strength to party and cabinet colleagues. It is not unusual for a Chancellor to have much wider support than his party has. For example, in May 1972, after his narrow victory in the constructive vote of non-confidence moved by the opposition, Chancellor Brandt was the choice of 49 percent of those polled, while Barzel's popularity had slipped to 28 percent. Yet at the same time both government and opposition stood equal in their respective popularity levels.

This is a kind of personalization of politics, which is matched by an overall decline in party identification. It is also a manifestation of a historical pattern in German politics. Not only has there been a "cult of the strong man" in politics, but those periods which are generally regarded by the electorate as having been most successful are linked with the rule of a forceful leader. The nadir always seemed to be associated with weak leadership. This propensity of the German electorate has created greater opportunities for an assertive and vigorous Chancellor. For Adenauer and at times for Brandt, it was a major asset. For Ludwig Erhard, who was unable to personify strength while Chancellor, it posed a fatal handicap.

Is this proclivity toward strong, one-man rule a healthy phenomenon? Given the dangerous excesses of the past, might it again prove corrosive of democratic politics? Here the institutional safeguards designed for the Federal Republic should be sufficient to contain the problem. To be sure, under Adenauer's tutelage, the powers of the Chancellor created some imbalance in the system. But this was checked by other forces that set limits on the extent of one-man rule. The federal system, the provision for judicial review, the capacity of the opposition to exercise some control in parliament, the power of interest groups identified with each of the two major parties, and the frequency of elections all pose substantial curbs on government prerogatives. It is not so much the potential abuse of power by the Chancellor as the incapacity of the system to operate well without a strong leader that remains a source of concern. The demise of Erhard in 1966 led directly to the establishment of a grand coalition of the two major parties, leaving the opposition inadequately represented by the Free Democrats, who represented less than 10 percent of the Bundestag.

More than the rise of the strong man, it is the decline of the opposition that is a serious problem in Germany today. This is not just a matter of the growing similarity of the major parties and the receding role of parliament. A far deeper cause is the decrease of viable alternatives as industrial societies grow more complex. The dissatisfaction of the voter with government has not diminished, but his capacity to discern meaningful alternate courses has decreased. Affluence, stability, and the growing complexity of controlling the conditions of modern life have reduced the options for consensus-seeking mass parties. Under these circumstances, opposition has lost much of its ideological sting. While controversy has not been muted, the personification of politics remains one of the few methods available for generating broad-based support in the political arena. In Germany this has worked for the government, not only because of the great visibility of the Chancellor, but also because of the preference for order and respect for office that remain an important heritage of the past. All this has served to create a system that is perhaps still best described as a "Chancellor democracy."

The President

The President's office has been very much reduced in power since the Weimar Republic. The Parliamentary Council felt that presidential politics under Weimar had served to weaken the Chancellor and had led to an easy abuse of the parliamentary system through recourse to emergency rule under Article 48 of the Weimar constitution. The drafters of the Basic Law also sought to place the symbol of the state above partisan politics, which meant removing the presidency from any important involvement in the political process.

As a result, the President has emerged as a relatively weak and rather symbolic figurehead, but as such, he has served well in the Federal Republic. While he is the head of state, his responsibilities are largely ceremonial, which relieves the Chancellor of a number of time-consuming formalities. The President has extensive powers to appoint and dismiss officials, including the Chancellor, but, in fact, these are dependent on decisions taken elsewhere. While he designates ambassadors, most federal judges, and senior civil servants, he does so at the behest of the Chancellor and the cabinet. Occasionally, he may forestall an appointment or promote his own candidate, but such instances are relatively rare. His cooperation, however, would be important if a Chancellor sought a dissolution of the Bundestag under Article 68, as was the case in September 1972.

The President exercises the right of pardon on behalf of the federation. He also represents the state in international relations and must consent to all treaties. A good portion of his time is spent in good-will travel abroad. But even where the President is given powers, they cannot be exercised autonomously. The Chancellor, for example, must countersign all presidential orders and decrees.

The President is elected for a five-year term by a special federal convention composed of the members of the Bundestag and an equal number of delegates from the various *Land* parliaments. In this case the votes cast by West Berlin do count. The President may serve for only two successive terms and must be elected by a secret vote requiring either a majority on the first two ballots or a plurality thereafter. Any German citizen over the age of forty who is entitled to vote in the Bundestag elections is eligible to stand as a candidate for the presidency, but the choice of nominees is predetermined by the parties represented in the federal convention.

The President may be impeached under Article 61. A motion for impeachment must carry one-fourth of the votes of either house of parliament. Trial by the Federal Constitutional Court must be sustained by a two-thirds majority in either the Bundestag or the Bundesrat.

For many, the President embodies the state above politics. He can serve as a symbolic moral force in the German political system if his qualifications lend themselves to such a role. Certainly in the case of the first incumbent, the distinguished academician and statesman Theodor Heuss, the President served an important educative function. But one of the problems of the position has been the difficulty of recruiting prestigious candidates in view of the weakness of the President's prerogatives. However, this may change, especially in view of the avowed candidacy for the post in 1974 of Walter Scheel, the very popular and powerful Foreign Minister and chairman of the Free Democrats.

While the President formally designates the Chancellor, the Bundestag can override his choice. Thus invariably his proposal reflects the views of the lower house, and his power is, therefore, very restricted. When in 1961 President Lübke sought to convey his preference for a grand coalition to the party leaders before the election, he was chided for intruding in the political process. Indeed, his contact with the Chancellor and cabinet, which was dominated by his own party, remained formal and distant. When in 1969 the election of the new President threatened to coincide with the Bundestag elections, Lübke was willing to resign before the end of his term so that the election of a successor could be kept out of the oncoming Bundestag election campaign.

This led to the election as President of a Social Democrat and former member of the C.D.U., Gustav Heinemann, by a narrow majority of four votes. Heinemann was supported by the F.D.P., which thereby signaled its preference for joining with the Social Democrats to form a government should the two together secure sufficient votes in the forthcoming Bundestag election. F.D.P. backing of the Social Democratic candidate was a significant political act that foreclosed some of the freedom of action of the F.D.P. in the electoral campaign.

The weakness of the presidency is very much influenced by history. It is an important factor in explaining the strength of the Chancellor and has contributed to the smooth functioning of the political system. The memory of the interference by Kaiser Wilhelm and President Hindenburg was too vivid to permit the ceding of any substantial powers to this post. Yet institutionally it remains useful to differentiate the head of state from the head of government. And while the division of functions strongly favors the latter, the distinction between the two positions has served a constructive purpose in the Federal Republic.

Indeed, it may be said that the political institutions designed for the new state in 1949 were well conceived. For the first time Germany stood possessed of a constitution that preserved individual rights, secured democratic processes, and provided for effective governance. In a country that gives such weight to the written law and attaches such importance to order, the success of the institutional provisions laid down in 1949 and amended since then has been of critical importance. While these institutions have revealed defects and substantial new problems have developed, the formal pattern of government has proved very workable and reasonably balanced. Yet this explains only one part of politics in the Federal Republic. To a large degree the real determinants of the political system rest with the parties and the informal pattern of interests that really control the institutions of government.

Six

The Party System

To gain an adequate understanding of the political system of the Federal Republic, it is essential to give close attention to important changes that have occurred since 1945 in the pattern of interests. It is always difficult when judging a parliamentary democracy, especially one as recent in origin as the Federal Republic, to know how much weight to assign to its political institutions and how much to the underlying social and economic forces. In a way the explanation always tends to be somewhat circular and interdependent. While well-designed institutions can set the framework for the effective articulation and integration of political demands, these demands remain very much the expression of basic social and economic factors. Between these two strata, the institutional framework and the socioeconomic base, rest the political parties and groups, which in a parliamentary democracy largely determine whether the government can function effectively.

Changes in these parties and groups are particularly important in explaining the apparent success of the Federal Republic as a political system. Here the heritage from the past was especially inauspicious. The party system before World War I was relatively weak. During the war it was largely ineffective, and then, during the Weimar Republic, it proved badly flawed and was an important contributing factor in the chronic instability of its regimes. As we have seen, the Weimar parties were ideological, divisive, and rent with factionalism. The Catholics, the industrialists, and the Bavarians sought to organize their own interest groups. The Left was torn by dissidence, while the Right was infused with animosity toward the parliamentary republic.

These features were reinforced by an electoral system that gave no incentive to consensus politics or to the emergence of strong individual leaders within the parties. Instead, it firmed the grip of the central party bureaucrats and reduced that of the parliamentary leadership. Narrow interests, reflecting a variety of rending social cleavages, prevailed, and it became increasingly difficult to integrate or harmonize such interests on a basis broad enough to command majority support. Thus the power represented by the parties could not be converted into a viable coalition government. The resulting pattern of instability, dissension, and turmoil undermined confidence in the party system, which seemed ever more impotent and nihilistic. *Parteipolitik* soon became a disreputable but ingrained feature of what was widely seen as a defective political system.

This helped create the conditions for an even more pernicious party system, the National Socialistic dictatorship. Twelve years of Nazi rule eradicated the roots of the old parties and replaced them with a single, totalitarian monolith, which was in turn destroyed through military defeat and occupation. By 1945 there was little in the German past on which to build a healthy and dynamic party system. Here, more than anywhere, a new beginning seemed essential. Remarkably, it was achieved.

The Reemergence of Political Parties

The reestablishment of political parties in occupied Germany came quickly. During the summer of 1945 a number were licensed by the Allied authorities. The first to organize was the Social Democratic party, which had been founded in 1863 and banned by the Nazis seventy years later. Some of its members returned from exile, while others emerged from the underground or from Nazi incarceration. In many respects it was much the same party as before, with a mass membership, a tight hierarchical structure, a working-class base, and a concentration of membership in the now war-ravaged cities. Its leader, Kurt Schumacher, had been one of the most courageous younger members of its Reichstag delegation who had spoken out vehemently against the Nazis in the early thirties. But he was also, in the tradition of his party, very wary of Communist intentions and control.

Germany in the immediate postwar period seemed fertile terrain for the reestablished Social Democrats. The enormity of the task of reconstruction made planning seem indispensable. The complicity of some industrialists in Hitler's rise to power and the sweeping reach of state control of the economy under Nazi rule made socialization of industrial assets a plausible undertaking. Shortages of food and displacement of much of the rural population suggested the timeliness of land reform. Both these objectives were proclaimed by the S.P.D. in its first postwar party program, in May 1946.

What is more, capitalism and the bourgeois parties seemed to be in disrepute because of the manner in which they had faltered in the last years of the Weimar Republic. The S.P.D. virtually alone among the democratic parties had voted against the legislation that had enabled Hitler to suspend parliamentary rights in 1933. The Social Democratic record seemed clean, and its leaders had little to fear from the denazification proceedings that the Allies had begun to impose.

But circumstances swiftly shifted in a direction that limited the opportunities available for the S.P.D. Most significant was the effort made by the Soviet authorities to force through a merger of the Social Democrats with the newly reestablished Communist party (K.P.D.). Schumacher immediately realized that this would mean Communist domination. He prevented an amalgamation of the two parties in the western zones, a move that reflected the overwhelming preference of his party cohorts. But this meant that the S.P.D. would be deprived of its eastern wing, for the Soviets compelled the merger of the two parties in their zone of occupation. Through this action the Social Democratic party lost many of its former strongholds in Prussia and Saxony. The division of Germany meant that the S.P.D. as it emerged after the war would at least initially remain a minority party in the western zones, despite the fortuitous circumstances that suggested that its program might find very broad acceptance.

A striking new development in 1945 was the establishment of the Christian Democratic Union (C.D.U.). This party was rather loosely structured at the federal level with strong local units, as in Bavaria, where the affiliated party was launched as the Christian Social Union (C.S.U.), a distinction that has remained to date. The early programmatic impetus within the C.D.U. was not dissimilar to the ethos of the postwar S.P.D. Especially under the influence of its Berlin wing, led by Jakob Kaiser and Ernst Lemmer, the C.D.U. at first adopted several Socialist objectives. It, too, was critical of capitalism and advocated limited state control of the giant firms that had dominated German industry. The C.D.U. favored codetermination, which offered to extend to organized labor an important voice in the control of the larger factories, and it sought support among the working class. This approach also characterized much of the western C.D.U., especially in the industrial Ruhr, where Karl Arnold became leader of the party. Arnold, like Kaiser, had been active before 1933 in the Catholic trade-union movement.

Indeed, the C.D.U. represented a rather variegated amalgam of political components. As such, it was a new phenomenon in German politics. It was the first successful effort to broaden a Christian party beyond the ranks of Catholicism; it derived as much from Protestant political forces as from Catholic. This was not just a postwar recrudescence of the old Center party, which, in fact, sought also to revive itself. Christian Democracy from the beginning attempted to reach out to a broader constituency. In this it paralleled developments in France and Italy. But it also remained emphatically conscious of a lesson from the German past, namely, that the divisiveness among the non-Socialist forces in the Weimar Republic had vitiated their efforts and had created insurmountable obstacles to stable government. This time these forces would have to coalesce.

As a mass movement Christian Democracy would emerge as a rather heterodox, loose-knit, and decentralized party. In attempting to integrate forces that had so long been divided, it had to make substantial concessions to each. The common denominator that remained was not clearly defined. Party organization initially was not tight or well formed. Instead, the C.D.U. remained a rather collegial federation that sought to embrace divergent elements, including the conservative Protestants of north Germany, the old liberals of southwest Germany, and the traditional Catholic forces from Bavaria and the Rhineland.

What gave the party form and definition and an opportunity for real success was the division of Germany. First, this removed a great Protestant bastion, leaving the Catholics, who comprised the more dynamic core of the C.D.U., almost a majority in the three western zones. Second, Soviet actions and the division provided the party with an effective, albeit negative, integrating ideology, that of anticommunism. Third, the division and the aggressiveness of Soviet policy gave credence to those forces within the C.D.U. which sought a pro-Western policy. This served to hasten the rise of Konrad Adenauer and to consolidate his position as leader of the new party. His foremost competitor was not, as many had expected, former Center Chancellor Heinrich Brüning, who had now returned to Germany; rather, it was Jakob Kaiser, the Catholic trade unionist in Berlin, who called for a neutral policy for Germany between East and West. But Soviet harassment of the C.D.U. in its zone and the expulsion of Kaiser undermined Kaiser's policy and destroyed his base, leaving Adenauer, the spokesman of a more conservative, free-enterprise–oriented, and emphatically pro-Western outlook, as the uncontested leader of the Christian Democrats.

By 1947 Adenauer had made his breakthrough, and two years later he was the first Chancellor of the Federal Republic. This success was critical for his party. Loosely federated and largely heterogeneous as it was, the C.D.U. was greatly assisted by the common purpose of constituting a government and by the prestige of office. These provided the cement to hold together what was originally a decentralized and unassimilated coalition of contending forces. Indeed, it was not until 1950, after the first C.D.U.-dominated government had been established, that the party was able to hold its first national convention. Even so, its Bavarian wing, the Christian Social Union, remained an independent affiliate.

The opportunities of office and the effectiveness of its leaders gave the C.D.U. a common incentive to cohere rather than splinter. This was the most significant factor in the postwar reconstruction of the German party system. By 1953 one party was almost able to command a majority of the seats in the Bundestag.[1] Four years later it would receive an absolute majority of the votes cast in the Bundestag elections. Never before in German history had this occurred. It was a singular achievement, but one that would not have been possible at the time without the division of Germany and the opportunities created by Soviet hostility.

Indeed, foreign policy was critical for the formation of the Federal Republic and for the success of its party system. While it created sudden opportunities for the Christian Democrats, the division of Germany effectively removed the extreme Left for the first two decades as a factor in West German politics and thereby freed the S.P.D. from one of its most onerous problems, a constant internecine battle with a formidable left-wing antagonist. Indeed, foreign policy had great impact on the position of the two major parties. Throughout the 1950s it tended to consolidate the position of the Christian Democrats. The Berlin blockade, the rising in East Berlin in 1953, and the brutal Soviet repression of the Hungarian revolution all closely preceded Bundestag elections that produced increasing C.D.U. victories. It was not until the mid-1960s, when the opportunities of détente and of rapprochement with the East became viable alternatives, that foreign policy began to favor the Social Democrats, who sought a more flexible and less antagonistic approach to the Soviet Union, Eastern Europe, and East Germany.

By that time the trend toward a two-party system was firmly developed, and the S.P.D. for the first time could seriously contemplate winning a plurality of the Bundestag votes and perhaps constituting a government. This was due to several substantial changes that had occurred within the major parties, especially within the S.P.D. It was also a consequence of the changing social and economic complexion of the Federal Republic by the mid-sixties. But above all, the emergence of large, unified parties and the stability of the political process were the result of changes in the electoral system.

The Electoral System

The electoral system has been a crucial factor in determining the pattern and success of party politics in the Federal Republic. The present system has evolved with a continuing awareness of the defects of the election law

---

[1]For the Bundestag election returns from 1949 through 1972, see Appendix A.

as defined in the past. From 1871 to 1918, members of the Reichstag were elected by majority vote, if necessary through a runoff second ballot, in single-member constituencies. During the Weimar Republic a strict proportional system of party lists was instituted, with one seat allocated for every 60,000 votes won.

The Parliamentary Council was divided on the electoral issue. The Christian Democrats preferred the British system of relative majorities in single-member constituencies. The Social Democrats, on the other hand, pressed for proportional representation. As a result of this division, the Parliamentary Council contented itself with drafting the law for the first Bundestag election only, leaving to that chamber the task of further legislation. Therefore, the Basic Law says little about the electoral system, stipulating only in Article 38 that elections to the Bundestag shall be universal, direct, free, equal, and secret; that any person having reached the age of eighteen be entitled to vote, and that those over the age of twenty-one may stand for election; and that all further details are to be determined by subsequent federal law.

Since 1949 there has been a substantial body of legislation dealing with the electoral process. Basically it has been guided by three aims. First, there has been an effort to correct the depersonalized pattern of the Weimar Republic by allocating to local constituencies one-half of the seats in the Bundestag. Second, the other half of the seats (originally only 40 percent) are filled from the party lists in such a way that each party receives a number of seats in proportion to the total number of votes cast for it. Third, only parties that either receive 5 percent of the list vote or win three constituencies outright are represented in the Bundestag. Votes for the parties that do not surmount this hurdle are reallocated to the parties that do, so that in the Bundestag each party may be represented by a slightly larger percentage of the seats than the votes it has gained in the election.

Each of the two major parties contests all 248 election districts. Through 1965 the C.D.U. (with its Bavarian affiliate) always outpolled the Social Democrats in these direct constituency elections. However, in 1969 this pattern was reversed for the first time, with the S.P.D. winning 127, or slightly over half, of these 248 seats. Three years later the S.P.D. was able to win 152 districts outright, while the C.D.U. fell to only 96.

The average population of these districts totals 225,000, two-thirds of whom are eligible to vote. The nomination of the candidates in the districts is left to the local constituency selection conference. In the larger cities several districts will combine to form one conference. But the size of these conferences has remained small, ranging from 25 to 360 party members. There are no primaries. This means that less than 3 percent of the 1.4 million members of the two larger parties actually participate in the selection of candidates.

There has been a real effort in constituency nominations to develop a strong link between the candidate and his locality. In 1969, of the 496 candidates nominated by the two major parties in constituencies, only 22 percent did not live in their districts, and of these over half maintained a nearby residence. The remaining candidates tended to be prominent national figures within their parties or experts whom the national party was eager to have elected to the Bundestag.

The compliance of the local selection conferences in this process is important because constituency nomination has become a more frequent prerequisite for safe placement on the party lists, which determine how the other 248 seats are allocated. This is particularly true for the S.P.D. It is less the case for the Christian Democrats, who elected forty-two members in 1969 on the basis of a list candidacy alone. This is explained by the greater influence within the C.D.U. of a diverse range of interest groups, whose support of the party may depend on receiving a safe seat, and thus on strong placement on the *Land* list. Generally, nomination in the S.P.D. depends more on a candidate's relations within the party, whereas in the C.D.U. a candidate's relations outside the party carry considerable weight. But overall the importance of a strong local party base is growing. Of the 156 new candidates elected to the sixth Bundestag in 1969, 60 percent held important party posts. Fifty-five percent of the Bundestag members elected since 1949 have entered politics at the local or community level, whereas in the Weimar Republic only 40 percent did so. This is an indicator of the decreased importance of the central party bureaucracy as compared to that of the local party organization, which is a natural concomitant of a direct constituency system.

The composition of the lists is quite complex. Here a variety of factors and calculations must be considered. First is the party's prospect for victory in the constituency elections. In those *Länder* where one of the two major parties tends to win more direct districts than its share of the total vote, placement on the list is meaningless for its candidates. Thus in Bremen, for example, the Social Democrats have won only through the constituencies, whereas in Bavaria or Baden-Württemberg they have little hope of winning any districts outside the larger cities and must depend on the lists. Other considerations involve the popularity of those heading a *Land* list; the allocation of safe seats to certain groups, especially to women; and the reinsurance of those candidates whom the party is particularly eager to place in the Bundestag and who are contesting difficult or hopeless constituencies. Thus Fritz Erler, for years the major foreign policy spokesman and deputy leader of the S.P.D. in the Bundestag, always failed to win in his district, but gained reelection through safe placement high on the *Land* list.

This system of dual election has worked reasonably well. No distinction has developed between those members directly elected and those who gain entry to the Bundestag through the lists, as was originally feared. The method of constituency candidate selection, which is the key process, has worked on a more democratic basis than in many other parliamentary systems. The lists also serve as a party reservoir in the case of death, removal, or resignation of a member of the Bundestag, thereby obviating by-elections. They can be used as an instrument to preserve party discipline. In the spring of 1972 Chancellor Brandt was able to restore briefly his narrow and precarious parliamentary majority when two Free Democrats, who had turned against the government in the constructive vote of non-confidence, resigned their seats and were replaced by two party loyalists who were next in line.

The two hurdles, 5 percent of the votes or three constituencies won, have been particularly important features of this system. Except in the case of regionally concentrated parties they have meant that the smaller parties can only win through the lists and, therefore, tend not to contest many constituencies. Since 1961 the process has eliminated all but one of the smaller parties from the Bundestag. Today only the Free Democrats (who fell as low as 5.8 percent of the vote in 1969) are still represented in the lower house. In fact, by the end of the shortened term of the sixth Bundestag, the F.D.P. had fallen to within one seat of the 5 percent margin due to the defection of four of its deputies.

This induced the S.P.D. to try to win votes for its weaker coalition partner in 1972. The effort apparently succeeded. The Free Democrats were able to obtain 8.4 percent of the second (or list) votes, which was 3.6 percent more than the first (or direct constituency) votes won by the party. This got the F.D.P. handily over the 5 percent hurdle, which is computed on the basis of second votes only. On the other hand, the Social Democrats had 3.1 percent more first votes than second, which helped the party to score such dramatic victories in the direct constituencies. Clearly, this ticket splitting served the interests of both parties in maximizing their respective parliamentary representation. It also reflected a fairly sophisticated electorate. Curiously, had the fourth party, the right-wing National Democrats (N.P.D.), secured but 226,000 more votes in 1969, the coalition between the Social Democrats and the F.D.P. would not have been possible since it was only through the reallocation of the 4.8 percent vote of the N.P.D. that these two parties obtained a narrow majority in the Bundestag.

Perhaps a more serious problem is a predilection to keep changing the electoral law. The entry requirements for the Bundestag have been successively tightened over the years. A recent constitutional amendment has extended the vote to all those between the ages of eighteen and twenty-one. State financing of parties has been redefined several times. More serious has been the attempt under the grand coalition of the C.D.U. and S.P.D. that came into office in 1966 to raise the issue of fundamental and radical reform of the electoral system, replacing the lists entirely with single member constituencies. There are many experts and forces in the Federal Republic who have been advocating this reform for many years. However, in 1966 when the grand coalition came into office, it had strongly partisan reasons for considering such a change: It would have permanently eliminated the two smaller parties, the F.D.P., which had demonstrated itself to be an illoyal coalition partner, and the N.D.P., which suggested too strong a revival of right-wing nationalism for inclusion in any government. As elsewhere, the foremost problem of a multiparty system in Germany has been that of assuring stable coalition government.

But even without electoral reform, it seems likely that a two-party system will emerge in the framework of the present system. The two major parties have consistently enlarged their joint share of the seats in the Bundestag, rising from 60 percent in 1949 to over 90 percent twenty-three years later. With 91.2 percent of the electorate voting in 1972, the S.P.D. and the C.D.U. together gained some 34 million votes of the 37.5 million that were cast. The turnout itself was a striking phenomenon. In past federal elections it had averaged 87 percent, which is very high for non-compulsory elections. But in 1972 approximately one-eighth of the electorate was voting for the first time because of the reduction of the minimum age for voters to eighteen. Generally, first-time voters score a poor turnout. Not so in Germany. Given the unusually charged atmosphere of the political confrontation of 1972 and the great popularity of Chancellor Brandt among the young, a remarkable turnout was recorded. The fact that it produced such an overwhelming vote on behalf of the two major parties is an impressive feat in view of Germany's record in the past. It is very largely the consequence of an electoral system designed to maximize the coalescing of votes (and interests) and the consolidation of the larger parties.

The Parties and the State

In the Federal Republic, state institutions and the government play a considerable role in determining important features of the party system. First of all, the Basic Law provides for their existence. Article 21 states explicitly that "the political parties shall participate in the forming of the political will of the people. They may be freely established. Their internal organization must conform to democratic principles. They must publicly account for the sources of their funds. Parties which, by reason of their aims or the behavior of their adherents, seek to impair or abolish the free democratic basic order or to endanger the existence of the Federal Republic of Germany, shall be unconstitutional."

It is the Federal Constitutional Court that holds the power to rule on the constitutionality of party practices. Its rulings have been very significant.

During the 1950s, two parties, the extreme right-wing Socialist Reich party (S.R.P.) and the Communists (K.P.D.), were decreed in violation of Article 21 and banned as unconstitutional. In the case of the former it was the fear of a renascent Nazi movement that motivated its prohibition. The case of the K.P.D. was more complex and controversial. It was explained in part by the desire of the court and the government to appear evenhanded in banning extremist parties on both Right and Left. However, the political efficacy of this action was widely challenged, because the Communists seemed such a negligible political force in the Federal Republic. By declaring their party illegal, the court actually helped to camouflage the electoral weakness of the K.P.D. This is the reason why several prominent politicians welcomed the reestablishment of a new Communist party (now labeled the D.K.P.) in 1968, hoping that it would secure scant support while removing a propaganda weapon of the East Germans. In fact, the party won only 114,000 votes, or 0.3 percent of the total cast, in the 1972 elections. An effort to have the court ban the new and radical Maoist Communist Party of Germany failed early in 1974.

The Federal Constitutional Court has also ruled frequently on matters of party finance. Here the relationship between the government and the parties has been a particularly close and somewhat unique one in the Federal Republic. The first decision of the court in 1958 merely declared that contributions to political parties were not to be considered tax exempt, which had been the practice up to that date. This judgment worsened the financial condition of the parties, though least of all the S.P.D., which derives the larger part of its income from the dues paid by its members. However, the two coalition parties, the C.D.U. and the F.D.P., were especially threatened and, therefore, pressed for new state subsidies to the parties for the "political education" work that they sponsored.

Beginning in 1959 and lasting for the next six years, the parties received a total of 131 million marks from the government, ostensibly for this purpose. Then, in July 1966, the court ruled again, forbidding this form of support. It did, however, sanction payments by the government to the parties to defray the costs of election campaigns. This has become a major source of party income. Each party is entitled to two-and-a-half marks for each vote won in a federal election for the Bundestag (and one-and-a-half marks per vote cast in elections for the *Land* parliaments). Only parties that receive half of 1 percent of the vote or more are eligible for such government subsidy. As there are now some 40 million enfranchised voters in Germany, the total amount available for the parties over a four year period is approaching 100 million marks, and, indeed, nearly this amount was paid out during the 1969 election. A further 60 million is available for the state elections held every four years. In the event of an interim election caused by the dissolution of parliament, this amount is paid out sooner.

This practice is very important for party development in the Federal

Republic. It has greatly eased the burden of financing the costly election campaigns and reduced the dependency of the parties on those interest groups and wealthy individuals who were, heretofore, an important source of monetary support. Up to 600 marks may be given annually on a tax exempt basis by an individual or firm to a political campaign. In contrast to the United States electoral law, companies may donate funds. All contributions above 20,000 marks must be reported by the recipients.

There has been a continuous cost inflation for party activities and electoral campaigns in the Federal Republic, as elsewhere. For example, it has been estimated that total party spending in 1968, in which there was no federal election, was about 150 million marks. But the contributions reported by the three major parties for that year only came to 11 million marks, or about 8 percent of the total. Even assuming substantial underreporting, it is clear that private contributions are a very secondary source of income for the parties—which is a healthy development. Dues tend to be more important. The S.P.D. reports that almost 40 percent of its income derives from this source, but for the other parties the figure is closer to 12 percent.

The great problem is the constantly escalating cost of elections. The first Bundestag campaign of 1949 is reported to have cost the three major parties about 7 million marks. In 1972, despite a shortened campaign, it is estimated that 200 million marks were spent. The major parties spent about five marks per vote won, half of which was recovered from the state. But because of the pressure of rising costs, the C.D.U. and the F.D.P. have been seeking an increase in the state subsidy to 3.5 marks per voter. The Social Democrats have been less eager to move to this higher figure, in part because of their more substantial dues, which are apportioned as a percentage of income among their 850,000 members.

There has been some voluntary interparty agreement to limit spending. Television time in Germany is free (as it is state-owned). But the size of the parties' professional apparatus and staff has swelled in recent years as electoral techniques have become more sophisticated. Germans are probably the most poll saturated people in the world. Literally dozens of polling institutes are testing public opinion, often on behalf of the parties, almost all the time. And the frequency of the *Land* elections, which have such bearing on federal politics, creates an almost continuous campaign atmosphere for the parties.

It has been argued that the practice of state subsidies poses dangers. It may create a greater susceptibility toward a state orientation within the parties. Conceivably, it also discriminates against new parties, which would find it difficult to amass one-half of 1 percent of the vote, the minimum requirement for eligibility for a subsidy. In 1972 only one of the four smaller parties contesting the election (the N.P.D.) received support from this source. Had parliament had its way and not been overruled by the Federal Constitutional Court, the cutoff actually would have been higher at 2.5 percent of the vote. But it is not really this hurdle as much as the 5 percent vote clause for entry into the Bundestag that is the major obstacle for any new political grouping.

In fact, state support actually is of greater advantage to the opposition. The provision of funds is more important for it in any election because the government parties have certain cost-free advantages available to them through the regular government public relations machinery. It is always more costly to popularize an opposition leader and usually more difficult to obtain contributions for an opposition party. Thus, state support serves as a kind of equalizer. But it can, occasionally, cause difficulties, as in 1969 when the Free Democrats polled less votes than they had expected and, as a result, found that they had substantially overspent in the campaign, having overcalculated the amount that would be available from government coffers. The loss by the party of 1.2 million voters cost it some 3 million marks of state subsidy.

Party Organization

The two major parties are organized along rather similar lines, although the S.P.D. has a more cohesive and integrated structure. The composition of each reflects its historical evolution, regional strength, and social bases. Initially, the C.D.U. was organized as a rather loose coalition, held together by the prerogatives, prestige, and patronage of the government that it had headed for twenty years. It yielded substantial influence to its various components, and especially to its Bavarian affiliate, the C.S.U., with which it caucuses in the Bundestag in order whenever possible to retain the privileges of the largest parliamentary party, until 1972 when the S.P.D. emerged as the largest party. In many ways the C.S.U. is really an autonomous component of the C.D.U., but it has utilized its independent position to maximum effect and, occasionally, has threatened to pursue its own course.

In other ways as well the C.D.U. structure has remained somewhat bizarre. For example, in North Rhine-Westphalia, Lower Saxony, and Baden-Württemberg, it has no statewide organizations, but rather operates through party units that do not encompass the entire state. Thus, in the largest *Land* there are separate organizations for Rhineland and for Westphalia, which adds to the problems of an overall coordination of policy. Furthermore, since the C.S.U. is organized more effectively than any other state unit, its leverage is all the greater on issues that concern the party nationally.

The C.D.U. also yields important powers to various groups that are represented within the party. The influence of the Protestant working group and of the social committees that derives from the Christian trade-union movement and from the socialism of the early postwar years has remained considerable. Recently the influence of this wing has grown, especially in the industrial bastion of North Rhine-Westphalia. Here, for example, the social committees were able to place sixteen of their candidates in safe positions on the *Land* list for the the 1972 elections, compared with only eleven in 1969. Likewise, in view of the importance of business and agrarian constituents within the party, the C.D.U. tends to incorporate their wishes in its programs and to allocate positions of influence to their delegates within party councils.

The greater homogeneity of the S.P.D., while limiting its electoral base, has eased its organizational problems. Its state-wide organizations, which exist in each *Land* except Hesse, tend to have less autonomous power within the party. It is only where there is a significant difference of outlook between a local unit and the national leadership that regional tensions tend to emerge. Controversies within the S.P.D. have dealt more with policy than with structure. Its greatest organizational problems have been in contending with its own left-wing dissidents, who, since the mid-1960s, have become more outspoken in their criticism of party policy. By 1973 one-third of the thirty-six man executive committee that determines S.P.D. policy belonged to the "new" left wing.

The S.P.D. has a substantially larger membership than the C.D.U., with some 850,000 to the latter's 450,000 (of whom less than one-fifth belong to the Bavarian C.S.U.). Party recruitment since 1971 has experienced a fairly dramatic increase. Traditionally, the number of Germans tempted to enroll in a party has been small. A recent poll revealed that only 14 percent of those asked saw party membership as part of the role of a good citizen. In fact, such enrollment comprises less than 4 percent of the electorate.

For both parties, the party congress, which is usually convened once or twice in every electoral period, is the highest organ, but for the Social Democrats the congress has greater significance in view of its role in debating programmatic issues. Actually the key governing body of each party is its executive committee. In 1972, that of the C.D.U. contained some thirty-one members, half of whom also comprised the leadership of the party in the Bundestag. Thus federal and state politicians were fairly evenly matched in numbers, although the former were more heavily represented on the smaller presidium, which is the inner core of the party leadership.

Roughly the same pertains to the S.P.D. Nineteen of the thirty-six members on its executive committee in 1972 were members of the Bundestag. As in the C.D.U., the executive committee had shown a high continuity of membership and relatively little mobility. Generally in the past it has been difficult and unusual for anyone under forty to penetrate these inner ranks of party leadership except from a base in the parties' youth organizations. This was less true for the Free Democrats, which had the youngest leadership.

The trend in the two major parties changed dramatically in 1973. The S.P.D. at its Hannover congress and, especially, the C.D.U. at its special congress in Bonn opened the ranks of party leadership to new and often younger figures. In the S.P.D. it was in particular the more vociferous left that was able to place its candidates and block a number of those who sought a more conservative course. In the case of the C.D.U., the party leader himself was changed due to the sudden resignation of Rainer Barzel as parliamentary floor leader. This led to his replacement as party chairman by Helmut Kohl, the forty-three-year-old governor of Rhineland-Palatinate. Kurt Biedenkopf, also forty-three and, like Kohl, holder of a doctoral degree, became the new secretary general of the party. Others close to Kohl, such as Bernhard Vogel and Heinrich Geissler, both members of his state cabinet, were also in their early forties.

The new leadership in both parties is likely to be increasingly preoccupied with issues of economic policy and social reform. In the S.P.D. there is strong pressure for a more radical program in these areas on the part of its youth organization, the *Jung Sozialisten* (or *Jusos,* as they are popularly known), and the trade unions. The *Jusos,* some quarter of a million strong, have become increasingly outspoken in challenging the party leadership. By comparison, the *Junge Union,* which is the youth organization of the C.D.U., or the *Jungdemokraten* of the F.D.P. have been less assertive.

But even within the more conservative C.D.U., the new leadership has already announced that its motto will call for a "compass set upon reform," (in the words of Helmut Kohl). This was reflected in its party conference in Hamburg in November, 1973. Critical problems of property law, tax reform, limits on capital accumulation, extension of worker codetermination and educational opportunity will be addressed by the C.D.U. in an effort to head off government initiatives that the party feels are misguided or overreaching in these areas. For the C.D.U. the foremost challenge of the immediate future rests in its capacity to become a forward-looking, modern party, offering constructive alternative solutions for the problems confronting Germany as an advanced industrial society. Precisely because the S.P.D., which has heretofore been the more programmatically-oriented party, can claim the more popular leader in Willy Brandt, the C.D.U. while in opposition must develop more attractive policies than it has in the past. Its difficulty derives from its internal division into rather equally balanced conservative and reformist wings. In June 1973, Norbert Blüm, the leader of the more left-wing social committees, and Alfred Dregger, the conservative state leader from Hesse, received about an equal number of votes for the party's executive committee. And the rather independent Bavarian affiliate of Christian Democracy, the

C.S.U., seems as set on a right-wing course as ever, which could mute the efforts on behalf of reform in the parent C.D.U.

All of this suggests the reemergence of more ideological disputes on the part of the major parties. It signals a reversal of the trend that persisted through the 1960s. For the S.P.D., which traces its origins and heritage to the last century, this transformation into a pragmatic party has been particularly painful. Its Marxist *Weltanschauung* had been a central feature of party ideology for almost a century. But a great deal had changed during this period, and by 1959, at Godesberg, the party found the lure of the electorate greater than the conceptions of its party theoreticians, many of which it jettisoned in its famous Godesberg Program.

The Composition of the Electorate

In changing its course, the S.P.D. has had to take into account shifts in the German electorate, some of which have posed special problems for the party. About 45 percent of all West Germans are Catholics. Only one-third of the population lives in cities of more than 100,000. Because of the decimation of the male population in the two world wars, women comprise 55 percent of the electorate in postwar Germany. They have tended to be more conservative, less class-conscious, more concerned with inflation than with social reform, and, generally, more religious than the male voter. This last factor is important, since several surveys have revealed that it is the intensity of the religious tie that is most relevant in determining voter preference. Until 1972 about two-thirds of those Catholics who attended church regularly voted for the C.D.U., while one-half of those who rarely attended opted for the S.P.D. However, in the elections of that year, the Social Democrats were able to score impressive gains among Catholic workers. For the first time the S.P.D. outpolled the C.D.U. in the Catholic industrial Saarland.

If the female voter has been an important asset to the C.D.U., so have in the past the growing number of employees and government officials who tend to prefer this party. With development and affluence, the percentage of the population that regards itself as working class has decreased, and with higher incomes and relatively full employment, the attitudes of the workers themselves have changed. This shift has been reflected in the changing composition of the S.P.D. In 1961 55 percent of its membership was working class. By the end of the sixties, this group represented less than 45 percent of the party membership. In 1972 the party was able to win 65 percent of the working class vote as against only 22 percent for the C.D.U. In the same period the party substantially increased its membership among the sectors of the population that were growing most rapidly in terms of employment and social position. Today, white-collar employees and government officials comprise almost one-third of its membership. It does least well among top management, where the C.D.U. and F.D.P. together captured 93 percent of the vote in 1972, whereas the S.P.D. won 48 percent of the middle managers. Farmers remain loyal to the C.D.U., which polled 81 percent in this sector in the elections to the seventh Bundestag.

In terms of income, the S.P.D. membership today conforms more closely to that of the Federal Republic as a whole. In 1970, 31 percent of its members had monthly incomes below 800 marks, and only 17 percent were above 1,400 marks. The national composite figures were 36 and 12 percent respectively, whereas those for the C.D.U. membership were considerably weighted in favor of the more affluent. Only 15 percent of its members received less than 800 marks a month, and over one-third earned more than 1,400.

These figures suggest that economic factors can be critical for the success of the Social Democrats. Any substantial downturn in the economy that threatened the large lower-income groups would broaden the appeal of the S.P.D. if it were in opposition. This was the cause for its major electoral victory in North Rhine-Westphalia in June 1966, in which it won almost 50 percent of the vote, a development which paved the way for the party's inclusion in the grand coalition that was established in Bonn five months later.

Other sociological and demographic factors seem to be favoring the S.P.D. The imbalance between male and female voters will in time correct itself. The new youth vote of those between eighteen and twenty-one may align itself more easily with a party advocating social reform, as the S.P.D. tends to do. Recent polls reveal that 42 percent of those under twenty-four prefer the S.P.D., while only one-third favor the Christian Democrats. It is estimated that the government parties (S.P.D. and F.D.P.) won as much as two-thirds of the new youth vote in the 1972 federal elections. For the S.P.D. to capitalize effectively on this advantage may require a process of rejuvenation within the party, only 18 percent of whose members are today under the age of thirty-four. In fact, one of the great inner problems of the S.P.D. has been the preponderance of the old *Parteigenossen* ("party comrades"). Over half of its membership is over fifty years of age, whereas in the C.D.U. this age group comprises only 40 percent of its smaller membership. However, the Social Democrats are trying to meet this problem in their recruiting of new members. Of the new members who have joined the party since 1967, four out of ten are under thirty, which represents a 30 percent increase in this category over a ten-year period.

The S.P.D. should also benefit from the increasing urbanization of Germany. The demise of the farmer and of the rural sectors will deplete an important reservoir of C.D.U. strength and will probably serve to weaken the religious factor in determining party preference. In fact, as the S.P.D.

moves away from its working-class base, the C.D.U. will have to readdress itself to the problems of a more modern, industrialized, and urban society, which will probably give greater weight to those groups within it that played such an important part in its establishment and that have always sought to emphasize social reform as a central credo of the party.

What seems clear is that these two parties have become more similar to each other over time. They have successfully reached out to broaden their constituency and to appeal to the uncommitted voters, who today represent between 15 and 20 percent of the electorate. In this process, both parties tend to appeal to an identical audience. Such is often the fate of two-party systems, and it can produce problems of disaffection, splintering, and antisystem politics if the range of choice between the major contending parties appears too narrow to a significant portion of the electorate. In the Federal Republic this problem has not yet become severe. The more extreme manifestations of political disaffection, such as the N.P.D. on the Right or the A.P.O. on the Left, have been epiphenomenal, brief, and often overrated. Indeed, it has been the success of the two major parties in integrating diverse political forces that has helped shape a stable pattern of politics, which is increasingly developing into a two-party system.

Toward a Two-Party System

The process of consolidation of the two major parties has been very consistent. During the 1950s it was the C.D.U. that steadily expanded its base, capitalizing on the popularity of its leader, the domestic appeal of its foreign policy, and the success of its economic efforts. The S.P.D., by contrast, was ineffectively led from 1952, after the death of Schumacher, until the selection of Willy Brandt as its Chancellor candidate and chairman of the party in the sixties. The key reversal for the party was its Godesberg program, adopted amid a great deal of shrill controversy, in 1959. Basically, the party congress meeting at Bad Godesberg jettisoned its Marxist program in favor of a program seeking a modern, mixed economy that combined free enterprise with state planning.

This shift in policy enabled the party to make a substantial breakthrough in its voter support, which rose from a low point of 32 percent in 1957 to almost 46 percent of the votes cast fifteen years later. It also meant that from the early sixties onward the possibility of a grand coalition spanning the C.D.U. and the S.P.D. was a reasonable possibility.

This option became important by the mid-1960s because of three factors: the leadership crisis within the C.D.U., the uncertainty of its continued coalition with the F.D.P., and the brief but sudden rise of the National Democrats. The C.D.U. found it difficult to hasten the retirement of Chancellor Adenauer, which seemed desirable in view of his long tenure in office and advanced age. After Adenauer's retirement in 1963, Ludwig Erhard, long identified with the brilliant economic recovery of Germany, became Chancellor. He faltered badly in 1966, which led important factions within his own party to favor a coalition with the S.P.D. in order to effect his removal.

For this purpose a renewed coalition of the Christian Democrats with the F.D.P., which had been a junior partner in all the cabinets since 1949, did not seem feasible. After seventeen years of partnership, relations between the two parties had eroded badly. This was reflected in the complex negotiations to establish a C.D.U./F.D.P. coalition in both 1961 and 1965, which had taken an average of seven weeks of intensive post-election interparty negotiation. Furthermore, the Free Democrats sustained substantial defeats in the Hessian and Bavarian *Landtag* elections that were held in November 1966, just at the time when the Erhard coalition had broken down. Under these circumstances the C.D.U. turned to the S.P.D. to establish a grand coalition under Chancellor Kurt Georg Kiesinger.

The rise of the right-wing N.P.D. was an important factor in the establishment of this coalition. Capitalizing on the economic recession of 1966, the National Democrats scored some impressive electoral gains, receiving more than 7 percent of the vote in both the Hessian and Bavarian *Landtag* elections. This prompted a sense of alarm about a further downturn in the economy. Many leaders spoke of an impending economic crisis. A grand coalition was deemed the only way to deal effectively with the situation.

As a transitory phenomenon the grand coalition was a success. It restored vitality to the economy and began a readjustment of foreign policy that seemed long overdue. Perhaps more importantly, it demonstrated that the S.P.D. was also highly competent to govern. Long castigated by the C.D.U. for its purportedly radical ideology, the S.P.D. seized the opportunity of partnership in government to shed this distorted image and present itself as a more skillful and expert, but not very different party from the C.D.U.

The weakness of the grand coalition was the enormous reduction in the size of the parliamentary opposition. Forty-nine Free Democrats, less than 10 percent of the Bundestag, became the minute voice of parliamentary opposition. This gave a boost to the right-wing N.P.D., which almost passed the 5 percent hurdle in the 1969 Bundestag elections. This was not a healthy situation. Yet it was one that was forced upon the system by the increasing weakness of the third party, the F.D.P. The role of this small party with a membership of only 80,000 is important disproportionately to its size. It can, barring a clear majority vote for one of the two giant parties, determine the composition of a coalition, as it did in 1969, when it refused to consider a renewed alliance with the C.D.U. Thus the power of the party was enormous, even though it had lost 38 percent of its voters over the previous four years. Rarely has a defeated party played so critical a role in the formation of a government. However, had the party done slightly worse, or the N.P.D. slightly better, the coalition that was constituted in the fall of 1969 between the S.P.D. and the F.D.P. would not have been possible. Indeed, the 5 percent hurdle for entry into the Bundestag remains a very significant factor in the political process.

The F.D.P., which shifted from a lengthy partnership with the C.D.U. from 1949 to 1966 to one with the S.P.D. since 1969, has found its own new base among the electorate. It has polled increasingly well among the growing new middle class of civil servants and white-collar employees. These represented 34 percent of its vote in 1953, but grew to 66 percent by 1972. By 1972 it seems to have made a transition from its former base, which was too dependent on declining sectors of the population, especially the self-employed. In the elections of the seventh Bundestag, one-fifth of the party's vote came from the working class (although they may well have been votes "borrowed" from the S.P.D.).

The growing similarity of the electoral base of the Free Democrats to that of the Social Democrats suggests a fairly stable foundation for a continued coalition between the two parties. However, should the S.P.D. feel confident that it could obtain an absolute majority of the seats in a Bundestag election, competition between the parties would intensify. It may also increase if the S.P.D. presses on with vigorous new legislation on controversial social and economic issues. More than half the F.D.P. voters expressed opposition to socialism when polled in 1973 (but so did 30 percent of the S.P.D. supporters). The party has styled itself as a kind of domestic brake on its more adventurous and ideologically inclined larger partner. Agreement between the two was easy during the first Brandt administration, which gave such priority to foreign affairs. It may become more difficult and elusive as domestic reform programs take center stage, and when the F.D.P.-leader Walter Scheel retires from the Foreign Ministry.

One of the important factors contributing to the stability of German politics has been the demise of all the other smaller parties, which was not foreseen in 1949. Originally, in the early fifties, when Allied licensing of political parties had ceased, there were over thirty parties competing for electoral support. Eleven were represented in the first Bundestag. By 1953 only five survived, and by 1957, when the C.D.U. won an absolute majority, only four parties remained in the Bundestag. After the 1961 elections, the number dropped to three. In the 1972 elections, the splinter parties were able to obtain a total of less than 1 percent of the vote.

Most of the vote of these small, special-interest parties was absorbed by the C.D.U. This has made the increasing success of the S.P.D. after its debacle in 1957 all the more remarkable. The 1972 elections, which were the most significant in the history of the Federal Republic, indicated that the prospects for the S.P.D. may be improving more rapidly than for the C.D.U., which it suddenly displaced as the largest party. Urban growth, industrial development, the decline of the rural sector, the weakening of religious ties, the end of the refugee vote, and the increase of young voters all seem to favor the S.P.D. This poses a fundamental challenge for the C.D.U. to become a more effective party.

If it does, the large ratio of independent voters should permit each of the two parties to vie for a majority vote over time or to appear as an attractive partner for the small F.D.P. if, as seems likely, it survives. An alternative possibility is that if one or both of the large parties fail to contain internal disagreement, they might subdivide. This poses a more immediate dilemma for the S.P.D., given the growing stridency of left-wing forces among its ranks. Still, this does not appear probable.

The development of a healthy three-party, and perhaps emerging two-party, system does seem rather remarkable in the context of Germany's past. It is partially the result of well-designed institutions and the capacity of the parties to develop as consensus-building, multi-interest mass movements. But it is also due to the decline of conflict-producing cleavages in German society. The homogeneity of the German electorate has made possible the hegemony of three parties alone.

Seven

Economic Progress and Problems

The absence of meaningful social cleavages in the Federal Republic is due to a number of factors. Foremost among these has been its striking economic recovery and transformation during the two-and-a-half decades since the war. No other country in Europe has experienced a comparable postwar economic resurgence. It is not surprising, therefore, that the West German achievement is often described as "miraculous." After the enormous destruction wrought by the war, the dislocations brought by division, the proscriptions enforced by the occupying authorities, and the massive influx of displaced refugees from the East, the prognosis for the German economy in the early 1950s was far from sanguine. Yet remarkably, the West German economy was able to grow at an average annual rate of more than 10 percent under conditions of controlled price inflation; succeeded in absorbing more than 11 million refugees in the fifteen postwar years and still achieved full employment by 1957; and was able to gain levels of affluence and an overall standard of living higher than that of either Britain or France by the end of the 1960s.

The Economic Miracle

How was all this achieved? What explains the German economic "miracle"? A number of factors must be cited to comprehend a process that has been fundamental to the social stability and political harmony that have characterized the first two decades of the Federal Republic and that have produced a seemingly durable equilibrium unknown in Germany's recent past.

First, it is important to note that the wartime destruction, while very extensive, seemed greater than it really was. Sixty-one percent of all industrial assets in prewar Germany were located in what was to become the Federal Republic. Many of these had been rationalized and modernized under National Socialism. While factories and mines were ravaged by the bombings, production in the later years of the war was actually greater than before. According to the economist Karl Roskamp, "West German industry actually had, in 1946, a greater industrial capacity than in 1936."[1] And what had been destroyed could be replaced in the postwar years by more modern and productive equipment. The rebuilding of German industry, which was concentrated during the first decade after the war, permitted widespread introduction of the most modern techniques and machine goods, many imported, together with massive economic assistance, from the United States.

American financial aid was of vital significance. In the first seven years after the termination of hostilities, Germany received more than 3.5 billion dollars from the United States, of which about one-third came in the form of Marshall Plan loans. Furthermore, in striking contrast to, but largely because of, the grim experience after World War I, reparations payments were initially deferred. It was not until after 1952, when the German economy had begun to recover, that reparations began to be made on a substantial basis. The dismantling of industry and the forced payment of goods and services, which was extracted on a vast level by the Soviet Occupation government in its zone, had quickly been brought to an end in the western zones.

The Federal Republic had certain special advantages when compared with its former occupying powers. It had no costly overseas or colonial commitments. Initially, there was no defense budget at all, only the payments for the costs of the Occupation, a substantial portion of which fed back into the German economy. Even after rearmament was begun in the mid-fifties, the cost of the German defense effort remained less than that of Britain or France. In 1958, for example, less than 3 percent of the German gross national product was allocated for military purposes, while the comparable figure for Britain was close to 7 percent. Ten years later the gap had narrowed, although, in the absence of a military nuclear program and foreign commitments, the German defense budget still remained smaller in proportion to gross national product than the defense budgets of most of its major N.A.T.O. allies.

A second asset of even greater importance was the availability of a

[1] Karl W. Roskamp, *Capital Formation in West Germany* (Detroit, 1965), p. 36.

skilled labor reservoir throughout the 1950s. Some economists, such as Charles Kindleberger, have seen this as the key factor in accounting for German growth since the war. During the sixteen years between the end of the war and the construction of the Berlin wall, some 12 million German expellees and refugees moved westward from Eastern Europe and East Germany to the Federal Republic. Of this number, 7 million eventually entered the work force. Initially, the refugees were seen as a potential burden upon the German economy. Destitute and often homeless, they had to be provided with basic social services: food, which was sometimes scarce; and housing. Many of them chose to settle in the poorer, rural areas of West Germany, in Bavaria, Lower Saxony, and Schlewsig-Holstein, creating additional pressures on the limited resources of these *Länder.*

But, in fact, the refugees proved to be a uniquely valuable resource. Speaking the same language and having sought refuge from oppressive conditions elsewhere, they were relatively easy to assimilate and to satisfy. What is more, they were usually willing to relocate and often had special skills. The latter was particularly the case among the 3 million refugees who fled from the German Democratic Republic before departure was barred in 1961.

The availability of a large reservoir of labor was doubtless a factor of vital importance for German economic recovery. Not only did it allow for a rapid increase in production; this pool of unemployed also contributed to the tempering of labor demands for wage increases and to the prevailing disinclination to strike. Indeed, the conditions under which postwar recovery began had a great impact on the labor movement, accounting for the docility and the common enterprise of the working force. The vivid memories of vast unemployment and uncontrolled inflation coupled with the experience of enormous postwar deprivation created conditions congenial to an unprecedented labor harmony, which in turn contributed significantly to the marked increase in productivity. It was not so much the purported German ethos, or national character, that accounted for the consistent record of hard work and increasing output. Rather, it was the absence of workdays lost through strikes. Here, the postwar German record was unmatched by any other industrial nation.

The low incidence of strikes can be attributed to a number of factors, several of which have already been enumerated. An important additional explanation can be found in the attitude of the trade unions. When the union movement was reorganized after the proscriptions of the Third Reich, it had special reasons to avoid strikes. First, the position of the German Trade Union Federation (*Deutscher Gewerkschafts Bund,* or D.G.B) was unchallenged, and, therefore, its leadership did not have to resort to strikes to assert its position against potential competitors. This was, to some degree, a change from the situation that prevailed before 1933. Second, union coffers were largely empty, so that the damage to the union membership of a prolonged strike would have been particularly severe. More importantly, the unions on the whole tended to seek objectives other than mere wage increases or social benefits. Much of their energy was directed toward achieving labor representation in the management of companies and other quasi-political goals.

The moderation of labor demands in terms of compensation was also the result of the widespread fear of inflation. In Germany alone of all the industrial nations of Europe, this prevalent attitude toward inflation, which was conditioned by the experiences of 1923 and 1947, greatly facilitated the task of the government in pursuing a growth-oriented policy while avoiding inordinate cost-and-price inflation. Monetary stability in Germany carried a very special value of its own, and compliance with antiinflationary actions could be assumed there, when it could not be elsewhere in Europe. Thus, while the German economy has grown faster than those of France and Britain, the rate of inflation in consumer goods, for which demand was even higher in Germany, has been less than half that of its western neighbors until recently.

This has been a great asset, especially in the period of increasing labor scarcity after 1957. It was critical for the success of the German drive for a major export market, which, in turn, was a key factor in stimulating growth. Export prices remained strongly competitive, while the domestic market was less attractive to foreign producers because of price restraints. This balance was achieved with a minimum of government-imposed controls. In short, the same factors that permitted accelerated growth with minimal inflation provided Germany with the opportunity to concentrate on policies conducive to continued expansion without fearing their consequences.

One of the ironies of German postwar experience was that consumer demand, which had been intensified by the privations of war and the Occupation, could be deferred in favor of a policy that emphasized investment in capital goods. In part this was the result of a determined government policy of providing a substantial amount of basic and urgently required social services and products, such as housing. This, in turn, was made possible by a stringent tax system. Since the war Germany has had the highest tax rate of any West European country. According to Andrew Shonfield, taxes in 1960 represented no less than 34 percent of the gross national product.[2] Public awareness of the need for state action in bringing about the economic recovery of Germany made such levies seem acceptable and rendered to the state a substantial role in the economy.

This public awareness was reflected in the widespread compliance with government efforts to encourage savings. By the late fifties, German public saving totaled about 8 percent of G.N.P., a figure roughly twice the level in France and Italy and about four times that in Britain. This made addi-

[2]Andrew Shonfield, *Modern Capitalism* (London, 1965), p. 265.

tional funds available for investment and helped further to reduce inflation.

Once the system began to work, it seemed to provide its own rewards. Well-placed investment in new machinery and capital goods made possible consistent increases in labor productivity. At an annual rate of increase of almost 6 percent throughout the 1950s, the productivity of labor grew far more rapidly in Germany than anywhere else in Europe. This, in turn, permitted wages to rise without creating inflationary pressures. Between 1950 and 1966 real wages rose by some 140 percent, while the work week was reduced by 10 percent. This was a sufficient reward for most of the labor force, sufficient at least to deter it from pursuing costly strikes.

German economic growth was indeed prodigious. For the first fifteen years after the establishment of the Federal Republic, annual growth averaged 7.5 percent. This compared to a rate of 4 percent in France and less than 3 percent in Britain, and it was exceeded only by the rate of recovery of the Japanese economy. This remarkable achievement took place in the context of an economic policy that rejected overall planning. Elsewhere in Europe governments adopted elaborate machinery to plan economic growth, but the German government, under a Christian Democratic–dominated coalition, adhered to an economic outlook of neoliberalism that strongly emphasized free enterprise. To be sure, capitalism was tempered with social-purpose policies, but planning and even national forecasting were mostly rejected. Instead, the policies long identified with Ludwig Erhard, who served as Minister of Economics for fourteen consecutive years, affirmed the virtues of competition and the free market mechanism and advocated the removal of government restraints and controls. It was a policy that worked extremely well for a decade and a half, taking Germany from the debacle of defeat to a position of economic leadership in Europe. When it finally began to fail, in the mid-sixties, it had run a uniquely successful course. This was a distinctive policy, an amalgam of various theories and impulses, and its aim came to be known as *Sozialmarktwirtschaft,* or "social-market economy."

The Social Market Economy

Erhard's liberal economic doctrine sought to create conditions of maximum freedom in the economy while simultaneously promoting certain limited social goals. A small dosage of social welfare was blended into an overall program designed to foster the resurgence of free enterprise. The fundamental premises of this program reflected a great faith in the virtues of competition and private ownership and in the incentives of an economic system geared to the maximization of profit. The policies that were pursued sought an overall reduction in the role of the state in direct management of the economy and the systematic removal of government controls on production, prices, and profits.

Although initially this course was vigorously opposed by the Social Democrats, it had special appeal in postwar Germany. In view of the experience of twelve years of stringent Nazi controls and planning and the subsequent restrictions placed on economic activity by the Allies, there was a strong sentiment against what was seen as excessive government intrusion into the economic sphere. This was reinforced by the growing antipathy in western Germany toward the state-imposed economic policies that the Soviet occupying authorities rigorously applied in their zone.

It was further strengthened by the perception in important quarters that the Americans very much favored a free enterprise system for Germany. As anticommunism became the ideological ethos of the Federal Republic, an economic doctrine that seemed to emphasize freedom and liberty seemed both congenial and efficacious. If the German business community—which was an important constituency of the C.D.U. and the F.D.P., the twin pillars of the ruling coalitions for the first seventeen years of the Federal Republic—was to expedite the process by which it regained control over the German economy, it made sense to reject extensive planning, which was largely antithetical to American thinking at the time. Thus the neoliberal approach of Erhard and his cohorts, with its apparent affirmation of laissez faire, seemed particularly attractive.

What is more, the policy soon proved itself remarkably successful in promoting growth and development. It therefore became increasingly difficult for the opposition to attack and reject it. Throughout the 1950s all the economic indicators suggested that Erhard had found the magic formula for a government economic policy. Removing controls, promoting capital formation, and encouraging investment, but otherwise restraining government intervention in the economy, seemed to fit the needs of the time. Even the S.P.D. began to acknowledge the effectiveness of this policy. At the Berlin party congress in 1954, Karl Schiller, a prominent economic theoretician of the party, proclaimed that Germany required a policy that sought "as much competition as possible, and only as much planning as was necessary."[3] Five years later at Bad Godesberg his party jettisoned its residual and waning commitment to a Marxist program. The astounding success of the *Sozialmarktwirtschaft* had overwhelmed the appeals of a Socialist program.

But while the government disclaimed any interest in planning and desisted from adopting an incomes policy (which was actually unnecessary in view of the temperance of labor's demands), its intervention in the economy was, in fact, rather substantial. First of all, there was extensive planning in various sectors. The government adopted "green plans" for agriculture, pursued medium-term planning in its railway and road-building

[3]Leo Brawand, "Gespräch mit Karl Schiller," in Leo Brawand, *Wohin steuert die deutsche Wirtschaft?* (Munich, 1971), p. 26.

programs, and set fixed targets in the ambitious provision of state-subsidized public housing. Extensive plans were developed for Berlin, the Saar, and lagging regional areas and territories bordering on the German Democratic Republic. Various kinds of subsidies were provided by the federal and *Länder* budgets, sometimes to reward important political constituencies but more often to achieve economic and social goals, such as effective integration of the continuing flood of refugees.

Monetary and fiscal policy was also carefully calibrated to curb the extreme gyrations of an uncontrolled business cycle. Usually in close collusion with the powerful central bank, established as an independent authority in 1957, interest rates were constantly readjusted either to spur or restrain the level of economic activity. Indeed, it is fair to summarize the policy of the fifties and early sixties as one of "positive, coordinated state intervention carefully moulded to achieve specific and limited objectives."[4]

This policy was designed not only to maximize stable growth but also to achieve certain other aims. A very conscious effort was made to encourage the development of a prosperous middle class. The government sought deliberately to support medium and small producers in trade, business, and agriculture. Public contracts often were placed with small or medium-sized firms. Several state-owned assets were distributed to small owners. The partial denationalization of giant government companies such as Volkswagen, Preüssag, Veba, and Lufthansa were part of this effort, which came to be known as *Mittelstandspolitik.* An anticartel law was passed, establishing a federal cartel office (Bundeskartellamt) in Berlin, although its effectiveness was substantially reduced by the successful efforts of business interests lobbying against it in Bonn.

A deliberate effort was made to support lagging sectors as well. Agriculture in particular was heavily subsidized, partially to ease the plight of the small farmers, but also because of the political influence of their well-organized pressure group, the Bauernverband, which regularly delivered substantial pluralities for C.D.U. candidates in rural districts. Nonetheless, the subsidies for agriculture, which rose to more than 5 billion marks in 1968, could not curb the exodus from the countryside nor improve the economic condition of the small farmer. More than one-third of the 1.5 million farms of less than ten hectares ceased to operate during the first two decades of the Federal Republic, while the farming population declined from almost 5 to less than 3 million.

Subsidies were also lavished on other depressed areas of the economy. The coal industry, threatened by American exports and cheaper fuel oil before 1973, was largely sustained by payments from Bonn. So were some

[4]Malcolm MacLennan, Murray Forsyth, and Geoffrey Denton, *Economic Planning and Policies in Britain, France, and Germany* (New York, 1968), p. 77.

other inefficient producers. With large tax revenues to distribute, the federal government displayed a predilection to use public finance to subsidize industry and trade, but without a coherent plan. By 1965 this pattern had begun to become enormously costly and highly political. Andrew Schonfeld has estimated that by that year no less than one-fourth of the federal budget was being used to support agriculture, industry, and commerce through subsidies, cheap loans, preferential tax allowances, and other procedures. This was a form of massive state intervention through ad hoc concessions, without any developed blueprint for structural reforms or purposeful reorientation of the lagging sectors.

The state has also intervened in the economy in other ways. Despite its emphatic preference for free enterprise, the C.D.U.-dominated governments of the fifties and early sixties did not dismantle the bulk of state-owned enterprise. Instead, the federal government has continued to own and operate about 50 billion marks' worth of assets, with occasional efforts to denationalize some of these. About one out of ten workers is employed by a state enterprise, if the railroad and postal systems are included. One-fourth of all coal mining, more than half of all iron ore production, 66 percent of all aluminum output, and one-third of all shipbuilding is undertaken by government-owned firms. State-run companies are among the giants in the German economy.

In addition the *Länder* and local communities control substantial assets of their own. Their role in controlling local savings and loan associations and institutions is particularly marked. Finally, the government, even under the more conservative Christian Democrats, exercises a major role in the provision of social services. Here the Federal Republic has followed upon a strongly developed German tradition that began more than a century ago. Indeed, Article 20 of the Basic Law refers to the Federal Republic as "a social federal state." This document is, in fact, rather specific, by comparison with other constitutions, in stipulating the social rights to which German citizens are entitled.

Toward a Social Welfare State

With a budget approaching 100 billion marks today (which represents a seven-fold increase over twenty years), about one-third of all federal spending is presently allocated for social services. The annual social budget of the government, begun in 1969, is a consolidated review and forecast of all social security programs projected forward for a half-decade. As Germany grows more affluent, a rising percentage of its wealth will be allocated for items in this social budget. Taken together, social welfare programs will total 18.5 percent of G.N.P. by 1975. This increase may seem surprising in view of the diminishing burden of the social costs (rehabilitation, indemnification, disability payments and unemployment insurance) that were caused by the suffering of the war. Beginning in 1952, a program to equalize burdens was introduced in the Federal Republic. By 1971, somewhat over 6 billion marks was provided annually for indemnification and support of war victims, who today still number some two and a half million. Large payments have also been made to the refugees who emigrated to West Germany in such large numbers after the war.

A peculiar innovation has also sought to redress imbalances among the *Länder*. Here the redistribution of certain revenues has benefitted the more indigent states. The *Länder* with relatively high per capita incomes, such as North Rhine-Westphalia, Baden-Württemberg, Hesse, and Hamburg, have provided assistance for those which are poorer. Under this arrangement, Lower Saxony received, for example, more than 500 million marks in 1965, or roughly 70 marks per inhabitant, many of whom were former refugees. In addition, a massive program of regional development assistance for backward areas was instituted in the sixties.

In 1952 government child support was introduced. In 1972 the scale provided twenty-five marks monthly for families with two children and annual incomes below 15,000 marks. Larger amounts up to one hundred marks were available for families with three or more children below the age of eighteen. While this assistance is less generous than that provided in France, the federal budget in 1971 allocated almost 3 billion marks for family allowances. This is in keeping with Article 6 of the Basic Law, which states that "marriage and family are under the special protection of the state" and that "every mother has a claim to the protection and assistance of the community."

By comparison with France work accident insurance is lower in the Federal Republic, while unemployment compensation is more comprehensive (but, since 1957, rarely required because there has been so little unemployment). On the whole, the Federal Republic today spends slightly more of its national income on social welfare than does France and far outdistances the United States and Britain in such expenditures. Indeed, the amount allocated for old age, sickness, and disability alone is close to 8 percent of national income in Germany, while less than 4 percent in the other three countries. And the percentage has been increasing. In 1950, despite the depressed condition of the economy and the enormity of the postwar burden, the Federal Republic spent 11.6 percent of its gross national product on social welfare. By 1970 this figure was close to 16 percent, and this of a G.N.P. that had swelled enormously.

A comparable increase has been registered in the provision of pensions. Here payments have increased by more than 350 percent since 1950, totaling almost 40 billion marks in 1971. The Pension Reform Bill adopted by parliament in that year extended eligibility to women who were not gainfully employed, dependents helping in family businesses, and the self-employed. A special bill in 1957 had extended old-age assistance to farmers, in part as an inducement to hasten their retirement from the land. Farmers who have lost their livelihood may apply for pension payments at the age of fifty-five.

These provisions have caused much of the increase in pension costs for the state. But even more important is the progressive system which links the rate of pension payment to the rise in the cost of living. This has been termed the "dynamic system" of pensions, which rise as wages and salaries do. Thus, for example, in 1957 the average monthly benefit for a person who had been employed for forty years amounted to 214 marks; in 1972 the amount had increased to 548 marks. The purpose of this program is to establish not only social equity but also a sort of political reinsurance. The government wants at all costs to avert the pauperization of the retired working and middle class, which took such a grievous toll and proved so destabilizing during the Weimar Republic.

In housing policy, too, the government has been particularly enterprising. Some 11 million dwellings were constructed during the first two decades of the Federal Republic. In those twenty years West Germany erected 192 units per 1,000 inhabitants. Comparable figures in France and Britain, which also experienced widespread wartime destruction, were 113 and 119 units per 1,000 persons. Even in the United States, with its large number of second homes and rapid urban growth, construction of new housing units lagged well behind, at about three-quarters of the German level.

Roughly 35 percent of German housing has been erected with state support. Here intervention has been wide-ranging but carefully measured. As a recent study concluded, "the restoration of market forces has been deliberately and systematically encouraged, though controls were maintained as long as the market was structurally out of balance; and social intervention has been such as to prevent those with low incomes from suffering, but carefully adapted so as to distort the market as little as possible."[5] But where the state has failed to act is in curbing land speculation. With 60 percent of all present-day housing constructed since 1950 and a massive influx of refugees and farm-leavers into the cities, urban land prices have soared, leading to a steep and continuous rise in rents. This has produced a loud clamor for government action to control land speculation and unjustified rent increases. Solving this problem is one of the many tasks that will fall to the new federal Ministry for Regional Planning and Urban Development, headed by the able former mayor of Munich (the city which has experienced the most intense land boom).

All these factors suggest that the neoliberal Erhard model of the German

[5] *Ibid.*, p. 58.

economy has ineluctably moved toward a social-welfare state. To be sure, the ethos of the system emphasizes free enterprise, the profit motive, and competition. But to a substantial degree, it has failed to realize these goals, for economic concentration, the reemergence of cartels, and the grip of oligopolistic firms have become characteristic of the system. Nonetheless, from the outset the outspoken capitalism of the Erhard years was tempered by a broadly developed social policy. The social-market economy has evolved as a mixed system. As Alfred Grosser has argued, "the German 'welfare state' is more reminiscent of the British Socialist model than of traditional liberalism."[6] Yet, curiously, this is a welfare state in which the Social Democrats, at least until 1966, played a relatively minor role. And when finally they entered the government, their prescriptions and policies were directed more toward refining and reforming the system that had been established, rather than seeking its replacement with a radically different program.

This made good sense given the major successes of the past two decades. Any fundamental redirection of course would have met much popular resistance. And Germany has emerged as a highly affluent society. Today 62 percent of German households own one car compared to 53 percent in Britain. Real wages increased an average of 5 percent annually through the 1960s, whereas in Britain they rose by just half that amount. Unemployment is nominal and social insurance very comprehensive. Germans today have close to the highest standard of living in the world. In fact, by July 1973, with the sudden momentary weakness of the dollar, German G.N.P. per inhabitant actually briefly overtook that of the United States by some one-hundred dollars. Although this is a distorted indicator it is still a remarkable achievement for a country that lay in ruins in 1945.

But while German economic policy over the past two decades has made enormous strides and gained unanticipated achievements, it has not been free of problems. Some of these have been the consequence of rapid growth. Others are the result of the kinds of policy that were pursued, of the compromises that were struck and of the accommodations that were made. For the future the resolution of these problems will be of critical significance.

Economic Problems

One of the more serious problems of the German economy is the restricted capacity and willingness of the government to control the private sector. This is largely the result of the continuous pattern of amalgamation and

[6]Alfred Grosser, *Germany in Our Time* (New York, 1971), p. 193.

concentration, which has rendered vast power to a relatively small number of giant firms. The initial postwar efforts of the Allies to break up the monolithic companies, especially in the steel, coal, and chemical industries, had no lasting effect. Many of the Allied edicts made little sense and were quickly set aside as Germany regained sovereign control over its own industry. The requirements of maximizing growth in the wake of the Cold War provided an acceptable rationale for suspending limitations on the size of firms. A trend toward concentration soon took hold. By 1960 four chemical companies (including the three firms into which the I.G. Farben trust had been divided) controlled 40 percent of all chemical production. Within the next decade their share of this sector had grown to 70 percent.

Similar figures reveal the pattern of concentration in iron and steel production. Originally, the Allies had subdivided the twelve giant heavy industrial firms concentrated in the Ruhr into twenty-eight companies. But within a decade of the establishment of the Federal Republic many of these had merged again. By 1960 the four largest steel companies controlled more than half of all German production. Today they produce 90 percent of all German steel. Four companies control 50 percent of the output of the electrical industry. Concentration in the automotive industry is even greater. And even in retailing the pattern of amalgamation is marked. Here fifteen giant chains control one-third of all retail sales.

In part the pattern of amalgamation may be attributed to the German aspiration to gain and preserve a strong, favorable balance of trade. The desire to remain competitive abroad and to protect domestic producers against foreign goods within Germany and the Common Market has reinforced the trend in favor of large firms. Here government preferences combined with those of industry. Today the 100 largest companies produce about 50 percent of all German exports, a fact which helps to explain the benevolent attitude of the government toward amalgamation. It is an attitude reminiscent of the past, for German governments have always sought to support industry in its efforts to protect its markets and to seek new ones. As tariffs tumbled, rationalization through concentration seemed a necessary measure to secure the competitive position of German industry.

Antitrust legislation has remained weak and ineffective. Since 1958 all companies seeking to merge must request permission from the Berlin Kartellamt if together they employ more than 10,000 workers, control 20 percent of the market, or have sales exceeding .5 billion marks annually. But because of the way in which the relevant legislation was drafted, it is difficult for the Kartellamt to withhold its permission. So the pattern toward concentration has continued and, in fact, recently has substantially accelerated. In the two-year period beginning in 1970, some 168 mergers were registered in Germany, representing a three-fold increase from the level of two years before. All together more than 100,000 firms have been liquidated since 1949. This suggests that the ostensible commitment of the

C.D.U. and the F.D.P. to maximum free competition may have been more theoretical than real.

Similarly, the reestablishment of cartels in the postwar period has been relatively unhindered. To date more than 230 cartels have been registered. Less than 10 percent of those that were proposed to the Kartellamt have been rejected by it. In part this has been the result of pressure from those business groups which sought cartel arrangements in restraint of trade. It seems apparent that where the government was confronted by a choice between assuring competition within Germany and strengthening German producers vis-à-vis foreign firms, it strongly favored the latter.

Most significant is the concentrated power within the banking system. Here the three giant banks, the Deutsche Bank, the Dresdner, and the Commerzbank, not only dominate the provision of credit but also exert an enormous influence on business activity in Germany. In part this is made possible by the voting of custodial shares held for customers by these banks. An exhaustive inquiry conducted in 1964 indicated that German banks held 70 percent of the voting power of the 425 quoted joint-stock companies. But 87 percent of the shares controlled by the banks were not actually owned by them but held in custody. For 58 firms, the banks actually held a majority of the voting shares. For 138 others, they retained more than a quarter interest, which is sufficient to exercise a veto power over decisions.

This pattern renders great power to the banks. For example, among the nineteen companies in which the Deutsche Bank alone holds more than one-quarter of the shares are such giants as Daimler-Benz, Hapag-Lloyd, Karstadt, and the Bavarian Electrical Works, each of which is dominant in its own sector. The Dresdner and the Commerzbank are in equivalent positions. Furthermore, the trend toward concentration among the banks is continuing. Some 150 private banks have been absorbed since 1949.

The federal government has resisted nationalizing privately owned assets, although the Basic Law clearly gives it the right to do so. Article 15 provides that "land, natural resources and means of production may for the purpose of socialization be transferred to public ownership or other forms of publicly controlled economy. . . ." Generally state intervention is conceived as a rescue operation. Firms under duress and industries in decline have benefited from government assistance. When, in 1967, the federal government helped Krupp to survive an acute liquidity crisis, it made no attempt to seize the assets of the firm. What afflicted Krupp was in part a structural dilemma of the loss-incurring coal industry concentrated in the Ruhr. With the ostensible purpose of securing jobs and safeguarding a domestic source of energy, the federal government, in effect, took over the mining operations of most of the Ruhr firms by placing them in a giant state-run company known as *Ruhrkohle.* But it did not obtain the very valuable land holdings of the financially threatened companies.

The efficiency and purpose of government action in the coal industry have been questioned and attacked. It is estimated that the government is providing a subsidy for this industry in the amount of 1 billion marks annually at the consumer end. This is done by subsidizing the cost of power for several new coal-fired power stations, which would otherwise not have been competitive with other sources of energy supply, at least prior to the 1973 energy crisis.

This has been a costly and not very coherent policy. Indigenous coal hardly supplies 25 percent of German energy needs today. Coal mining remains very labor intensive, and labor is scarce in Germany. Over time a more comprehensive energy policy will have to be developed, which might expedite the rationalization or closure of the Ruhr coal mines.

The shipbuilding industry has been another major beneficiary of government intervention. In 1968 German shipyards were ranked third in the world. By 1972, with only 5 percent of world tonnage on order, they were ranked sixth. With two-thirds of their output going for export, the industry suffered severely from the successive revaluation of the mark, which made German prices less competitive abroad. As a result, the federal government appointed a special team of experts to inquire into the problems of the shipyards. Upon its recommendation a threefold policy was developed, featuring government subsidies, an export finance program, and stringent guidelines for internal reorganization on the part of the major private firms involved.

Government assistance may also be required by those sectors of industry particularly dependent on foreign sales. The combined effect of high domestic inflation and the upward revaluation of the German currency may have a severe impact on export demand. As Germany is one of the world's largest traders, its economy is substantially dependent on a stable export market. Thirty-one percent of all manufactured goods are sold abroad. In some industries the figure is higher. Forty-four percent of German machine goods are exported, and this industry is the largest single employer of labor in the Federal Republic. Foreign sales of automobiles comprise 52 percent of production.

While the government has been cautious about intervening in the private sector of the economy, it has been quite enterprising in providing programs for the development of low income regions scattered throughout the Federal Republic. These include areas that depend heavily on declining industries or dominant industries that are threatened. Some are areas where there are large numbers of expected farm-leavers (or, in the past, where there were heavy concentrations of refugees). Finally, the 40-kilometer-wide strip running along the frontier with the G.D.R. and, of course, West Berlin, have benefited from special federal programs. Backward areas are designated for regional action programs, which are a mixture of federal and state direct investment and tax relief. In addition, special incentives for private industry are created by government under the so-called *Ge-*

meinschaftsaufgabe (Cooperative Task) program, which has sought to develop 460,000 new jobs and secure 240,000 existing ones by the mid-seventies through a combination of private investment, municipal and community projects, and federal and *Land* subsidies. Several hundred stress points have been selected for this employment-inducing program.

The most serious economic problem of all in West Germany today may be posed by soaring inflation. Until 1972 Germany experienced a relatively low rate. The increase in consumer prices between 1968 and 1972 was 20 percent, compared to 33 percent in Britain and 27 percent in France. In certain sectors it was higher. The cost of housing, for example, rose 63 percent in the eight-year period following 1962.

By 1974 the Federal Republic seemed headed for a solid 8 percent inflation, which was likely to be further aggravated by the sharp rise in fuel costs. This was particularly disturbing for three special reasons. First, as has been seen, the degree of dependence on export markets is high. This means that continued rapid inflation can quickly curb sales, which is obviously less of a problem in countries which absorb a larger portion of their own production. Second, as has also been seen, wage and price increases in Germany automatically trigger increases in pension and indemnification payments and other social security programs. This means that inflation in Germany has a somewhat self-stimulating circular effect, which can only accelerate its impact and increase its scope. Finally, historical memory of the hyperinflation of the early twenties and chronic insecurity about financial infirmity in the years thereafter have sensitized public opinion on this issue. Opinion polls taken in 1973 confirm that inflation is the foremost source of concern on the part of the German public.

It is not clear that the magic formula for a successful antiinflationary policy (without unacceptable side effects) exists today. But it is also not clear that the federal government in Germany has the freedom and authority to act in ways which would effectively combat inflationary developments. There are a number of economic constraints on the government. One is the concentration and power of industry, which is also well organized in its interest group representation. Directing the banks and major industrial firms to pursue a desired economic course is not an easy task for the federal government. There are other limits as well. First among these is the entrenched fiscal powers of the states. Article 109 cedes substantial taxing authority to the *Länder*. This accords with the postwar Allied preference to strengthen centrifugal and local forces in the Federal Republic, but it can impair the effectiveness of central government policy. Originally, personal income and corporate taxes, property taxes, and some additional revenues were assigned to the *Länder,* although Article 106 allowed the federal government to claim a certain portion of these receipts. This arrangement has had two adverse consequences. First, it has led to continuous disputes between Bonn and the *Länder.* Second, it has left the federal government with insufficient revenue and has conferred substantial fiscal power on the *Länder* in a way that may impede overall coordination, especially when opposition parties at the federal level constitute the government in several states. This can be critical in those instances when fiscal policy is pursued to achieve an anticyclical effect. The relatively small size of the central government sectors as compared to other sectors is "by itself an obstacle to demand management by means of the budget."[7] The imbalance is becoming more pronounced. Whereas the role of the federation in total state expenditure was 48 percent in 1955, it stood at less than 42 percent ten years later.

This is in part because of the heavy social-service burden carried by the *Länder.* But it is also a reflection of the inadequate sources of revenue for the federal budget. As tariffs have declined, the federal government has become more dependent on the added-value and excise taxes and on obtaining a larger portion of the income taxes collected by the *Länder.* Its share has increased steadily from one-third to some 43 percent of income tax receipts.

Even so, federal revenues have been insufficient. This is particularly critical because the Basic Law does not permit budgetary deficits. Article 110 stipulates that "revenue and expenditure must be balanced." This is a strange proviso in a constitution and may be explained by the abiding fear of the kind of deficit spending that characterized German government policy at the beginning and the end of the Weimar Republic. Nonetheless, since 1963 government expenditure has been rising more rapidly than income. This has created particular problems for the government in periods of economic slowdown, such as occurred in 1966 and 1971. At such times it is especially difficult to reduce spending without further adverse effects on the level of economic activity, yet a substantial decline in the economy will, of course, reduce available government revenues.

This dilemma has led the federal government in recent years to move further in the direction of middle-range planning and to give greater attention to accurate forecasting. The government was substantially assisted by the establishment of the central bank (the Bundesbank), which replaced the more decentralized Bank deutscher Länder in 1957. While the Bundesbank has retained great independence of action, it has sought on the whole to develop precise forecasts regarding the direction of the economy and has been amenable to close cooperation with the federal government.

A five-member Council of Economic Advisors (Wirtschaftsrat) was established in 1964 to render advice to the central government. But the most significant development was the adoption by the grand coalition three

[7] Bent Hansen, *Fiscal Policy in Seven Countries 1955–65* (Paris, 1969), p. 210.

years later of a program of middle-range financial planning, which requires projections of budgetary planning over a five-year period. This has made possible the anticipation of future deficits several years before they arise. Indeed, it was an awareness of the enormity of the deficit projected for 1975 that caused the federal Finance Minister, Alex Möller, to resign his post in May 1971, when the federal cabinet refused to invoke the reduction in expenditure that he had urged. This resulted in the hasty consolidation of the ministries of finance and economics, which had traditionally remained separate in the German cabinet system. The resulting "superministry" under Karl Schiller and then Helmut Schmidt was regarded as a somewhat unwieldy instrument, which, its critics argue, possesses too much power within the cabinet as a whole. The two ministries were again separated, but reorganized, after the 1972 elections.

Nevertheless, these institutional innovations and programs have moved Germany far in the direction of a planned economy. Andrew Shonfield has argued that in Germany "the basic bits of apparatus which are required for systematic economic planning are more readily available than in many other countries."[8] In his view, the German system lends itself better than the British to collective economic planning because of the size and concentration of firms; the pattern of collaboration within the private sector; the powerful role of the banks; and the high priority of, and past experience with, rationalization within the economy to make it more efficient. Thus there is a kind of tension between the doctrinal predilection in favor of free enterprise and the gradual movement toward planning. If the recent decline of the rate of growth of the economy persists, it is likely that, despite all the stated inhibitions, German economic policy will continue to move further in the direction of central planning, although it remains unclear whether the federal government is in fact equipped with the powers necessary to effect its will and its plans in the present system.

[8]Shonfield, *op. cit.*, p. 296.

Eight

Social Development and Dilemmas

German society has changed a great deal since the war. The social leveling that occurred during the twelve years of National Socialism created a more fluid situation and a more open society. To be sure, important continuities and patterns of social differentiation persisted from the past. But the fundamental social cleavages that had stood in the way of modernization and change had been eradicated, or at least greatly enfeebled, by 1945.

The new cult that characterized German society was the pursuit of economic growth, beginning with recovery and extending to the higher reaches of an affluent society. This was a profoundly modern goal and one which was in no sense exclusive. Everyone could feel himself a participant, although some, as George Orwell might say, participated more favorably than others.

At the core of the prodigious German postwar economic development stands the German workingman. Labor, many have argued, was the key input in the economic miracle. Labor, and in particular organized labor, was the most important societal factor in the process of change in the period since the war.

Labor and the Unions

The trade unions were quickly reorganized after the war. Although the Basic Law does not specifically refer to the unions, Article 9 provides that "the right to form associations to safeguard and improve working and economic conditions is guaranteed to everyone." By 1949 a single, mammoth labor federation, the Deutsche Gewerkschaftsbund, had been established under the able leadership of Hans Böckler. The D.G.B. was actually an amalgamation of sixteen individual unions, which continued to retain their autonomy as unions do in the American system. As a result the D.G.B. has had much less direct control over its member unions.

This is necessary in part because of the great discrepancies in power and size among the member unions. Total D.G.B. membership numbers close to 7 million and represents 29.7 percent of all workers. Several of its affiliated unions are minuscule. The three for art, forestry, and leather have less than 150,000 members among them. On the other hand, the membership of the largest component, the giant I.G. Metall, comprises almost one-third of the total D.G.B. enrollment. Indeed, the metalworkers union —with more than 2 million members, many of them foreign "guest" workers—is by far the largest union in Europe. Its long-time leader, the recently deceased Otto Brenner, was the most powerful figure within the German labor movement, much more so than Ludwig Rosenberg, who headed the D.G.B. at the time.

German unions today possess substantial wealth. Each member contributes the equivalent of one hour's wages per week as dues. The low past incidence of strikes has enabled the unions to amass fortunes, which have been invested with impressive ingenuity. For example, the union-owned Bank für Gemeinwirtschaft, organized in 1958, is the fourth largest non-government bank in Germany. The D.G.B. owns a quarter of a million housing units, a large shipping fleet, and more than 6,000 cooperative stores. It has a close connection with the giant German cooperative movement, which maintains some 17,500 cooperatives and has 12 million members. German trade unions operate specialized schools and maintain an elaborate educational system for their workers. A host of union leaders sits on the boards of German enterprises. Otto Brenner, for example, was a member of the boards of both Krupp and Volkswagen.

German unions have fought vigorously for the right of codetermination, or *Mitbestimmung,* in the management of German industry. The notion of a shared responsibility for directing major industry derives from the early part of the century. The experiments of the Weimar Republic, both the *Zentralarbeitsgemeinschaft* and the formation of the shop councils *(Betriebsräte)* proved sadly abortive. However, after World War II labor was determined to wrest for itself the right to participate in the management of private industry. *Mitbestimmung* was one of the four central planks of the original D.G.B. platform drafted in 1949.

Initially, union efforts met with some success. In May 1951, under the threat of a massive strike, the Bundestag passed legislation with the acquiescence of the C.D.U., which provided that both the employees and the shareholders would be equally represented on the supervisory board (Aufsichtsrat) of the major companies in the mining, iron, and steel industries. Elsewhere in larger firms workers were given the right to appoint one-third of the members of the supervisory board. This was hailed as a great victory by the unions. It was also seen as a novel innovation in the German system. However, the union members of the supervisory boards rarely intervene in the ordinary conduct of business. Instead, they concentrate on issues that affect employment and the conditions of work. Especially important for the unions was the right awarded to them to nominate the personnel director, who is responsible for welfare questions and the training department of the firm. *Mitbestimmung* has served as a useful way to associate labor with management decisions at a relatively early stage in the decision-making process, which has contributed to labor harmony. Seen another way, "codetermination basically resulted in a sort of cartel of all those involved in the production process directed against the consumers."[1] But while codetermination has been a modest success where it was attempted, its impact on the German economy as a whole has been relatively marginal.

More recently the unions have pressed for an expansion of the scope of *Mitbestimmung.* The D.G.B. would like to extend the parity arrangement, so far limited to the iron, steel, and coal industries, to other sectors. It also seeks a larger role for the unions in selecting the workers' representatives from outside the enterprise. The D.G.B. would also like legislation safeguarding codetermination in firms that merge with non-German companies. The 1971 amalgamation of Hoesch, the giant German iron firm, with the Dutch Hoogovens group (which produced the third largest steel concern in western Europe) did not lead to a satisfactory resolution of this problem from the German unions' point of view.

The D.G.B. demand for new legislation has encountered the resistance not only of the powerful employers' association, but also growing concern on the part of the F.D.P., whose support is required for passage in parliament. The Free Democrats are eager to protect the rights of white-collar employees and middle management against worker domination.

Although the unions to date have been unable to prevail in their quest to extend codetermination on the supervisory boards, they did score a substantial victory in the passage of the Works Constitution Act in 1971, which relates to codetermination on the shop floor. This act produced great strain within the S.P.D.–F.D.P. coalition, but did find the support of twenty-one prolabor C.D.U. deputies. The act substantially enlarged the role of the works councils.

The idea of works councils dates back as far as 1848 in Germany. Major

[1]Gustav Stolper, Karl Häuser, and Knut Borchardt, *The German Economy: 1870 to the Present* (New York, 1967), p. 293.

initial legislation derived from the Weimar Republic. In 1952 parliament passed a first comprehensive law delineating the role of the councils. Their members were given an important say in matters of hiring and firing, transfer of labor to other plants, regulation of shifts, the preparation of holiday schedules, and related issues. These questions dealt basically with the quality of work and working conditions. It was widely accepted even by employers that the councils, which were elected by the plant workers, had a legitimate right to share in decision making in these areas.

The new act passed in 1971 gives the councils more substantial powers. The law also increased the size and effectiveness of the councils. At a large firm with more than 50,000 employees the council will have more than fifty members, most of whom are paid on a full-time basis for their work as councillors by the employer, who must also provide office accomodations and secretarial staff for the council.

In cases of dispute between a council and the management, each side must resort to a conciliation committee and, as a last resort, to a Labor Court. Larger firms are also required to establish a finance committee, one of whose members is a works councillor. This committee is meant to consult with the management on financial matters, amalgamation schemes, changes in organization, market planning, and even pricing. Many employers resent this arrangement, which some have labelled "dictatorship by functionaries."

But for the D.G.B. and for the union leadership, it represents a further accretion in their power. Some 90 percent of councillors are union members, even though only one of every three workers belongs to a union. This is a professional cadre which gives the unions a further grip in sharing in company decision making. About 25 percent of the works council chairmen have occupied their posts since 1952. They, together with the 200,000 members of the councils throughout German industry, give the unions an elaborate mechanism with which to monitor and contest company practice.

While the unions have fared well in sharing decision making within German firms, they have achieved less on other fronts. Originally, the D.G.B. had called for the nationalization of major industry, especially in the mining, metal, and energy fields. This endeavor proved unsuccessful. Indeed, the government has systematically sought to sell off certain assets in the form of *Volksaktien,* or small-holding "people's shares," thereby to further the spread of capitalism. The unions also failed in their efforts in the early fifties to combat the C.D.U. on such issues as rearmament and German entry into N.A.T.O.

The failure of such political action had several causes and consequences. In part, the inability of the unions to succeed with a political program derived from the substantial political apathy characteristic of the German public after years of totalitarian rule, war, and occupation. But also, union acquiescence was secured in place of political confrontation by the economic success that began to take hold in the mid-fifties. Wages grew rapidly, even at a time when there was still considerable unemployment. Real wages by 1970 were at a level almost twice that of two decades before. They have increased more rapidly than than elsewhere in Europe under conditions of full employment, and the number of those gainfully employed has risen from 14 million to 23 million. Today the average work week for an industrial laborer is 43.5 hours, which is less than in Britain. German workers also have more days off, with an average of 37 paid holidays, compared to 34 in France and only 21 in Britain. Such growth offered sufficient incentives and rewards to labor to satisfy important economic demands, even in the absence of major political concessions.

This led to a situation in which the D.G.B. began to temper its more radical political prescriptions. A policy of political activism was toned down in favor of "compliance with the political realities of the Federal Republic with a residue of radical rhetoric."[2] In this course, the unions followed the lead of the S.P.D. At its 1963 congress in Düsseldorf, the D.G.B. basically adopted the non-Marxist Godesberg program of political conciliation that the Social Democrats had accepted four years before.

This reflected the close symbiosis between the unions and the S.P.D. This relationship may become strained as the unions intensify their new demand for more radical policies. The D.G.B. is particularly eager for legislation to redistribute industrial wealth. It has proposed a plan to the S.P.D. for the reallocation of private capital assets *(Vermögensbildung)* in the Federal Republic. All companies earning more than 400,000 marks annually would be required by law—according to the D.G.B. model—to contribute a portion of their profits to an annual fund totaling 5 billion marks, which would be redistributed to all those gainfully employed and earning less than 48,000 marks annually (which is three times the average income of an industrial worker). Beneficiaries in the program would receive certificates worth about 200 marks a year in a general fund, which would be redeemable in seven years without interest.

Controversial issues of this sort may place renewed strain on the S.P.D. coalition with the Free Democrats, who take a more moderate position. On this issue and others dealing with domestic reform, the unions may try to build strength within the C.D.U. to obtain the necessary votes, in addition to those of the S.P.D., required for a legislative majority. The labor wing of the C.D.U. has been growing in force and is likely to take a more outspoken position in the years ahead. There are D.G.B. members within the party and close to its leadership. This has meant, in turn, that a separate Catholic union movement has not developed as a strong, independent

[2]Theo Pirker, *Die SPD nach Hitler* (Munich, 1965), p. 197.

force in the Federal Republic. The one effort to organize a Christian union movement, in the form of the *Christliche Gewerkschaftsbund* (or C.G.B.) in 1955, has been of little consequence. Its membership has not exceeded 200,000 and poses no threat to the monolithic D.G.B.

The separate organizations for employees (*Deutsche Angestellten-Gewerkschaft,* or D.A.G.) and for civil servants (*Deutscher Beamtenbund,* or D.B.B.), which together contain some 1.1 million members, also pose no threat to the D.G.B. Twelve percent of the D.G.B. membership consists of white-collar employees, which is more than the entire number in the D.A.G. The D.G.B. also counts almost as many civil servants in its ranks (550,000) as the total in the *Beamtenbund* (720,000). In fact, the two compete rather assiduously and somewhat along partisan lines.

There are also a number of smaller unaffiliated unions, including a separate organization for the police. The *Gewerkschaft der Polizei,* with some 120,000 members, is the largest police union in Europe. A novel feature in the German system is the fact that union recruitment is also permitted among the 200,000 regular servicemen in the armed forces. Virtually the only group poorly organized is composed of German women. They comprise less than one-sixth of the D.G.B. membership, which is a much smaller share than their participation in the working force as a whole.

The unions have not been particularly successful in recruiting an enlarged membership to keep pace with the increasing numbers of the working force. In part this is a consequence of the full employment and high wages that have characterized German growth in the fifties and early sixties, which created less need for union action. It is also a consequence of the growth of employment in service industries, where the unions have never been as well represented. More recently, new difficulties have emerged. Since 1965, the German economy has experienced two recessions. Second, price inflation has begun to manifest itself as a serious problem since the late sixties. These problems, taken together, have posed new dilemmas for the management of the economy and for the policy pursued by the unions. By 1971, union demands for wage increases began to exceed growth in the G.N.P. by a considerable amount. During 1970 Lufthansa employees received a wage increase of almost 16 percent upon threat of strike. In that year the printers' union demanded a 23 percent increase. By 1971, when growth in the economy had slowed considerably, the metalworkers, armed with a strike chest of almost 500 million marks, closed down the automotive industry in Baden-Württemberg with a demand for an 11 percent rise in wages—a figure that had been achieved before, but only in years of substantial boom.

The observation that the Federal Republic is blessed with a strike-free labor posture may no longer be valid. In the absence of continued prodigious strides in economic growth and with the waning of effective centralized control within the unions, a pattern of wildcat strikes and local restiveness has developed in certain sectors.

A more serious problem may be posed by the presence in Germany of a massive number of foreign workers. This is not, in fact, a totally new phenomenon. Even before World War I, almost 1 million non-Germans found employment in the Reich. Today there are more than twice that number working in Germany. Of these, the largest nationality groups are Turks, Yugoslavs, Italians, and Greeks. Their numbers have increased steadily from some 70,000 in 1954 to more than 2.2 million in 1973, one-fourth of whom are women. These "guest" workers, as they are known, are highly concentrated at the lower end of the labor scale. They tend to be manual workers, street cleaners, waiters, and maintenance men, and they are particularly heavily represented in the metal, construction, and textile industries.

The foreign workers, an indispensable source of labor supply in the period after the waning of the refugee influx, now pose very special problems. They are more difficult to assimilate, rarely speak German well, and tend to live under more deprived conditions. While they annually send some 5 billion marks of their earnings to their home countries, many have chosen to remain in Germany for years on end, and often they develop skills for which there is no market in their native lands. Increasingly, they have joined German unions, for which they present a particular problem because of their vulnerability to unemployment in periods of recession, as occurred in 1967. Officially, most of them enter Germany on a rotation system permitting a stay of only two years. In fact, more than one-quarter have now been in the Federal Republic for over seven years. This means that they are not content with temporary quarters, require services which are more comparable to those available to German workers, and often seek to have their families join them. There were in 1973 more than a million dependents of guest workers living in Germany. A continuation of this trend will compel the government to spend large amounts to integrate and service the needs of this large alien population, for they cannot remain second-class residents forever.

Freedom of labor movement within the Common Market makes this problem more acute. The planned association of Turkey with the Common Market as of 1985 would create a crisis. But the problem will have to be resolved long before that date. In a poll taken in October 1972, 71 percent of the respondents, all German citizens, indicated that they favored a reduction in the number of foreign workers living in Germany. In some industrial areas such as Stuttgart, where non-Germans represent one-fifth of the working force, feeling against them has swelled. For the first time since the war, problems of ethnic discrimination may be returning to Germany. Under these circumstances, the government will have to take measures to restrict freedom of entry and length of stay for the guest workers. In the years that lie ahead the mitigation of serious ethnic strife between German-born and foreign workers will pose a challenge for the unions and the government, as will the effects of the energy crisis, which may substantially reduce employment opportunities.

Social Patterns and Problems

The Federal Republic has emerged as a remarkably homogeneous society in view of the deep cleavages and bitter strife of the past. In part this is the result of the social leveling that occurred during the Third Reich. Furthermore, defeat and postwar impoverishment created a brief period in which a kind of social and economic equalization was imposed upon the entire population. The uprooting and transferring of population that followed, and especially the vast influx of refugees from the east, further eradicated historic factors of social differentiation. Many members of the old, landowning aristocracy from the lands east of the Elbe suddenly found themselves not only geographically, but also socially, dispossessed.

It was to a very large degree Germany's remarkable economic recovery that created the means and conditions for effective integration of the many potentially discordant and socially diverse forces. The primacy of economic recovery as an overall objective, the increasing opportunity of securing material gains, and the political weariness and apathy that characterized public opinion, all eased the process of social integration. So did the prevailing sense of animosity toward communism and Soviet policy in the 1950s. The resulting pattern suggests that Germany, at least in that portion which remains in the Federal Republic, has come a long way in developing a reasonably harmonious domestic social setting.

Still, it would be wrong to overlook important structural problems that remain. First, there is the issue of the lagging sectors. Agriculture has been in steady decline. By 1970, the agricultural sector was producing less than 4 percent of the gross national product, yet it was still employing about one out of every ten members of the working force. Meanwhile, as has been seen, subventions from Bonn have risen to more than 5 billion marks annually. This pattern is an unhealthy one and seriously in need of basic reform.

Today farmers still comprise 7 percent of the population (compared to 3 percent in Britain). The number of farms remains too numerous. While there has been a 26 percent reduction since 1960, more than 1.1 million farms continue to be operated, many of them inefficiently. The critical problem is that of the small, marginal farmer. Agricultural holdings are much smaller than in France. In all of the Federal Republic there are only 3,000 farms with more than 250 acres. Their numbers, encouraged by a government policy favoring concentration, have actually been increasing. It is the small farm with less than 25 acres which is disappearing. In the past twelve years 40 percent have ceased operating.

This is the result of a deliberate government policy. Subsidies are provided to induce the large farmers to expand their production. Support is available only for those farms which can generate an annual net income of not less than 16,000 marks within a four-year period. Farmers who fall below this level are encouraged to lease their land and are eligible for early retirement assistance. This has led many farmers into part-time farming. In fact, more than half the farm population does not work full time on the farm. The government has sought to bring industry or other forms of employment to areas where there are large numbers of small holdings. Despite these efforts, however, the family farm in West Germany is a dying entity and the small farmer remains anxious and insecure.

While the trend toward social homogeneity has increased in the Federal Republic, important factors of differentiation remain. It has been said by the German sociologist Helmut Schelsky and others that an important attribute of modern German society has been the "leveling" of its middle class. With the decline of the self-employed craftsman, shopkeeper, or farmer has come the rise of the affluent worker. However, if overall similarities have increased, fundamental inequalities persist. The pattern of income distribution has remained uneven. While overall taxes are high, ceilings are not. The maximum income tax of 53 percent, is well below the highest rate in Britain. Similarly, there has been an almost total neglect of inheritance taxation. Indeed, it may be argued that virtually from the outset, the very wealthy have been favored. The currency reform of 1948 greatly increased the value of real assets, while reducing that of savings. The subsequent effort to encourage capital reinvestment created unusual opportunities for the amassing of wealth by private industry. Today, some 16,000 industrialists, businessmen, bankers, and landowners have annual incomes in excess of 1 million marks.

Inequities also persist in the distribution of jobs. Educational opportunity has served as a critical filter. For example, in the 1960s only 8 percent of the sons of workers and farmers attended university. Yet higher education is a prerequisite for advancement at the higher echelons of business and government. A sample of only those who hold law degrees indicates how narrow the recruitment process tends to be. Twenty-two percent of all members of the Bundestag hold law degrees, and the same figure pertains for managers in industry. The percentage of law graduates within the federal cabinet is twice as high. And no less than 85 percent of the higher civil service, which controls the administration of government, is trained in law. Self-recruitment is also high. For example, 24 percent of all cabinet members, 30 percent of all managers, and 43 percent of all professors are the sons of higher civil servants. By contrast, the lower classes, Catholics, and women are substantially underrepresented in this elite work force.

Yet membership in the German upper class does not imply a combination of power, wealth, and respect. It is not a homogeneous group like the

British and French upper classes; it is not an establishment. For the Federal Republic lacks the elite schools, the great cosmopolitan capital, and the historical tradition of closely shared values and habits that are features of the British and French social systems. Class rule in Germany has always left competing groups at the helm. Today, it is a more open society, but clearly more open for some than for others. Women in particular have been denied a fair opportunity in the system. For example, of some 300,-000 students enrolled at German universities in 1968, less than one-fifth were women.

The pressing need to reform education and to create more equitable arrangements that will guarantee equal opportunity has led to an enlarged role for the federal government in educational planning, long a rather exclusive prerogative of the *Länder.* Efforts at comprehensive national educational planning have mapped out needed investments and resource development through 1985 under the so-called *Bildungsgesamtplan,* which requires the approval not only of parliament, but also of three-fourths of the states.

In science and technology as well the federal government has taken a larger role in planning new programs, especially for environmental control. Federal spending for science and technology has more than doubled since 1968. It has been successful in producing a high volume of task-oriented research. Perhaps the most striking achievement has been in the field of nuclear development for peaceful purposes. (The federal government long ago banned any nuclear research with military applications.) By 1980 Germany will draw 27 percent of its electricity from nuclear plants, a figure which exceeds those of Britain and the United States. Similar efforts today are being directed towards the development of super high-speed trains, new waste disposal systems, and a host of modern programs designed to improve the quality of life in a society so densely populated and the victim of such intensive growth as that of the Federal Republic.

Nine

Modernity Facing the Future

During the past century, the German people have lived under an extraordinary diversity of regimes. The Kaiserreich was succeeded briefly by the military dictatorship of General Ludendorff. This was followed in turn by the abortive revolution of 1918 and the establishment of the Weimar Republic. Fifteen years of chaotic republicanism brought on twelve of totalitarian frenzy. Then came the four-year hiatus of Allied Occupation with its several zones of administration. Even after 1949, Germany remained divided into two states, shorn of much of its former territory and with a separate and special status for its traditional capitol, Berlin. No other European people has experienced so much impermanence of boundaries or such frequent and extensive transfigurations of its political way of life.

For Germany it has been a century of prodigious growth and vast destruction. No other country grew as fast during the period of industrialization, nor was any other as completely militarized during World War I. No other suffered as bitter a disappointment in its first experiment with democratic institutions nor experienced as deep an economic dislocation in the wake of the Depression. Certainly nowhere else has totalitarianism produced so monolithic a system in so short a period of time, nor one that was based to such a degree on war, genocide, terror, and destructive megalomania. No other European nation was left as dismembered by World War II, nor did any other confront as massive a postwar forced transfer of population. Yet since the war, no European country has had an economic recovery comparable to that achieved by the Federal Republic.

A pattern of recurrent instability and of constant change has characterized German experience in the hundred years since unification. It was as though the forces unleashed by nationhood had created pressures so powerful that they could not be effectively controlled or contained. And yet while Germany appeared to be in motion all the time, its population seemed to yearn for nothing so much as order and stability. In a way, that which was most ardently sought was least available. A manifestly traditional society could not easily cope with such frequent and often radical change.

Virtually from the outset Germany as a unified nation was confronted by a dual dilemma. Internally, it had somehow to modernize its institutions and political system if it was successfully to integrate the forces of change. Externally, the German nation had to make certain that its quest for unity did not unsettle and threaten the rest of Europe. However, it failed from the start in achieving either of these tasks.

The intense scope and speed of industrialization had rapidly transformed the structure of German society. It suddenly produced a host of new claimants for participation in the political process. This further reinforced the need for overdue political reforms. Yet the capacity of the German system to modernize did not extend to the political realm. Deep social cleavages, entrenched special interests, an inept monarchy, and the grip of authoritarian habits stood in the way of an evolutionary transformation of the political way of life.

Unable and unwilling to effect reform from within, Germany's leaders sought gains abroad that might quell internal dissension and deflect pressure for political change at home. Nation, state, and *Volk* were held above the pursuit of pluralistic rights and liberal values. The cult of the military, the quest for economic expansion, and the fostering of a shrill, romantic nationalism were the components of an ideology that was meant to unify a restive and divided nation. This seemed to require tension abroad, so gradually, an aggressive foreign policy became a pillar of the domestic peace. But this produced a dangerous and highly unstable situation that could not long endure. In 1914 it led to a war from which Germany was never fully to recover.

When Germany took the path of reform during the Weimar Republic, conditions were extremely inauspicious. It was a noble experiment, but one that faltered very early. By 1920, with the abortive Kapp Putsch, the forces of the Right were able to mount the first onslaught of their counterrevolution. But it was less the conspiracies of the Right than the failings of the system that signaled the demise of this venture in democracy. Long before Hitler seized power, the Weimar Republic had ceased to function as a democratic, parliamentary system. This is not to say that Nazism was inevitable or somehow immanent in the German soul or system. Rather, events had created a situation in which the most pathological and authoritarian factors and forces became predominant.

Twelve years of macabre Nazi rule served as a kind of catharsis for Germany. Its vicious fanaticism and destructive mania removed a great deal of that which had been traditional in the German system. It not only consumed the forces of constructive change, but also obliterated the fundamental elements of the old order. Thus, when the regime was itself eradicated through the total defeat of 1945, the opportunity for a new beginning was at hand.

This brief review suggests how critical foreign policy has been in shaping the course of German history since the separate German states were first unified. To a large degree it was the international situation prevailing in the years just after World War II that led to the establishment of the Federal Republic and that created important opportunities for its regaining of sovereign powers. For Konrad Adenauer and Willy Brandt, the two most effective leaders among the four postwar German Chancellors, foreign policy played a central role in the consolidation of their domestic political positions. But in stark contrast to the past, this course did not prove unsettling and destablizing to Germany's neighbors. For in the postwar epoch Germany was no longer in a position to dominate others in Europe. The changed nature of the international system precluded an independent, aggressive policy pursued by any one European state. And in the case of Germany, its own division, becoming increasingly permanent over time, and its limited sovereignty greatly reduced the power available for the pursuit of an autonomous foreign policy.

This was a very significant change. For the first time in almost a century Germany was no longer a predominant military power. Although some irredentist claims and aspirations were kept alive, the Federal Republic did not pose an actual threat to any of its neighbors. Foreign policy still remained an important domestic factor, but no longer in the virulent and pernicious sense of the past. Indeed, despite its longtime official pretensions and pronouncements in favor of reunification, the Federal Republic has hardly, at least until recently, played a major independent political role in international affairs.

Ironically, this may have been a factor greatly to its advantage. While Britain and France had to cope with costly and cumbersome problems of decolonization and dwindling empires, the Federal Republic could concentrate on the tasks of domestic reconstruction. Having foresworn nuclear weapons and the maintenance of an independent military force outside the N.A.T.O. Alliance, it has been able to economize substantially on defense costs. In a period in which the pursuit of sovereign foreign-policy aims brought few gains and ample frustrations to other European nations, the Federal Republic seemed blessed by the postwar restrictions placed on its own freedom to maneuver.

Instead of pursuing purely national aims abroad, the Federal Republic has sought to mute its regained sovereign powers within the context of a larger European entity. The movement toward European integration created an entirely new framework for German aspirations. The Federal Republic alone among the six signatories of the Treaty of Rome regarded itself at the time as a somewhat provisional state. It was difficult to engender a real sense of permanent West German separateness. In part this was because the German nation remained divided into two states. But it was also the consequence of the fact that at the time of its entry into the Common Market, the Federal Republic was still not a fully sovereign state. Thus, it surrendered less and stood to gain more from the process of western integration.

To the degree that the Common Market has been a success, the Federal Republic has been able to derive a real sense of achievement from its foreign policy. Its efforts in the East have been less successful. Not until the late 1960s did the Federal Republic embark on a policy of détente toward the Soviet Union and Eastern Europe. This was accelerated under the government of Chancellor Brandt, whose efforts on behalf of *Ostpolitik* rendered to the Federal Republic a new sense of initiative in the realm of foreign policy. Suddenly, what had seemed to be a restrictive burden upon the Bonn government—namely its relations with the East—was transformed into a sense of special opportunity. But even so, German *Ostpolitik* has remained clearly subordinate to the primary purposes of achieving futher integration in the West and of maintaining the close alliance with the United States.

In the postwar epoch, foreign policy has served to reinforce the pattern of stable and liberal democratic politics within the Federal Republic. Whereas in the past external tensions were utilized to justify the thwarting of domestic reform, the Federal Republic has pursued policies of accommodation and cooperation. This has removed the traditional isolation of Germany from its Western neighbors. Instead, a powerful sense of transnational identification and symbiosis emerged, which has helped to consolidate the liberal, democratic parliamentary system in the Federal Republic. Today, despite the division of Germany, the special status of Berlin, and the continuing limited Allied rights with reference to issues of German reunification, the problems of the Federal Republic have come more and more to resemble those of other countries in Europe. There is no longer the acute sense of an ominous and intractable "German problem" that prevailed throughout the first half of this century. To be sure, there are issues still to be resolved, especially with regard to the relationship between the two German states and the matters of access to, and the status of, West Berlin. But German attitudes toward these issues are far more temperate than would have been conceivable several decades ago. The belligerent nationalism that sought the regaining of the Polish corridor or

Alsace-Lorraine in the years following World War I does not exist today. It may be unpalatable for West Germans to recognize the Oder-Neisse frontier separating the German Democratic Republic from Poland. But there are no responsible leaders or groups who would advocate the use of force to regain the lost territories of the East, which are far greater in size than those lost after 1918. And for the first time in a century, relations with France have become amicable. This is indeed a profound and salutary development.

In many other ways the Federal Republic has proven a rather remarkable success. Its political system, despite the parliamentary crisis of 1972, has emerged as relatively stable. The tenure in office of Chancellors and cabinets has been relatively long. Not once has a government resorted to emergency measures, despite the frequent stress produced by Soviet machinations in the past. Parliament has only once been dissolved and has not yet removed a Chancellor through a constructive vote of no confidence. Indeed, until the spring of 1972, no motion of constructive nonconfidence had ever been introduced in the Bundestag. Federalism seems to have worked well, allowing a useful interchange between state and national governments. The party system, too, has functioned relatively well. Coalitions have been unusually stable, and if the pattern of consolidation continues, it is likely that only the two major parties will soon remain, precluding the necessity, in most cases, of coalition government at all.

In terms of economic development and social transformation, the Federal Republic has also come a long way. Its growth rate is unmatched in Europe and has rendered to West Germany a position of leadership in trade and a high standard of living. The process of social integration has been highly successful. As Juan Linz has shown, in the 1950s "the crosscutting of group affiliations and the absence of overly organized and closed subcultures" already characterized the political system of the Federal Republic.[1] This was a striking departure from the patterns of the past. It was the more surprising insofar as a number of groups—including labor, industry, the farmers, and the refugees—were extremely well organized in this period. However, each had a sufficient capacity to identify with the common purposes and aims of the system as a whole to accept compromise and to acquiesce in favor of national priorities and prescriptions. Ironically, the Federal Republic, with a very weak symbolic manifestation of the national interest, was able to secure much greater compliance from a diversity of groups than its more outspokenly nationalistic predecessors.

In large part this was because material reconstruction was broadly accepted as the primary task of the Federal Republic. It proved easier to

[1]Juan J. Linz, "Cleavage and Consensus in West German Politics: The Early Fifties," in Seymour M. Lipset and Stein Rokkan, *Party Systems and Voter Alignments* (New York, 1967), p. 316.

integrate diverse social forces in pursuit of economic growth than on behalf of a highly articulated definition of German nationalism. But this was only possible because economic growth was so successfully achieved. The sheer quantity of material betterment was sufficiently great to provide concrete rewards even for those most opposed to acceptance of the political status quo. This was a great asset in the quest for political stability in the Federal Republic.

Will this success endure? To be sure, important problems remain. They are not so much those of the division of Germany, but rather uncertainties about the quality of change that has occurred within the Federal Republic. Ralf Dahrendorf has expressed his concern that "German society has not yet accepted the reality of conflict and the necessity of its rational regulation. Many of the most striking changes in the structure of the economy and society in the Federal Republic are, therefore, most liable to be undone again."[2] This is entirely possible. The great emphasis on material values poses dangers. First, it may falsely accustom the population to a continuous improvement in the standard of living, which can lead to abrupt and exaggerated disappointment such as occurred during the brief recession of 1966. Second, material satisfaction in itself should not be mistaken for a fundamental reorientation of political values.

In a sense public values seem to be largely missing, or at least poorly articulated, in the Federal Republic. There is a marked absence of any ideological commitment or vision. A kind of prosaic political culture has resulted. Even the scope of the nation is not clearly resolved. And, as Sidney Verba has observed, "the politics of Germany reflects a pragmatism and passivity to governmental authority."[3] Thus, a great deal depends on how that authority is used.

So far, it has been used with constructive effect. But the past record has been one of uninterrupted economic growth and a firm Western presence and pattern of continued integration. If one or the other were to be seriously thwarted, substantial instability might reemerge in German politics. Even with continued economic prosperity and success in foreign policy, it is not certain that the past pattern of stability will endure.

The prospect of political polarization is a serious one. This could manifest itself in a splintering of the two major parties or in a significant decline in party loyalty and an increase in extra-party activity. The vociferous challenge of the S.P.D. leadership by new, militant forces within the party, and especially among its younger members, has posed grave problems for the Social Democratic leaders. While the decade following the adoption

---

[2]Dahrendorf, *Society and Democracy in Germany* (London, 1967), pp. 446–447.

[3]Sidney Verba, "Germany: The Remaking of Political Culture," in Lucien W. Pye and Sidney Verba, *Political Culture and Development* (Princeton, 1969), p. 153.

of the Godesberg Program in 1959 was one of consensus-building movement toward the political center for the party, it seems that in the years ahead the S.P.D. will be confronted with a vigorous internal challenge by those seeking a more radical and ideological definition of the party program. How this movement of radical dissent will be absorbed or resisted by the party will be of critical importance for the development and success of the S.P.D. in the decade ahead.

Similarly, the C.D.U./C.S.U. must contend with increasingly vocal forces on the Right. The success of the German political system in containing the appeals of the N.P.D. and other right-wing parties in the past has, in part, been due to the capacity of the C.D.U./C.S.U. to absorb the reservoir of right-wing voters. But here, too, further polarization would pose serious dilemmas. The potential force of a right-wing reaction against some of the manifestations of modern, industrial life may grow among those social groups which are threatened or which still yearn for a more traditional social order and cannot accept the demise of effective national symbols in present-day Germany. And here the extremism of the Left, fostered by a small minority and manifested in a series of violent acts, can contribute to a dangerous overreaction on the Right.

The catalogue of potential social problems is large as well. Rancor against the foreigners working within the Federal Republic, the prospect of further rural stagnation, the radicalization of the universities, the persistence of educational imbalances, and the growth of crime are new problems that may well continue to afflict the Federal Republic in the years ahead. But they are in no sense unique to Germany. Rather, they are to a substantial degree the products of a highly advanced industrial society. Germany today is certainly not problem-free. But its foremost problems are mostly also common to other countries. There is still a great deal that is peculiar to the German system, but its predominant concerns are not so much of German origin as they are the result of processes of modernization. The Federal Republic today is in this sense a more "normal" society than any of its predecessors have been. To be afflicted by common ailments is, in the German case, symptomatic of a state of comparative good health—given the diseased record of the past.

Appendix A German Parliamentary Election Results (Selected Elections 1871–1912; All Elections 1919–1972)* Percent Share of Party Vote

Year	Social Democratic Party	Regional Parties	Center Party (Catholic)	German People's Party	Progressives (Liberal Parties)	National Liberal Party	Conservative Parties	Other Parties
1871	3.2	6.6	18.6	0.5	7.2	30.0	23.0	2.0
1881	6.1	8.8	23.2	2.0	21.1	14.6	23.7	0.5
1890	19.7	6.6	18.6	2.0	16.0	16.3	19.8	1.0
1903	31.7	6.0	19.7	1.0	8.3	13.9	16.1	3.5
1912	34.8	5.7	16.4	——— 12.3 ———		13.7	12.6	4.5

Year	Communist Party (K.P.D.)	Social Democratic Party	Bavarian People's Party	Center Party	German People's Party	German State Democratic Party	Special Interest Parties	National People's Party	National Socialists	Other Parties
1919		45.5		19.7	4.4	18.6	1.1	10.3		0.4
1920	2.1	39.5	4.4	13.6	13.9	8.3	1.7	14.9		1.6
1924[1]	12.6	20.5	3.2	13.4	9.2	5.7	5.3	19.5	6.5	4.0
1924[2]	9.0	26.0	3.7	13.6	10.1	6.3	5.7	20.5	3.0	2.0
1928	10.6	29.8	3.0	12.1	8.7	4.9	8.9	14.2	2.6	4.8
1930	13.1	24.5	3.0	11.8	4.5	3.8	11.3	7.0	18.3	3.1
1932[3]	14.6	21.6	3.2	12.5	1.2	1.0	2.3	5.9	37.4	0.9
1932[4]	16.9	20.4	3.1	11.9	1.9	1.0	2.5	8.8	33.1	2.2
1933[5]	12.3	18.3	2.7	11.7	1.1	0.8	1.6	8.0	43.9	0.3
1933[6]									92.2	

	Communist Party	Social Democratic Party	Christian Democratic Union/Christian Social Union	German Party	Free Democratic Party	Extreme Right Parties	Other Parties
1949	5.7	29.2	31.0	4.0	11.9	1.1	17.1
1953	2.2	28.8	45.2	3.2	9.5		11.1
1957		31.8	50.2	3.4	7.7		6.9
1961		36.2	45.3	12.8	12.8		2.9
1965		39.3	47.6		9.5	2.0	1.6
1969		42.7	46.1		5.8	4.3	1.2
1972	0.3	45.9	44.8		8.4	0.6	0.1

*Figures for 1949–1972 are second [list] votes.
[1]May 1924
[2]December 1924
[3]July 1932
[4]November 1932
[5]March 1933
[6]November 1933

DATA SOURCES: Walter Tormin, *Geschichte der deutschen Parteien seit 1848* (Stuttgart: 1964); *Statistisches Jahrbuch fur das deutsche Reich, 1933; Statistisches Jahrbuch fur die Bundesrepublik Deutschland, 1970; Das Parlament* (Bonn), 25 November 1972.

The Statistical Appendix was prepared by Glenn A. Robinson.

Appendix B THE *LÄNDER* IN THE FEDERAL REPUBLIC OF GERMANY

1. Baden-Württemberg
Capital: Stuttgart
Area: 13,739 sq. mi.
Inhabitants: 9.0 million
Bundesrat seats: 5

2. Bavaria
Capital: Munich
Area: 27,114 sq. mi.
Inhabitants: 10.6 million
Bundesrat seats: 5

3. Bremen
City-state
Area: 155 sq. mi.
Inhabitants: 0.8 million
Bundesrat seats: 3

4. Hamburg
City-state
Area: 287 sq. mi.
Inhabitants: 1.8 million
Bundesrat seats: 3

5. Hesse
Capital: Wiesbaden
Area: 8,113 sq. mi.
Inhabitants: 5.5 million
Bundesrat seats: 4

6. Lower Saxony
Capital: Hannover
Area: 18,217 sq. mi.
Inhabitants: 7.1 million
Bundesrat seats: 5

7. North Rhine-Westphalia
Capital: Düsseldorf
Area: 13,084 sq. mi.
Inhabitants: 17.2 million
Bundesrat seats: 5

8. Rhineland-Palatinate

Capital: Mainz
Area: 7,621 sq. mi.
Inhabitants: 3.7 million
Bundesrat seats: 4

9. Saarland

Capital: Saarbrücken
Area: 987 sq. mi.
Inhabitants: 1.1 million
Bundesrat seats: 3

10. Schleswig-Holstein

Capital: Kiel
Area: 6,018 sq. mi.
Inhabitants: 2.6 million
Bundesrat seats: 4

11. West Berlin

City-state (special status)
Area: 184 sq. mi.
Inhabitants: 2.1 million
Bundesrat seats: 4 (advisory)

Appendix C THE BASIC LAW FOR THE FEDERAL REPUBLIC OF GERMANY

(Promulgated on May 23, 1949 as amended up to and including May 31, 1971)

ANNOUNCEMENT BY THE PARLIAMENTARY COUNCIL

The Parliamentary Council, meeting in public session at Bonn am Rhein on 23 May 1949, confirmed the fact that the Basic Law for the Federal Republic of Germany, which was adopted by the Parliamentary Council on 8 May 1949, was ratified in the week of 16 to 22 May 1949 by the diets of more than two thirds of the participating constituent states (Länder).

By virtue of this fact the Parliamentary Council, represented by its Presidents, has signed and promulgated the Basic Law.

The Basic Law is hereby published in the Federal Law Gazette pursuant to paragraph (3) of Article 145.

PREAMBLE

The German People in the *Länder* of Baden, Bavaria, Bremen, Hamburg, Hesse, Lower Saxony, North Rhine-Westphalia, Rhineland-Palatinate, Schleswig-Holstein, Wuerttemberg-Baden and Wuerttemberg-Hohenzollern,

Conscious of their responsibility before God and men,

Animated by the resolve to preserve their national and political unity and to serve the peace of the world as an equal partner in a united Europe,

Desiring to give a new order to political life for a transitional period,

Have enacted, by virtue of their constituent power, this Basic Law for the Federal Republic of Germany. They have also acted on behalf of those Germans to whom participation was denied. The entire German people are called upon to achieve in free self-determination the unity and freedom of Germany.

I. BASIC RIGHTS

Article 1 (Protection of human dignity)

(1) The dignity of man shall be inviolable. To respect and protect it shall be the duty of all state authority.

(2) The German people therefore acknowledge inviolable and inalienable human rights as the basis of every community, of peace and of justice in the world.

(3) The following basic rights shall bind the legislature, the executive and the judiciary as directly enforceable law.

Article 2 (Rights of liberty)

(1) Everyone shall have the right to the free development of his personality in so far as he does not violate the rights of others or offend against the constitutional order or the moral code.
(2) Everyone shall have the right to life and to inviolability of his person. The liberty of the individual shall be inviolable. These rights may only be encroached upon pursuant to a law.

Article 3 (Equality before the law)

(1) All persons shall be equal before the law.
(2) Men and women shall have equal rights.
(3) No one may be prejudiced or favoured because of his sex, his parentage, his race, his language, his homeland and origin, his faith, or his religious or political opinions.

Article 4 (Freedom of faith and creed)

(1) Freedom of faith, of conscience, and freedom of creed, religious or ideological *(weltanschaulich),* shall be inviolable.
(2) The undisturbed practice of religion is guaranteed.
(3) No one may be compelled against his conscience to render war service involving the use of arms. Details shall be regulated by a federal law.

Article 5 (Freedom of expression)

(1) Everyone shall have the right freely to express and disseminate his opinion by speech, writing and pictures and freely to inform himself from generally accessible sources. Freedom of the press and freedom of reporting by means of broadcasts and films are guaranteed. There shall be no censorship.
(2) These rights are limited by the provisions of the general laws, the provisions of law for the protection of youth, and by the right to inviolability of personal honour.
(3) Art and science, research and teaching, shall be free. Freedom of teaching shall not absolve from loyalty to the constitution.

Article 6 (Marriage, Family, Illegitimate children)

(1) Marriage and family shall enjoy the special protection of the state.
(2) The care and upbringing of children are a natural right of, and a duty primarily incumbent on, the parents. The national community shall watch over their endeavours in this respect.
(3) Children may not be separated from their families against the will

of the persons entitled to bring them up, except pursuant to a law, if those so entitled fail or the children are otherwise threatened with neglect.
(4) Every mother shall be entitled to the protection and care of the community.
(5) Illegitimate children shall be provided by legislation with the same opportunities for their physical and spiritual development and their place in society as are enjoyed by legitimate children.

Article 7 (Education)

(1) The entire educational system shall be under the supervision of the state.
(2) The persons entitled to bring up a child shall have the right to decide whether it shall receive religious instruction.
(3) Religious instruction shall form part of the ordinary curriculum in state and municipal schools, except in secular *(bekenntnisfrei)* schools. Without prejudice to the state's right of supervision, religious instruction shall be given in accordance with the tenets of the religious communities. No teacher may be obliged against his will to give religious instruction.
(4) The right to establish private schools is guaranteed. Private schools, as a substitute for state or municipal schools, shall require the approval of the state and shall be subject to the laws of the *Länder.* Such approval must be given if private schools are not inferior to the state or municipal schools in their educational aims, their facilities and the professional training of their teaching staff, and if segregation of pupils according to the means of the parents is not promoted thereby. Approval must be withheld if the economic and legal position of the teaching staff is not sufficiently assured.
(5) A private elementary school shall be permitted only if the education authority finds that it serves a special pedagogic interest, or if, on the application of persons entitled to bring up children, it is to be established as an interdenominational or denominational or ideological school and a state or municipal elementary school of this type does not exist in the commune *(Gemeinde).*
(6) Preparatory schools *(Vorschulen)* shall remain abolished.

Article 8 (Freedom of assembly)

(1) All Germans shall have the right to assemble peaceably and unarmed without prior notification or permission.
(2) With regard to open-air meetings this right may be restricted by or pursuant to a law.

Article 9 (Freedom of association)

(1) All Germans shall have the right to form associations and societies.
(2) Associations, the purposes or activities of which conflict with criminal laws or which are directed against the constitutional order or the concept of international understanding, are prohibited.
(3) The right to form associations to safeguard and improve working and economic conditions is guaranteed to everyone and to all trades, occupations and professions. Agreements which restrict or seek to impair this right shall be null and void; measures directed to this end shall be illegal. Measures taken pursuant to Article 12a, to paragraphs (2) and (3) of Article 35, to paragraph (4) of Article 87a, or to Article 91, may not be directed against any industrial conflicts engaged in by associations within the meaning of the first sentence of this paragraph in order to safeguard and improve working and economic conditions.

Article 10 (Privacy of posts and telecommunications)

(1) Privacy of posts and telecommunications shall be inviolable.
(2) This right may be restricted only pursuant to a law. Such law may lay down that the person affected shall not be informed of any such restriction if it serves to protect the free democratic basic order or the existence or security of the Federation or a *Land,* and that recourse to the courts shall be replaced by a review of the case by bodies and auxiliary bodies appointed by Parliament.

Article 11 (Freedom of movement)

(1) All Germans shall enjoy freedom of movement throughout the federal territory.
(2) This right may be restricted only by or pursuant to a law and only in cases in which an adequate basis of existence is lacking and special burdens would arise to the community as a result thereof, or in which such restriction is necessary to avert an imminent danger to the existence or the free democratic basic order of the Federation or a *Land,* to combat the danger of epidemics, to deal with natural disasters or particularly grave accidents, to protect young people from neglect or to prevent crime.

Article 12 (Right to choose trade, occupation, or profession)

(1) All Germans shall have the right freely to choose their trade, occupation, or profession, their place of work and their place of training. The practice of trades, occupations, and professions may be regulated by or pursuant to a law.

(2) No specific occupation may be imposed on any person except within the framework of a traditional compulsory public service that applies generally and equally to all.
(3) Forced labour may be imposed only on persons deprived of their liberty by court sentence.

Article 12a (Liability to military and other service)

(1) Men who have attained the age of eighteen years may be required to serve in the Armed Forces, in the Federal Border Guard, or in a Civil Defence organization.
(2) A person who refuses, on grounds of conscience, to render war service involving the use of arms may be required to render a substitute service. The duration of such substitute service shall not exceed the duration of military service. Details shall be regulated by a law which shall not interfere with the freedom of conscience and must also provide for the possibility of a substitute service not connected with units of the Armed Forces or of the Federal Border Guard.
(3) Persons liable to military service who are not required to render service pursuant to paragraph (1) or (2) of this Article may, when a state of defence (Verteidigungsfall) exists, be assigned by or pursuant to a law to specific occupations involving civilian services for defence purposes, including the protection of the civilian population; it shall, however, not be permissible to assign persons to an occupation subject to public law except for the purpose of discharging police functions or such other functions of public administration as can only be discharged by persons employed under public law. Persons may be assigned to occupations —as referred to in the first sentence of this paragraph—with the Armed Forces, including the supplying and servicing of the latter, or with public administrative authorities; assignments to occupations connected with supplying and servicing the civilian population shall not be permissible except in order to meet their vital requirements or to guarantee their safety.
(4) If, while a state of defence exists, civilian service requirements in the civilian public health and medical system or in the stationary military hospital organization cannot be met on a voluntary basis, women between eighteen and fifty-five years of age may be assigned to such services by or pursuant to a law. They may on no account render service involving the use of arms.
(5) During the time prior to the existence of any such state of defence, assignments under paragraph (3) of this Article may be effected only if the requirements of paragraph (1) of Article 80a are satisfied. It shall be admissible to require persons by or pursuant to a law to attend training courses in order to prepare them for the performance of such services

in accordance with paragraph (3) of this Article as presuppose special knowledge or skills. To this extent, the first sentence of this paragraph shall not apply.
(6) If, while a state of defence exists, the labour requirements for the purposes referred to in the second sentence of paragraph (3) of this Article cannot be met on a voluntary basis, the right of a German to give up the practice of his trade or occupation or profession, or his place of work, may be restricted by or pursuant to a law in order to meet these requirements. The first sentence of paragraph (5) of this Article shall apply mutatis mutandis prior to the existence of a state of defence.

Article 13 (Inviolability of the home)

(1) The home shall be inviolable.
(2) Searches may be ordered only by a judge or, in the event of danger in delay, by other organs as provided by law and may be carried out only in the form prescribed by law.
(3) In all other respects, this inviolability may not be encroached upon or restricted except to avert a common danger or a mortal danger to individuals, or, pursuant to a law, to prevent imminent danger to public safety and order, especially to alleviate the housing shortage, to combat the danger of epidemics or to protect endangered juveniles.

Article 14 (Property, Right of inheritance, Expropriation)

(1) Property and the right of inheritance are guaranteed. Their content and limits shall be determined by the laws.
(2) Property imposes duties. Its use should also serve the public weal.
(3) Expropriation shall be permitted only in the public weal. It may be effected only by or pursuant to a law which shall provide for the nature and extent of the compensation. Such compensation shall be determined by establishing an equitable balance between the public interest and the interests of those affected. In case of dispute regarding the amount of compensation, recourse may be had to the ordinary courts.

Article 15 (Socialization)

Land, natural resources and means of production may for the purpose of socialization be transferred to public ownership or other forms ot publicly controlled economy by a law which shall provide for the nature and extent of compensation. In respect of such compensation the third and fourth sentences of paragraph (3) of Article 14 shall apply mutatis mutandis.

Article 16 (Deprivation of citizenship, Extradition, Right of asylum)

(1) No one may be deprived of his German citizenship. Loss of citizenship may arise only pursuant to a law, and against the will of the person affected only if such person does not thereby become stateless.
(2) No German may be extradited to a foreign country. Persons persecuted on political grounds shall enjoy the right of asylum.

Article 17 (Right of petition)

Everyone shall have the right individually or jointly with others to address written requests or complaints to the appropriate agencies and to parliamentary bodies.

Article 17a (Restriction of basic rights for members of the Armed Forces, etc.)

(1) Laws concerning military service and substitute service may, by provisions applying to members of the Armed Forces and of substitute services during their period of military or substitute service, restrict the basic right freely to express and to disseminate opinions by speech, writing and pictures (first half-sentence of paragraph (1) of Article 5), the basic right of assembly (Article 8), and the right of petition (Article 17) in so far as this right permits the submission of requests or complaints jointly with others.
(2) Laws for defence purposes including the protection of the civilian population may provide for the restriction of the basic rights of freedom of movement (Article 11) and inviolability of the home (Article 13).

Article 18 (Forfeiture of basic rights)

Whoever abuses freedom of expression of opinion, in particular freedom of the press (paragraph (1) of Article 5), freedom of teaching (paragraph (3) of Article 5), freedom of assembly (Article 8), freedom of association (Article 9), privacy of posts and telecommunications (Article 10), property (Article 14), or the right of asylum (paragraph (2) of Article 16) in order to combat the free democratic basic order, shall forfeit these basic rights. Such forfeiture and the extent thereof shall be pronounced by the Federal Constitutional Court.

Article 19 (Restriction of basic rights)

(1) In so far as a basic right may, under this Basic Law, be restricted by or pursuant to a law, such law must apply generally and not solely to an individual case. Furthermore, such law must name the basic right, indicating the Article concerned.

(2) In no case may the essential content of a basic right be encroached upon.
(3) The basic rights shall apply also to domestic juristic persons to the extent that the nature of such rights permits.
(4) Should any person's right be violated by public authority, recourse to the court shall be open to him. If jurisdiction is not specified, recourse shall be to the ordinary courts. The second sentence of paragraph (2) of Article 10 shall not be affected by the provisions of this paragraph.

II. THE FEDERATION AND THE CONSTITUENT STATES *(LÄNDER)*

Article 20 (Basic principles of the Constitution—Right to resist)

(1) The Federal Republic of Germany is a democratic and social federal state.
(2) All state authority emanates from the people. It shall be exercised by the people by means of elections and voting and by specific legislative, executive, and judicial organs.
(3) Legislation shall be subject to the constitutional order; the executive and the judiciary shall be bound by law and justice.
(4) All Germans shall have the right to resist any person or persons seeking to abolish that constitutional order, should no other remedy be possible.

Article 21 (Political parties)

(1) The political parties shall participate in the forming of the political will of the people. They may be freely established. Their internal organization must conform to democratic principles. They must publicly account for the sources of their funds.
(2) Parties which, by reason of their aims or the behaviour of their adherents, seek to impair or abolish the free democratic basic order or to endanger the existence of the Federal Republic of Germany, shall be unconstitutional. The Federal Constitutional Court shall decide on the question of unconsitutionality.
(3) Details shall be regulated by federal laws.

Article 22 (Federal flag)

The federal flag shall be black-red-gold.

Article 23 (Jurisdiction of the Basic Law)

For the time being, this Basic Law shall apply in the territory of the *Länder* of Baden, Bavaria, Bremen, Greater Berlin, Hamburg, Hesse, Lower Saxony, North Rhine-Westphalia, Rhineland-Palatinate, Schleswig-Holstein, Wuerttemberg-Baden, and Wuerttemberg-Hohenzollern. In other parts of Germany it shall be put into force on their accession.

Article 24 (Entry into a collective security system)

(1) The Federation may by legislation transfer sovereign powers to intergovernmental institutions.
(2) For the maintenance of peace, the Federation may enter a system of mutual collective security; in doing so it will consent to such limitations upon its rights of sovereignty as will bring about and secure a peaceful and lasting order in Europe and among the nations of the world.
(3) For the settlement of disputes between states, the Federation will accede to agreements concerning international arbitration of a general, comprehensive and obligatory nature.

Article 25 (International law integral part of federal law)

The general rules of public international law shall be an integral part of federal law. They shall take precedence over the laws and shall directly create rights and duties for the inhabitants of the federal territory.

Article 26 (Ban on war of aggression)

(1) Acts tending to and undertaken with the intent to disturb the peaceful relations between nations, especially to prepare for aggressive war, shall be unconstitutional. They shall be made a punishable offence.
(2) Weapons designed for warfare may not be manufactured, transported or marketed except with the permission of the Federal Government. Details shall be regulated by a federal law.

Article 27 (Merchant fleet)

All German merchant vessels shall form one merchant fleet.

Article 28 (Federal guarantee of *Länder* constitutions)

(1) The constitutional order in the *Länder* must conform to the principles of republican, democratic and social government based on the rule of law, within the meaning of this Basic Law. In each of the *Länder,* counties *(Kreise),* and communes *(Gemeinden),* the people must be represented by a body chosen in general, direct, free, equal, and secret elections. In the communes the assembly of the commune may take the place of an elected body.
(2) The communes must be guaranteed the right to regulate on their own responsibility all the affairs of the local community within the limits set

by law. The associations of communes *(Gemeindeverbaende)* shall also have the right of self-government in accordance with the law and within the limits of the functions assigned to them by law.
(3) The Federation shall ensure that the constitutional order of the *Länder* conforms to the basic rights and to the provisions of paragraphs (1) and (2) of this Article.

Article 29 (Reorganization of the federal territory)

(1) The federal territory shall be reorganized by federal legislation with due regard to regional ties, historical and cultural connections, economic expediency and social structure. Such reorganization should create *Länder* which by their size and capacity are able effectively to fulfil the functions incumbent upon them.
(2) In areas which became, upon the reorganization of the *Länder* after 8 May 1945, part of another *Land* without the holding of a plebiscite, a definite change of the decision regarding such incorporation may be demanded by popular initiative within one year of the coming into force of this Basic Law. Such popular initiative shall require the assent of one tenth of the people entitled to vote in *Land* diet *(Landtag)* elections.
(3) If a popular initiative has received the assent required under paragraph (2) of this Article, a referendum shall be held in the area concerned not later than 31 March 1975, or in the Baden area of the *Land* of Baden-Wuerttemberg not later than 30 June 1970, on whether or not the proposed transfer shall be made. If the transfer is approved by a majority comprising at least one quarter of the people entitled to vote in *Land* diet elections, the territorial position of the area concerned shall be regulated by a federal law within one year after the referendum has been held. Where several areas within the same *Land* demand to be transferred to another *Land,* the necessary regulations shall be consolidated in one law.
(4) Such federal law shall be based upon the result of the referendum from which it may depart only to the extent necessary to achieve the purposes of reorganization as specified in paragraph (1) of this Article. Such law shall require the assent of a majority of Bundestag members. If it provides for a transfer, not demanded by a referendum, of an area from one *Land* to another, the law shall require approval by referendum in the entire area to be transferred; this shall not apply if in the event of the separation of areas from an existing *Land* the remaining areas are to continue as a *Land* in themselves.
(5) Following the adoption of a federal law on the reorganization of the federal territory by a procedure other than that laid down in paragraphs (2) to (4) of this Article, a referendum shall be held in every area to be transferred from one *Land* to another, on those provisions of the law

which concern that area. If such provisions are rejected in at least one of the areas concerned, the law must be reintroduced in the Bundestag. Should it be enacted again, the relevant provisions shall require approval by referendum throughout the federal territory.
(6) A referendum shall be decided by the majority of votes cast; this shall, however, not affect paragraph (3) of this Article. The pertinent procedure shall be laid down by a federal law. Should reorganization become necessary as a result of the accession of another part of Germany, such reorganization should be concluded within two years of such accession.
(7) The procedure regarding any other change in *Land* boundaries shall be established by a federal law requiring the consent of the Bundesrat and of the majority of the members of the Bundestag.

Article 30 (Functions of the *Länder)*

The exercise of governmental powers and the discharge of governmental functions shall be incumbent on the *Länder* in so far as this Basic Law does not otherwise prescribe or permit.

Article 31 (Priority of federal law)

Federal law shall override *Land* law.

Article 32 (Foreign relations)

(1) Relations with foreign states shall be conducted by the Federation.
(2) Before the conclusion of a treaty affecting the special circumstances of a *Land,* that *Land* must be consulted in sufficient time.
(3) In so far as the *Länder* have power to legislate, they may, with the consent of the Federal Government, conclude treaties with foreign states.

Article 33 (All Germans have equal political status)

(1) Every German shall have in every *Land* the same political *(staatsbuergerlich)* rights and duties.
(2) Every German shall be equally eligible for any public office according to his aptitude, qualifications, and professional achievements.
(3) Enjoyment of civil and political rights, eligibility for public office, and rights acquired in the public service shall be independent of religious denomination. No one may suffer any disadvantage by reason of his adherence or non-adherence to a denomination or ideology.
(4) The exercise of state authority as a permanent function shall as a rule be entrusted to members of the public service whose status, service and loyalty are governed by public law.

(5) The law of the public service shall be regulated with due regard to the traditional principles of the professional civil service.

Article 34 (Liability in the event of malfeasance)

If any person, in the exercise of a public office entrusted to him, violates his official obligations to a third party, liability shall rest in principle on the state or the public body which employs him. In the event of wilful intent or gross negligence the right of recourse shall be reserved. In respect of the claim for compensation or the right of recourse, the jurisdiction of the ordinary courts must not be excluded.

Article 35 (Legal, administrative, and police assistance)

(1) All federal and *Land* authorities shall render each other legal and administrative assistance.
(2) In order to deal with a natural disaster or an especially grave accident, a *Land* may request the assistance of the police forces of other *Länder* or of forces and facilities of other administrative authorities or of the Federal Border Guard or the Armed Forces.
(3) If the natural disaster or the accident endangers a region larger than a *Land,* the Federal Government may, in so far as this is necessary effectively to deal with such danger, instruct the *Land* governments to place their police forces at the disposal of other *Länder,* and may commit units of the Federal Border Guard or the Armed Forces to support the police forces. Measures taken by the Federal Government pursuant to the first sentence of this paragraph must be revoked at any time upon the request of the Bundesrat, and in any case without delay upon removal of the danger.

Article 36 (Personnel of the federal authorities)

(1) Civil servants employed in the highest federal authorities shall be drawn from all *Länder* in appropriate proportion. Persons employed in other federal authorities should, as a rule, be drawn from the *Land* in which they serve.
(2) Military laws shall, inter alia, take into account both the division of the Federation into *Länder* and the regional ties of their populations.

Article 37 (Federal enforcement)

(1) If a *Land* fails to comply with its obligations of a federal character imposed by this Basic Law or another federal law, the Federal Government may, with the consent of the Bundesrat, take the necessary measures to enforce such compliance by the *Land* by way of federal enforcement.

(2) To carry out such federal enforcement the Federal Government or its commissioner shall have the right to give instructions to all *Länder* and their authorities.

III. THE FEDERAL PARLIAMENT (BUNDESTAG)

Article 38 (Elections)

(1) The deputies to the German Bundestag shall be elected in general, direct, free, equal, and secret elections. They shall be representatives of the whole people, not bound by orders and instructions, and shall be subject only to their conscience.
(2) Anyone who has attained the age of eighteen years shall be entitled to vote; anyone who has attained full legal age shall be eligible for election.
(3) Details shall be regulated by a federal law.

Article 39 (Assembly and legislative term)

(1) The Bundestag shall be elected for a four-year term. Its legislative term shall end four years after its first meeting or on its dissolution. The new election shall be held during the last three months of the term or within sixty days after dissolution.
(2) The Bundestag shall assemble within thirty days after the election, but not before the end of the term of the previous Bundestag.
(3) The Bundestag shall determine the termination and resumption of its meetings. The President of the Bundestag may convene it at an earlier date. He must do so if one third of its members or the Federal President or the Federal Chancellor so demand.

Article 40 (President, Rules of procedure)

(1) The Bundestag shall elect its President, vice-presidents, and secretaries. It shall draw up its rules of procedure.
(2) The President shall exercise the proprietary and police powers in the Bundestag building. No search or seizure may take place in the premises of the Bundestag without his permission.

Article 41 (Scrutiny of elections)

(1) The scrutiny of elections shall be the responsibility of the Bundestag. It shall also decide whether a deputy has lost his seat in the Bundestag.
(2) Complaints against such decisions of the Bundestag may be lodged with the Federal Constitutional Court.
(3) Details shall be regulated by a federal law.

Article 42 (Proceedings, Voting)

(1) The meetings of the Bundestag shall be public. Upon a motion of one tenth of its members, or upon a motion of the Federal Government, the public may be excluded by a two-thirds majority. The decision on the motion shall be taken at a meeting not open to the public.
(2) Decisions of the Bundestag shall require a majority of the votes cast unless this Basic Law provides otherwise. The rules of procedure may provide exceptions for elections to be made by the Bundestag.
(3) True and accurate reports on the public meetings of the Bundestag and of its committees shall not give rise to any liability.

Article 43 (Presence of the Federal Government)

(1) The Bundestag and its committees may demand the presence of any member of the Federal Government.
(2) The members of the Bundesrat or of the Federal Government as well as persons commissioned by them shall have access to all meetings of the Bundestag and its committees. They must be heard at any time.

Article 44 (Committees of investigation)

(1) The Bundestag shall have the right, and upon the motion of one fourth of its members the duty, to set up a committee of investigation which shall take the requisite evidence at public hearings. The public may be excluded.
(2) The rules of criminal procedure shall apply mutatis mutandis to the taking of evidence. The privacy of posts and telecommunications shall remain unaffected.
(3) Courts and administrative authorities shall be bound to render legal and administrative assistance.
(4) The decisions of committees of investigation shall not be subject to judicial consideration. The courts shall be free to evaluate and judge the facts on which the investigation is based.

Article 45 (Standing Committee)

(1) The Bundestag shall appoint a Standing Committee which shall safeguard the rights of the Bundestag as against the Federal Government in the intervals between any two legislative terms. The Standing Committee shall also have the rights of a committee of investigation.
(2) Wider powers, such as the right to legislate, to elect the Federal Chancellor, or to impeach the Federal President, shall not be within the competence of the Standing Committee.

Article 45a (Committees on Foreign Affairs and Defense)

(1) The Bundestag shall appoint a Committee on Foreign Affairs and a Committee on Defense. Both committees shall function also in the intervals between any two legislative terms.
(2) The Committee on Defense shall also have the rights of a committee of investigation. Upon the motion of one fourth of its members it shall have the duty to make a specific matter the subject of investigation.
(3) Paragraph (1) of Article 44 shall not be applied in matters of defense.

Article 45b (Defense Commissioner of the Bundestag)

A Defense Commissioner of the Bundestag shall be appointed to safeguard the basic rights and to assist the Bundestag in exercising parliamentary control. Details shall be regulated by a federal law.

Article 46 (Indemnity and immunity of deputies)

(1) A deputy may not at any time be prosecuted in the courts or subjected to disciplinary action or otherwise called to account outside the Bundestag for a vote cast or a statement made by him in the Bundestag or any of its committees. This shall not apply to defamatory insults.
(2) A deputy may not be called to account or arrested for a punishable offense except by permission of the Bundestag, unless he is apprehended in the commission of the offence or in the course of the following day.
(3) The permission of the Bundestag shall also be necessary for any other restriction of the personal liberty of a deputy or for the initiation of proceedings against a deputy under Article 18.
(4) Any criminal proceedings or any proceedings under Article 18 against a deputy, any detention or any other restriction of his personal liberty shall be suspended upon the request of the Bundestag.

Article 47 (Right of deputies to refuse to give evidence)

Deputies may refuse to give evidence concerning persons who have confided facts to them in their capacity as deputies, or to whom they have confided facts in such capacity, as well as concerning these facts themselves. To the extent that this right to refuse to give evidence exists, no seizure of documents shall be permissible.

Article 48 (Entitlements of deputies)

(1) Any candidate for election to the Bundestag shall be entitled to the leave necessary for his election campaign.

(2) No one may be prevented from accepting and exercising the office of deputy. He may not be given notice of dismissal nor dismissed from employment on this ground.
(3) Deputies shall be entitled to a remuneration adequate to ensure their independence. They shall be entitled to the free use of all state-owned means of transport. Details shall be regulated by a federal law.

Article 49 (Interim between legislative terms)

In respect of the members of the Presidency, the Standing Committee, the Committee on Foreign Affairs, and the Committee on Defense, as well as their principal substitutes, Articles 46, 47, and paragraphs (2) and (3) of Article 48, shall apply also in the intervals between any two legislative terms.

IV. THE COUNCIL OF CONSTITUENT STATES (BUNDESRAT)

Article 50 (Function)

The *Länder* shall participate through the Bundesrat in the legislation and administration of the Federation.

Article 51 (Composition)

(1) The Bundesrat shall consist of members of the *Land* governments which appoint and recall them. Other members of such governments may act as substitutes.
(2) Each *Land* shall have at least three votes; *Länder* with more than two million inhabitants shall have four, *Länder* with more than six million inhabitants five votes.
(3) Each *Land* may delegate as many members as it has votes. The votes of each *Land* may be cast only as a block vote and only by members present or their substitutes.

Article 52 (President, Rules of procedure)

(1) The Bundesrat shall elect its President for one year.
(2) The President shall convene the Bundesrat. He must convene it if the members for at least two *Länder* or the Federal Government so demand.
(3) The Bundesrat shall take its decisions with at least the majority of its votes. It shall draw up its rules of procedure. Its meetings shall be public. The public may be excluded.
(4) Other members of, or persons commissioned by, *Land* governments may serve on the committees of the Bundesrat.

Article 53 (Participation of the Federal Government)

The members of the Federal Government shall have the right, and on demand the duty, to attend the meetings of the Bundesrat and of its committees. They must be heard at any time. The Bundesrat must be currently kept informed by the Federal Government of the conduct of affairs.

IVa. THE JOINT COMMITTEE

Article 53a

(1) Two thirds of the members of the Joint Committee shall be deputies of the Bundestag and one third shall be members of the Bundesrat. The Bundestag shall delegate its deputies in proportion to the sizes of its parliamentary groups; such deputies must not be members of the Federal Government. Each *Land* shall be represented by a Bundesrat member of its choice; these members shall not be bound by instructions. The establishment of the Joint Committee and its procedures shall be regulated by rules of procedure to be adopted by the Bundestag and requiring the consent of the Bundesrat.
(2) The Federal Government must inform the Joint Committee about its plans in respect of a state of defence. The rights of the Bundestag and its committees under paragraph (1) of Article 43 shall not be affected by the provision of this paragraph.

V. THE FEDERAL PRESIDENT

Article 54 (Election by the Federal Convention)

(1) The Federal President shall be elected, without debate, by the Federal Convention *(Bundesversammlung).* Every German shall be eligible who is entitled to vote for Bundestag candidates and has attained the age of forty years.
(2) The term of office of the Federal President shall be five years. Reelection for a consecutive term shall be permitted only once.
(3) The Federal Convention shall consist of the members of the Bundestag and an equal number of members elected by the diets of the *Länder* according to the principles of proportional representation.
(4) The Federal Convention shall meet not later than thirty days before the expiration of the term of office of the Federal President or, in the case of premature termination, not later than thirty days after that date. It shall be convened by the President of the Bundestag.
(5) After the expiration of a legislative term, the period specified in the

first sentence of paragraph (4) of this Article shall begin with the first meeting of the Bundestag.
(6) The person receiving the votes of the majority of the members of the Federal Convention shall be elected. If such majority is not obtained by any candidate in two ballots, the candidate who receives the largest number of votes in the next ballot shall be elected.
(7) Details shall be regulated by a federal law.

Article 55 (No secondary occupation)

(1) The Federal President may not be a member of the government nor of a legislative body of the Federation or of a *Land.*
(2) The Federal President may not hold any other salaried office, nor engage in a trade or occupation, nor practise a profession, nor belong to the management or the board of directors of an enterprise carried on for profit.

Article 56 (Oath of office)

On assuming his office the Federal President shall take the following oath before the assembled members of the Bundestag and the Bundesrat:

> "I swear that I will dedicate my efforts to the well-being of the German people, enhance its benefits, ward harm from it, uphold and defend the Basic Law and the laws of the Federation, fulfil my duties conscientiously, and do justice to all. So help me God."

The oath may also be taken without religious affirmation.

Article 57 (Representation)

If the Federal President is prevented from acting, or if his office falls prematurely vacant, his powers shall be exercised by the President of the Bundesrat.

Article 58 (Countersignature)

Orders and decrees of the Federal President shall require for their validity the countersignature of the Federal Chancellor or the appropriate Federal Minister. This shall not apply to the appointment and dismissal of the Federal Chancellor, the dissolution of the Bundestag under Article 63 and the request under paragraph (3) of Article 69.

Article 59 (Authority to represent Federation in international relations)

(1) The Federal President shall represent the Federation in its international relations. He shall conclude treaties with foreign states on behalf of the Federation. He shall accredit and receive envoys.

(2) Treaties which regulate the political relations of the Federation or relate to matters of federal legislation shall require the consent or participation, in the form of a federal law, of the bodies competent in any specific case for such federal legislation. As regards administrative agreements, the provisions concerning the federal administration shall apply mutatis mutandis.

Article 60 (Appointment of federal civil servants and officers)

(1) The Federal President shall appoint and dismiss the federal judges, the federal civil servants, the officers and noncommissioned officers, unless otherwise provided for by law.
(2) He shall exercise the right of pardon in individual cases on behalf of the Federation.
(3) He may delegate these powers to other authorities.
(4) Paragraphs (2) to (4) of Article 46 shall apply *mutatis mutandis* to the Federal President.

Article 61 (Impeachment before the Federal Constitutional Court)

(1) The Bundestag or the Bundesrat may impeach the Federal President before the Federal Constitutional Court for wilful violation of this Basic Law or any other federal law. The motion for impeachment must be brought forward by at least one fourth of the members of the Bundestag or one fourth of the votes of the Bundesrat. The decision to impeach shall require a majority of two thirds of the members of the Bundestag or of two thirds of the votes of the Bundesrat. The impeachment shall be substantiated by a person commissioned by the impeaching body.
(2) If the Federal Constitutional Court finds the Federal President guilty of a wilful violation of this Basic Law or of another federal law, it may declare him to have forfeited his office. After impeachment, it may issue an interim order preventing the Federal President from exercising his functions.

VI. THE FEDERAL GOVERNMENT

Article 62 (Composition)

The Federal Government shall consist of the Federal Chancellor and the Federal Ministers.

Article 63 (Election of the Federal Chancellor—Dissolution of the Bundestag)

(1) The Federal Chancellor shall be elected, without debate, by the Bundestag upon the proposal of the Federal President.

(2) The person obtaining the votes of the majority of the members of the Bundestag shall be elected. The person elected must be appointed by the Federal President.
(3) If the person proposed is not elected, the Bundestag may elect within fourteen days of the ballot a Federal Chancellor by more than one half of its members.
(4) If no candidate has been elected within this period, a new ballot shall take place without delay, in which the person obtaining the largest number of votes shall be elected. If the person elected has obtained the votes of the majority of the members of the Bundestag, the Federal President must appoint him within seven days of the election. If the person elected did not obtain such a majority, the Federal President must within seven days either appoint him or dissolve the Bundestag.

Article 64 (Appointment of Federal Ministers)

(1) The Federal Ministers shall be appointed and dismissed by the Federal President upon the proposal of the Federal Chancellor.
(2) The Federal Chancellor and the Federal Ministers, on assuming office, shall take before the Bundestag the oath provided for in Article 56.

Article 65 (Distribution of responsibility)

The Federal Chancellor shall determine, and be responsible for, the general policy guidelines. Within the limits set by these guidelines, each Federal Minister shall conduct the affairs of his department autonomously and on his own responsibility. The Federal Government shall decide on differences of opinion between Federal Ministers. The Federal Chancellor shall conduct the affairs of the Federal Government in accordance with rules of procedure adopted by it and approved by the Federal President.

Article 65a (Power of command over Armed Forces)

Power of command in respect of the Armed Forces shall be vested in the Federal Minister of Defense.

Article 66 (No secondary occupation)

The Federal Chancellor and the Federal Ministers may not hold any other salaried office, nor engage in a trade or occupation, nor practice a profession, nor belong to the management or, without the consent of the Bundestag, to the board of directors of an enterprise carried on for profit.

Article 67 (Vote of no-confidence)

(1) The Bundestag can express its lack of confidence in the Federal Chancellor only by electing a successor with the majority of its members and by requesting the Federal President to dismiss the Federal Chancellor. The Federal President must comply with the request and appoint the person elected.
(2) Forty-eight hours must elapse between the motion and the election.

Article 68 (Vote of confidence—Dissolution of the Bundestag)

(1) If a motion of the Federal Chancellor for a vote of confidence is not assented to by the majority of the members of the Bundestag, the Federal President may, upon the proposal of the Federal Chancellor, dissolve the Bundestag within twenty-one days. The right to dissolve shall lapse as soon as the Bundestag with the majority of its members elects another Federal Chancellor.
(2) Forty-eight hours must elapse between the motion and the vote thereon.

Article 69 (Deputy of the Federal Chancellor)

(1) The Federal Chancellor shall appoint a Federal Minister as his deputy.
(2) The tenure of office of the Federal Chancellor or a Federal Minister shall end in any event on the first meeting of a new Bundestag; the tenure of office of a Federal Minister shall also end on any other termination of the tenure of office of the Federal Chancellor.
(3) At the request of the Federal President the Federal Chancellor, or at the request of the Federal Chancellor or of the Federal President a Federal Minister, shall be bound to continue to transact the affairs of his office until the appointment of a successor.

VII. LEGISLATIVE POWERS OF THE FEDERATION

Article 70 (Legislation of the Federation and the *Länder*)

(1) The *Länder* shall have the right to legislate in so far as this Basic Law does not confer legislative power on the Federation.
(2) The division of competence between the Federation and the *Länder* shall be determined by the provisions of this Basic Law concerning exclusive and concurrent legislative powers.

Article 71 (Exclusive legislation of the Federation, definition)

In matters within the exclusive legislative power of the Federation the *Länder* shall have power to legislate only if, and to the extent that, a federal law explicitly so authorizes them.

Article 72 (Concurrent legislation of the Federation, definition)

(1) In matters within concurrent legislative powers the *Länder* shall have power to legislate as long as, and to the extent that, the Federation does not exercise its right to legislate.
(2) The Federation shall have the right to legislate in these matters to the extent that a need for regulation by federal legislation exists because:

1. a matter cannot be effectively regulated by the legislation of individual *Länder,* or
2. the regulation of a matter by a *Land* law might prejudice the interests of other *Länder* or of the people as a whole, or
3. the maintenance of legal or economic unity, especially the maintenance of uniformity of living conditions beyond the territory of any one *Land,* necessitates such regulation.

Article 73 (Exclusive legislation, catalogue)

The Federation shall have exclusive power to legislate in the following matters:

1. foreign affairs as well as defence, including the protection of the civilian population;
2. citizenship in the Federation;
3. freedom of movement, passport matters, immigration, emigration, and extradition;
4. currency, money and coinage, weights and measures, as well as the determination of standards of time;
5. the unity of the customs and commercial territory, treaties on commerce and on navigation, the freedom of movement of goods, and the exchanges of goods and payments with foreign countries, including customs and other frontier protection;
6. federal railroads and air transport;
7. postal and telecommunication services;
8. the legal status of persons employed by the Federation and by federal corporate bodies under public law;
9. industrial property rights, copyrights and publishers' rights;
10. cooperation of the Federation and the *Länder* in matters of crimi-

nal police and of protection of the constitution, establishment of a Federal Criminal Police Office, as well as international control of crime;

11. statistics for federal purposes.

Article 74 (Concurrent legislation, catalogue)

Concurrent legislative powers shall extend to the following matters:

1. civil law, criminal law and execution of sentences, the organization and procedure of courts, the legal profession, notaries, and legal advice *(Rechtsberatung);*
2. registration of births, deaths, and marriages;
3. the law of association and assembly;
4. the law relating to residence and establishment of aliens;
5. the protection of German cultural treasures against removal abroad;
6. refugee and expellee matters;
7. public welfare;
8. citizenship in the *Länder;*
9. war damage and reparations;
10. benefits to war-disabled persons and to dependants of those killed in the war as well as assistance to former prisoners of war;

10a. war graves of soldiers, graves of other victims of war and of victims of despotism;

11. the law relating to economic matters (mining, industry, supply of power, crafts, trades, commerce, banking, stock exchanges, and private insurance);

11a. the production and utilization of nuclear energy for peaceful purposes, the construction and operation of installations serving such purposes, protection against hazards arising from the release of nuclear energy or from ionizing radiation, and the disposal of radioactive substances;

12. labor law, including the legal organization of enterprises, protection of workers, employment exchanges and agencies, as well as social insurance, including unemployment insurance;
13. the regulation of educational and training grants and the promotion of scientific research;
14. the law regarding expropriation, to the extent that matters enumerated in Articles 73 and 74 are concerned;
15. transfer of land, natural resources and means of production to public ownership or other forms of publicly controlled economy;
16. prevention of the abuse of economic power;

17. promotion of agricultural and forest production, safeguarding of the supply of food, the importation and exportation of agricultural and forest products, deep sea and coastal fishing, and preservation of the coasts;
18. real estate transactions, land law and matters concerning agricultural leases, as well as housing, settlement and homestead matters;
19. measures against human and animal diseases that are communicable or otherwise endanger public health, admission to the medical profession and to other health occupations or practices, as well as trade in medicines, curatives, narcotics, and poisons;

19a. the economic viability of hospitals and the regulation of hospitalization fees;

20. protection regarding the marketing of food, drink and tobacco, of necessities of life, fodder, agricultural and forest seeds and seedlings, and protection of plants against diseases and pests, as well as the protection of animals;
21. ocean and coastal shipping as well as aids to navigation, inland navigation, meteorological services, sea routes, and inland waterways used for general traffic;
22. road traffic, motor transport, construction and maintenance of long-distance highways as well as the collection of charges for the use of public highways by vehicles and the allocation of revenue therefrom;
23. nonfederal railroads, except mountain railroads.

Article 74a (Wider competence of Federation for pay scales)

(1) Concurrent legislation shall further extend to the pay scales and pensions of members of the public service whose service and loyalty are governed by public law, in so far as the Federation does not have exclusive power to legislate pursuant to item 8 of Article 73.

(2) Federal laws enacted pursuant to paragraph (1) of this Article shall require the consent of the Bundesrat.

(3) Federal laws enacted pursuant to item 8 of Article 73 shall likewise require the consent of the Bundesrat, in so far as they prescribe for the structure and computation of pay scales and pensions, including the appraisal of posts, criteria or minimum or maximum rates other than those provided for in federal laws enacted pursuant to paragraph (1) of this Article.

(4) Paragraphs (1) and (2) of this Article shall apply mutatis mutandis to the pay scales and pensions for judges in the *Länder*. Paragraph (3) of this Article shall apply mutatis mutandis to laws enacted pursuant to paragraph (1) of Article 98.

Article 75 (General provisions of the Federation, catalogue)

Subject to the conditions laid down in Article 72 the Federation shall have the right to enact skeleton provisions concerning:

1. the legal status of persons in the public service of the *Länder,* communes, or other corporate bodies under public law, in so far as Article 74a does not provide otherwise;

1a. the general principles governing higher education;

2. the general legal status of the press and the film industry;
3. hunting, protection of nature, and care of the countryside;
4. land distribution, regional planning, and water management;
5. matters relating to the registration of changes of residence or domicile *(Meldewesen)* and to identity cards.

Article 76 (Bills)

(1) Bills shall be introduced in the Bundestag by the Federal Government or by members of the Bundestag or by the Bundesrat.
(2) Bills of the Federal Government shall be submitted first to the Bundesrat. The Bundesrat shall be entitled to state its position on such bills within six weeks. A bill exceptionally submitted to the Bundesrat as being particularly urgent by the Federal Government may be submitted by the latter to the Bundestag three weeks later, even though the Federal Government may not yet have received the statement of the Bundesrat's position; such statement shall be transmitted to the Bundestag by the Federal Government without delay upon its receipt.
(3) Bills of the Bundesrat shall be submitted to the Bundestag by the Federal Government within three months. In doing so, the Federal Government must state its own view.

Article 77 (Procedure concerning adopted bills—Objection of the Bundesrat)

(1) Bills intended to become federal laws shall require adoption by the Bundestag. Upon their adoption they shall, without delay, be transmitted to the Bundesrat by the President of the Bundestag.
(2) The Bundesrat may, within three weeks of the receipt of the adopted bill, demand that a committee for joint consideration of bills, composed of members of the Bundestag and members of the Bundesrat, be convened. The composition and the procedure of this committee shall be regulated by rules of procedure to be adopted by the Bundestag and requiring the consent of the Bundesrat. The members of the Bundesrat on this committee shall not be bound by instructions. If the consent of the Bundesrat is required for a bill to become a law, the convening of this committee may also be demanded by the Bun-

destag or the Federal Government. Should the committee propose any amendment to the adopted bill, the Bundestag must again vote on the bill.
(3) In so far as the consent of the Bundesrat is not required for a bill to become a law, the Bundesrat may, when the proceedings under paragraph (2) of this Article are completed, enter an objection within two weeks against a bill adopted by the Bundestag. This period shall begin, in the case of the last sentence of paragraph (2) of this Article, on the receipt of the bill as readopted by the Bundestag, and in all other cases on the receipt of a communication from the chairman of the committee provided for in paragraph (2) of this Article, to the effect that the committee's proceedings have been concluded.
(4) If the objection was adopted with the majority of the votes of the Bundesrat, it can be rejected by a decision of the majority of the members of the Bundestag. If the Bundesrat adopted the objection with a majority of at least two thirds of its votes, its rejection by the Bundestag shall require a majority of two thirds, including at least the majority of the members of the Bundestag.

Article 78 (Conditions for passing of federal laws)

A bill adopted by the Bundestag shall become a law if the Bundesrat consents to it, or fails to make a demand pursuant to paragraph (2) of Article 77, or fails to enter an objection within the period stipulated in paragraph (3) of Article 77, or withdraws such objection, or if the objection is overridden by the Bundestag.

Article 79 (Amendment of the Basic Law)

(1) This Basic Law can be amended only by laws which expressly amend or supplement the text thereof. In respect of international treaties the subject of which is a peace settlement, the preparation of a peace settlement, or the abolition of an occupation regime, or which are designed to serve the defence of the Federal Republic, it shall be sufficient, for the purpose of clarifying that the provisions of this Basic Law do not preclude the conclusion and entry into force of such treaties, to effect a supplementation of the text of this Basic Law confined to such clarification.
(2) Any such law shall require the affirmative vote of two thirds of the members of the Bundestag and two thirds of the votes of the Bundesrat.
(3) Amendments of this Basic Law affecting the division of the Federation into *Länder,* the participation on principle of the *Länder* in legislation, or the basic principles laid down in Articles 1 and 20, shall be inadmissible.

Article 80 (Issue of ordinances having force of law)

(1) The Federal Government, a Federal Minister or the *Land* governments may be authorized by a law to issue ordinances having the force of law (Rechtsverordnungen). The content, purpose, and scope of the authorization so conferred must be set forth in such law. This legal basis must be stated in the ordinance. If a law provides that such authorization may be delegated, such delegation shall require another ordinance having the force of law.
(2) The consent of the Bundesrat shall be required, unless otherwise provided by federal legislation, for ordinances having the force of law issued by the Federal Government or a Federal Minister concerning basic rules for the use of facilities of the federal railroads and of postal and telecommunication services, or charges therefor, or concerning the construction and operation of railroads, as well as for ordinances having the force of law issued pursuant to federal laws that require the consent of the Bundesrat or that are executed by the *Länder* as agents of the Federation or as matters of their own concern.

Article 80a (State of tension)

(1) Where this Basic Law or a federal law on defence, including the protection of the civilian population, stipulates that legal provisions may only be applied in accordance with this Article, their application shall, except when a state of defence exists, be admissible only after the Bundestag has determined that a state of tension *(Spannungsfall)* exists or if it has specifically approved such application. In respect of the cases mentioned in the first sentence of paragraph (5) and the second sentence of paragraph (6) of Article 12a, such determination of a state of tension and such specific approval shall require a two-thirds majority of the votes cast.
(2) Any measures taken by virtue of legal provisions enacted under paragraph (1) of this Article shall be revoked whenever the Bundestag so requests.
(3) In derogation of paragraph (1) of this Article, the application of such legal provisions shall also be admissible by virtue of, and in accordance with, a decision taken with the consent of the Federal Government by an international organ within the framework of a treaty of alliance. Any measures taken pursuant to this paragraph shall be revoked whenever the Bundestag so requests with the majority of its members.

Article 81 (State of legislative emergency)

(1) Should, in the circumstances of Article 68, the Bundestag not be dissolved, the Federal President may, at the request of the Federal

Government and with the consent of the Bundesrat, declare a state of legislative emergency with respect to a bill, if the Bundestag rejects the bill although the Federal Government has declared it to be urgent. The same shall apply if a bill has been rejected although the Federal Chancellor had combined with it the motion under Article 68.
(2) If, after a state of legislative emergency has been declared, the Bundestag again rejects the bill or adopts it in a version stated to be unacceptable to the Federal Government, the bill shall be deemed to have become a law to the extent that the Bundesrat consents to it. The same shall apply if the bill is not passed by the Bundestag within four weeks of its reintroduction.
(3) During the term of office of a Federal Chancellor, any other bill rejected by the Bundestag may become a law in accordance with paragraphs (1) and (2) of this Article within a period of six months after the first declaration of a state of legislative emergency. After the expiration of this period, a further declaration of a state of legislative emergency shall be inadmissible during the term of office of the same Federal Chancellor.
(4) This Basic Law may not be amended nor repealed nor suspended in whole or in part by a law enacted pursuant to paragraph (2) of this Article.

Article 82 (Promulgation and effective date of laws)

(1) Laws enacted in accordance with the provisions of this Basic Law shall, after countersignature, be signed by the Federal President and promulgated in the Federal Law Gazette. Ordinances having the force of law shall be signed by the agency which issues them, and, unless otherwise provided by law, shall be promulgated in the Federal Law Gazette.
(2) Every law or every ordinance having the force of law should specify its effective date. In the absence of such a provision, it shall become effective on the fourteenth day after the end of the day on which the Federal Law Gazette containing it was published.

VIII. THE EXECUTION OF FEDERAL LAWS AND THE FEDERAL ADMINISTRATION

Article 83 (Execution of federal laws by the *Länder*)

The *Länder* shall execute federal laws as matters of their own concern in so far as this Basic Law does not otherwise provide or permit.

Article 84 (*Land* administration and Federal Government supervision)

(1) Where the *Länder* execute federal laws as matters of their own concern, they shall provide for the establishment of the requisite authorities and the regulation of administrative procedures in so far as federal laws consented to by the Bundesrat do not otherwise provide.
(2) The Federal Government may, with the consent of the Bundesrat, issue pertinent general administrative rules.
(3) The Federal Government shall exercise supervision to ensure that the *Länder* execute the federal laws in accordance with applicable law. For this purpose the Federal Government may send commissioners to the highest *Land* authorities and with their consent or, if such consent is refused, with the consent of the Bundesrat, also to subordinate authorities.
(4) Should any shortcomings which the Federal Government has found to exist in the execution of federal laws in the *Länder* not be corrected, the Bundesrat shall decide, on the application of the Federal Government or the *Land* concerned, whether such *Land* has violated applicable law. The decision of the Bundesrat may be challenged in the Federal Constitutional Court.
(5) With a view to the execution of federal laws, the Federal Government may be authorized by a federal law requiring the consent of the Bundesrat to issue individual instructions for particular cases. They shall be addressed to the highest *Land* authorities unless the Federal Government considers the matter urgent.

Article 85 (Execution by *Länder* as agents of the Federation)

(1) Where the *Länder* execute federal laws as agents of the Federation, the establishment of the requisite authorities shall remain the concern of the *Länder* except in so far as federal laws consented to by the Bundesrat otherwise provide.
(2) The Federal Government may, with the consent of the Bundesrat, issue pertinent general administrative rules. It may regulate the uniform training of civil servants *(Beamte)* and other salaried public employees *(Angestellte)*. The heads of authorities at the intermediate level shall be appointed with its agreement.
(3) The *Land* authorities shall be subject to the instructions of the appropriate highest federal authorities. Such instructions shall be addressed to the highest *Land* authorities unless the Federal Government considers the matter urgent. Execution of the instructions shall be ensured by the highest *Land* authorities.
(4) Federal supervision shall extend to conformity with law and appropriateness of execution. The Federal Government may, for this purpose,

require the submission of reports and documents and send commissioners to all authorities.

Article 86 (Direct federal administration)

Where the Federation executes laws by means of direct federal administration or by federal corporate bodies or institutions under public law, the Federal Government shall, in so far as the law concerned contains no special provision, issue pertinent general administrative rules. The Federal Government shall provide for the establishment of the requisite authorities in so far as the law concerned does not otherwise provide.

Article 87 (Matters of direct federal administration)

(1) The foreign service, the federal finance administration, the federal railroads, the federal postal service, and, in accordance with the provisions of Article 89, the administration of federal waterways and of shipping shall be conducted as matters of direct federal administration with their own administrative substructures. Federal frontier protection authorities and central offices for police information and communications, for the compilation of data for the purpose of protecting the constitution, and for the criminal police, may be established by federal legislation.
(2) Social insurance institutions whose sphere of competence extends beyond the territory of one *Land* shall be administered as federal corporate bodies under public law.
(3) In addition, autonomous federal higher authorities as well as federal corporate bodies and institutions under public law may be established by federal legislation for matters in which the Federation has the power to legislate. If new functions arise for the Federation in matters in which it has the power to legislate, federal authorities at the intermediate and lower levels may be established, in case of urgent need, with the consent of the Bundesrat and of the majority of the members of the Bundestag.

Article 87a (Build-up, strength, use, and functions of the Armed Forces)

(1) The Federation shall build up Armed Forces for defense purposes. Their numerical strength and general organizational structure shall be shown in the budget.
(2) Apart from defence, the Armed Forces may only be used to the extent explicitly permitted by this Basic Law.
(3) While a state of defence or a state of tension exists, the Armed

Forces shall have the power to protect civilian property and discharge functions of traffic control in so far as this is necessary for the performance of their defence mission. Moreover, the Armed Forces may, when a state of defence or a state of tension exists, be entrusted with the protection of civilian property in support of police measures; in this event the Armed Forces shall cooperate with the competent authorities.

(4) In order to avert any imminent danger to the existence or to the free democratic basic order of the Federation or a *Land,* the Federal Government may, should conditions as envisaged in paragraph (2) of Article 91 obtain and the police forces and the Federal Border Guard be inadequate, use the Armed Forces to support the police and the Federal Border Guard in the protection of civilian property and in combatting organized and militarily armed insurgents. Any such use of Armed Forces must be discontinued whenever the Bundestag or the Bundesrat so requests.

Article 87b (Administration of the Armed Forces)

(1) The Federal Armed Forces Administration shall be conducted as a direct federal administration with its own administrative substructure. Its function shall be to administer personnel matters and directly to meet the material requirements of the Armed Forces. Tasks connected with benefits to injured persons or with construction work shall not be assigned to the Federal Armed Forces Administration except by federal legislation requiring the consent of the Bundesrat. Such consent shall also be required for any laws to the extent that they empower the Federal Armed Forces Administration to interfere with rights of third parties; this shall, however, not apply in the case of laws concerning personnel.

(2) Moreover, federal laws concerning defense including recruitment for military service and protection of the civilian population may, with the consent of the Bundesrat, provide that they shall be carried out, wholly or in part, either by means of direct federal administration having its own administrative substructure or by the *Länder* acting as agents of the Federation. If such laws are executed by the *Länder* acting as agents of the Federation, they may, with the consent of the Bundesrat, provide that the powers vested in the Federal Government or appropriate highest federal authorities by virtue of Article 85 shall be transferred wholly or in part to higher federal authorities; in such an event it may be enacted that these authorities shall not require the consent of the Bundesrat in issuing general administrative rules as referred to in the first sentence of paragraph (2) of Article 85.

Article 87c (Production and utilization of nuclear energy)

Laws enacted under item 11a of Article 74 may, with the consent of the Bundesrat, provide that they shall be executed by the *Länder* acting as agents of the Federation.

Article 87d (Aviation Administration)

(1) The Aviation Administration shall be conducted as a direct federal administration.
(2) By means of federal legislation requiring the consent of the Bundesrat, functions of the Aviation Administration may be delegated to the *Länder* acting as agents of the Federation.

Article 88 (Federal Bank)

The Federation shall establish a note-issuing and currency bank as the Federal Bank.

Article 89 (Federal waterways)

(1) The Federation shall be the owner of the former Reich waterways.
(2) The Federation shall administer the federal waterways through its own authorities. It shall exercise those governmental functions relating to inland shipping which extend beyond the territory of one *Land,* and those governmental functions relating to maritime shipping which are conferred on it by law. Upon request, the Federation may transfer the administration of federal waterways, in so far as they lie within the territory of one *Land,* to that *Land* as its agent. If a waterway touches the territories of several *Länder,* the Federation may designate one *Land* as its agent if so requested by the *Länder* concerned.
(3) In the administration, development, and new construction of waterways the needs of soil cultivation and of water management shall be safeguarded in agreement with the *Länder.*

Article 90 (Federal highways)

(1) The Federation shall be the owner of the former Reich motorways *(Reichsautobahnen)* and Reich highways.
(2) The *Länder,* or such self-governing corporate bodies as are competent under *Land* law, shall administer as agents of the Federation the federal motorways and other federal highways used for long-distance traffic.
(3) At the request of a *Land,* the Federation may take under direct federal administration federal motorways and other federal highways

used for long-distance traffic, in so far as they lie within the territory of that *Land.*

Article 91 (Aversion of dangers to the existence of the Federation or of a *Land*)

(1) In order to avert any imminent danger to the existence or to the free democratic basic order of the Federation or a *Land,* a *Land* may request the services of the police forces of other *Länder,* or of the forces and facilities of other administrative authorities and of the Federal Border Guard.
(2) If the *Land* where such danger is imminent is not itself willing or able to combat the danger, the Federal Government may place the police in that *Land* and the police forces of other *Länder* under its own instructions and commit units of the Federal Border Guard. The order for this shall be rescinded after the removal of the danger or else at any time upon the request of the Bundesrat. If the danger extends to a region larger than a *Land,* the Federal Government may, in so far as is necessary for effectively combatting such danger, issue instructions to the *Land* governments; the first and second sentences of this paragraph shall not be affected by this provision.

VIIIa. JOINT TASKS

Article 91a (Definition of joint tasks)

(1) The Federation shall participate in the discharge of the following responsibilities of the *Länder,* provided that such responsibilities are important to society as a whole and that federal participation is necessary for the improvement of living conditions (joint tasks):

1. expansion and construction of institutions of higher education including university clinics;
2. improvement of regional economic structures;
3. improvement of the agrarian structure and of coast preservation.

(2) Joint tasks shall be defined in detail by federal legislation requiring the consent of the Bundesrat. Such legislation should include general principles governing the discharge of joint tasks.
(3) Such legislation shall provide for the procedure and the institutions required for joint overall planning. The inclusion of a project in the overall planning shall require the consent of the *Land* in which it is to be carried out.
(4) In cases to which items 1 and 2 of paragraph (1) of this Article apply, the Federation shall meet one half of the expenditure in each *Land.* In cases to which item 3 of paragraph (1) of this Article applies, the

Federation shall meet at least one half of the expenditure, and such proportion shall be the same for all the *Länder*. Details shall be regulated by legislation. Provision of funds shall be subject to appropriation in the budgets of the Federation and the *Länder*.

(5) The Federal Government and the Bundesrat shall be informed about the execution of joint tasks, should they so demand.

Article 91b (Cooperation of Federation and *Länder* in educational planning and in research)

The Federation and the *Länder* may pursuant to agreements cooperate in educational planning and in the promotion of institutions and projects of scientific research of supraregional importance. The apportionment of costs shall be regulated in the pertinent agreements.

IX. THE ADMINISTRATION OF JUSTICE

Article 92 (Court organization)

Judicial power shall be vested in the judges; it shall be exercised by the Federal Constitutional Court, by the federal courts provided for in this Basic Law, and by the courts of the *Länder*.

Article 93 (Federal Constitutional Court, competency)

(1) The Federal Constitutional Court shall decide:

1. on the interpretation of this Basic Law in the event of disputes concerning the extent of the rights and duties of a highest federal organ or of other parties concerned who have been vested with rights of their own by this Basic Law or by rules of procedure of a highest federal organ;
2. in case of differences of opinion or doubts on the formal and material compatibility of federal law or *Land* law with this Basic Law, or on the compatibility of *Land* law with other federal law, at the request of the Federal Government, of a *Land* government, or of one third of the Bundestag members;
3. in case of differences of opinion on the rights and duties of the Federation and the *Länder*, particularly in the execution of federal law by the *Länder* and in the exercise of federal supervision;
4. on other disputes involving public law, between the Federation and the *Länder*, between different *Länder* or within a *Land*, unless recourse to another court exists;

4a. on complaints of unconstitutionality, which may be entered by any person who claims that one of his basic rights or one of his rights under paragraph (4) of Article 20, under Article 33, 38, 101, 103, or 104 has been violated by public authority;

4b. on complaints of unconstitutionality, entered by communes or associations of communes on the ground that their right to self-government under Article 28 has been violated by a law other than a *Land* law open to complaint to the respective *Land* constitutional court;

5. in the other cases provided for in this Basic Law.

(2) The Federal Constitutional Court shall also act in such other cases as are assigned to it by federal legislation.

Article 94 (Federal Constitutional Court, composition)

(1) The Federal Constitutional Court shall consist of federal judges and other members. Half of the members of the Federal Constitutional Court shall be elected by the Bundestag and half by the Bundesrat. They may not be members of the Bundestag, the Bundesrat, the Federal Government, nor of any of the corresponding organs of a *Land.*
(2) The constitution and procedure of the Federal Constitutional Court shall be regulated by a federal law which shall specify in what cases its decisions shall have the force of law. Such law may require that all other legal remedies must have been exhausted before any such complaint of unconstitutionality can be entered, and may make provision for a special procedure as to admissibility.

Article 95 (Highest courts of justice of the Federation—Joint Panel)

(1) For the purposes of ordinary, administrative, fiscal, labour, and social jurisdiction, the Federation shall establish as highest courts of justice the Federal Court of Justice, the Federal Administrative Court, the Federal Fiscal Court, the Federal Labour Court, and the Federal Social Court.
(2) The judges of each of these courts shall be selected jointly by the competent Federal Minister and a committee for the selection of judges consisting of the competent *Land* Ministers and an equal number of members elected by the Bundestag.
(3) In order to preserve uniformity of jurisdiction, a Joint Panel *(Senat)* of the courts specified in paragraph (1) of this Article shall be set up. Details shall be regulated by a federal law.

Article 96 (Federal courts)

(1) The Federation may establish a Federal Court for matters concerning industrial property rights.
(2) The Federation may establish military criminal courts for the Armed

Forces as federal courts. They shall exercise criminal jurisdiction while a state of defence exists, and otherwise only over members of the Armed Forces serving abroad or on board warships. Details shall be regulated by a federal law. These courts shall be within the competence of the Federal Minister of Justice. Their full-time judges must be persons qualified to exercise the functions of a judge.
(3) The highest court of justice for appeals from the courts mentioned in paragraphs (1) and (2) of this Article shall be the Federal Court of Justice.
(4) The Federation may establish federal courts for disciplinary proceedings against, and for proceedings in pursuance of complaints by, persons in the federal public service.
(5) In respect of criminal proceedings under paragraph (1) of Article 26 or involving the protection of the State, a federal law requiring the consent of the Bundesrat may provide that *Land* courts shall exercise federal jurisdiction.

Article 97 (Independence of the judges)

(1) The judges shall be independent and subject only to the law.
(2) Judges appointed permanently on a full-time basis in established positions cannot against their will be dismissed or permanently or temporarily suspended from office or given a different function or retired before the expiration of their term of office except by virtue of a judicial decision and only on the grounds and in the form provided for by law. Legislation may set age limits for the retirement of judges appointed for life. In the event of changes in the structure of courts or in districts of jurisdiction, judges may be transferred to another court or removed from office, provided they retain their full salary.

Article 98 (Legal status of judges)

(1) The legal status of the federal judges shall be regulated by a special federal law.
(2) If a federal judge, in his official capacity or unofficially, infringes the principles of this Basic Law or the constitutional order of a *Land,* the Federal Constitutional Court may decide by a two-thirds majority, upon the request of the Bundestag, that the judge be given a different function or retired. In a case of intentional infringement, his dismissal may be ordered.
(3) The legal status of the judges in the *Länder* shall be regulated by special *Land* laws. The Federation may enact general provisions, in so far as paragraph (4) of Article 74a does not provide otherwise.
(4) *Länder* may provide that the *Land* Minister of Justice together with a committee for the selection of judges shall decide on the appointment of judges in the *Länder.*

(5) The *Länder* may, in respect of *Land* judges, enact provisions corresponding to those of paragraph (2) of this Article. Existing *Land* constitutional law shall remain unaffected. The decision in a case of impeachment of a judge shall rest with the Federal Constitutional Court.

Article 99 (Assignment of competencies to Federal Constitutional Court and highest federal courts in matters involving *Land* law)

The decision on constitutional disputes within a *Land* may be assigned by *Land* legislation to the Federal Constitutional Court, and the decision of last instance in matters involving the application of *Land* law, to the highest courts of justice referred to in paragraph (1) of Article 95.

Article 100 (Compatibility of statutory law with Basic Law)

(1) If a court considers unconstitutional a law the validity of which is relevant to its decision, the proceedings shall be stayed, and a decision shall be obtained from the *Land* court competent for constitutional disputes if the constitution of a *Land* is held to be violated, or from the Federal Constitutional Court if this Basic Law is held to be violated. This shall also apply if this Basic Law is held to be violated by *Land* law or if a *Land* law is held to be incompatible with a federal law.
(2) If, in the course of litigation, doubt exists whether a rule of public international law is an integral part of federal law and whether such rule directly creates rights and duties for the individual (Article 25), the court shall obtain a decision from the Federal Constitutional Court.
(3) If the constitutional court of a *Land,* in interpreting this Basic Law, intends to deviate from a decision of the Federal Constitutional Court or of the constitutional court of another *Land,* it must obtain a decision from the Federal Constitutional Court.

Article 101 (Ban on extraordinary courts)

(1) Extraordinary courts shall be inadmissible. No one may be removed from the jurisdiction of his lawful judge.
(2) Courts for special fields may be established only by legislation.

Article 102 (Abolition of capital punishment)

Capital punishment shall be abolished.

Article 103 (Basic rights in the courts)

(1) In the courts everyone shall be entitled to a hearing in accordance with the law.
(2) An act can be punished only if it was an offence against the law before the act was committed.

(3) No one may be punished for the same act more than once under general penal legislation.

Article 104 (Legal guarantees in the event of deprivation of liberty)

(1) The liberty of the individual may be restricted only by virtue of a formal law and only with due regard to the forms prescribed therein. Detained persons may not be subjected to mental nor to physical ill-treatment.
(2) Only judges may decide on the admissibility or continuation of any deprivation of liberty. Where such deprivation is not based on the order of a judge, a judicial decision must be obtained without delay. The police may hold no one on their own authority in their own custody longer than the end of the day after the day of apprehension. Details shall be regulated by legislation.
(3) Any person provisionally detained on suspicion of having committed an offence must be brought before a judge not later than the day following the day of apprehension; the judge shall inform him of the reasons for the detention, examine him, and give him an opportunity to raise objections. The judge must, without delay, either issue a warrant of arrest setting forth the reasons therefor or order his release from detention.
(4) A relative or a person enjoying the confidence of the person detained must be notified without delay of any judicial decision ordering or continuing his deprivation of liberty.

X. FINANCE

Article 104a (Apportionment of expenditure, Financial assistance)

(1) The Federation and the *Länder* shall meet separately the expenditure resulting from the discharge of their respective tasks in so far as this Basic Law does not provide otherwise.
(2) Where the *Länder* act as agents of the Federation, the Federation shall meet the resulting expenditure.
(3) Federal laws to be executed by the *Länder* and involving the disbursement of funds may provide that such funds shall be contributed wholly or in part by the Federation. Where any such law provides that the Federation shall meet one half of the expenditure or more, the *Länder* shall execute it as agents of the Federation. Where any such law provides that the *Länder* shall meet one quarter of the expenditure or more, it shall require the consent of the Bundesrat.
(4) The Federation may grant the *Länder* financial assistance for particularly important investments by the *Länder* or communes or associations of communes, provided that such investments are necessary to avert a

disturbance of the overall economic equilibrium or to equalize differences of economic capacities within the federal territory or to promote economic growth. Details, especially concerning the kinds of investments to be promoted, shall be regulated by federal legislation requiring the consent of the Bundesrat, or by administrative arrangements based on the federal budget.
(5) The Federation and the *Länder* shall meet the administrative expenditure incurred by their respective authorities and shall be responsible to each other for ensuring proper administration. Details shall be regulated by a federal law requiring the consent of the Bundesrat.

Article 105 (Customs duties, Monopolies, Taxes—legislation)

(1) The Federation shall have exclusive power to legislate on customs matters and fiscal monopolies.
(2) The Federation shall have concurrent power to legislate on all other taxes the revenue from which accrues to it wholly or in part or where the conditions provided for in paragraph (2) of Article 72 apply.
(2a) The *Länder* shall have power to legislate on local excise taxes as long and in so far as they are not identical with taxes imposed by federal legislation.
(3) Federal laws relating to taxes the receipts from which accrue wholly or in part to the *Länder* or communes or associations of communes shall require the consent of the Bundesrat.

Article 106 (Apportionment of tax revenue)

(1) The yield of fiscal monopolies and the revenue from the following taxes shall accrue to the Federation:

1. customs duties,
2. excise taxes in so far as they do not accrue to the *Länder* pursuant to paragraph (2) of this Article, or jointly to the Federation and the *Länder* in accordance with paragraph (3) of this Article, or to the communes in accordance with paragraph (6) of this Article,
3. the road freight tax,
4. the capital transfer taxes, the insurance tax and the tax on drafts and bills of exchange,
5. nonrecurrent levies on property, and contributions imposed for the purpose of implementing the equalization of burdens legislation,
6. income and corporation surtaxes,
7. charges imposed within the framework of the European Communities.

(2) Revenue from the following taxes shall accrue to the *Länder:*

1. property (net worth) tax,
2. inheritance tax,
3. motor-vehicle tax,
4. such taxes on transactions as do not accrue to the Federation pursuant to paragraph (1) of this Article or jointly to the Federation and the *Länder* pursuant to paragraph (3) of this Article,
5. beer tax,
6. taxes on gambling establishments.

(3) Revenue from income taxes, corporation taxes and turnover taxes shall accrue jointly to the Federation and the *Länder* (joint taxes) to the extent that the revenue from income tax is not allocated to the communes pursuant to paragraph (5) of this Article. The Federation and the *Länder* shall share equally the revenues from income taxes and corporation taxes. The respective shares of the Federation and the *Länder* in the revenue from turnover tax shall be determined by federal legislation requiring the consent of the Bundesrat. Such determination shall be based on the following principles:

1. The Federation and the *Länder* shall have an equal claim to coverage from current revenues of their respective necessary expenditures. The extent of such expenditures shall be determined within a system of pluri-annual financial planning;
2. the coverage requirements of the Federation and of the *Länder* shall be coordinated in such a way that a fair balance is struck, any overburdening of taxpayers precluded, and uniformity of living standards in the federal territory ensured.

(4) The respective shares of the Federation and the *Länder* in the revenue from the turnover tax shall be apportioned anew whenever the relation of revenues to expenditures in the Federation develops substantially differently from that of the *Länder.* Where federal legislation imposes additional expenditures on, or withdraws revenue from, the *Länder,* the additional burden may be compensated by federal grants under federal laws requiring the consent of the Bundesrat, provided such additional burden is limited to a short period. Such laws shall lay down the principles for calculating such grants and distributing them among the *Länder.*

(5) A share of the revenue from income tax shall accrue to the communes, to be passed on by the *Länder* to their communes on the basis of income taxes paid by the inhabitants of the latter. Details shall be regulated by a federal law requiring the consent of the Bundesrat. Such law may provide that communes shall assess communal percentages of the communal share.

(6) Revenue from taxes on real property and businesses shall accrue to the communes; revenue from local excise taxes shall accrue to the communes or, as may be provided for by *Land* legislation, to associations of communes. Communes shall be authorized to assess the communal percentages of taxes on real property and businesses within the framework of existing laws. Where there are no communes in a *Land,* revenue from taxes on real property and businesses as well as from local excise taxes shall accrue to the *Land.* The Federation and the *Länder* may participate, by assessing an impost, in the revenue from the trade tax. Details regarding such impost shall be regulated by a federal law requiring the consent of the Bundesrat. Within the framework of *Land* legislation, taxes on real property and businesses as well as the communes' share of revenue from income tax may be taken as a basis for calculating the amount of such impost.
(7) An overall percentage, to be determined by *Land* legislation, of the *Land* share of total revenue from joint taxes shall accrue to the communes and associations of communes. In all other respects *Land* legislation shall determine whether and to what extent revenue from *Land* taxes shall accrue to communes and associations of communes.
(8) If in individual *Länder* or communes or associations of communes the Federation causes special facilities to be established which directly result in an increase of expenditure or a loss of revenue (special burden) to these *Länder* or communes or associations of communes, the Federation shall grant the necessary compensation, if and in so far as such *Länder* or communes or associations of communes cannot reasonably be expected to bear such special burden. In granting such compensation, due account shall be taken of third-party indemnities and financial benefits accruing to the *Länder* or communes or associations of communes concerned as a result of the institution of such facilities.
(9) For the purpose of this Article, revenues and expenditures of communes and associations of communes shall be deemed to be *Land* revenues and expenditures.

Article 107 (Financial equalization)

(1) Revenue from *Land* taxes and the *Land* share of revenue from income and corporation taxes shall accrue to the individual *Länder* to the extent that such taxes are collected by revenue authorities within their respective territories (local revenue). Federal legislation requiring the consent of the Bundesrat may provide in detail for the delimitation as well as the manner and scope of allotment of local revenue from corporation and wage taxes. Legislation may also provide for the delimitation and allotment of local revenue from other taxes. The *Land* share of revenue from the turnover tax shall accrue to the individual *Länder*

on a per-capita basis; federal legislation requiring the consent of the Bundesrat may provide for supplemental shares not exceeding one quarter of a *Land* share to be granted to *Länder* whose per-capita revenue from *Land* taxes and from the income and corporation taxes is below the average of all the *Länder* combined.

(2) Federal legislation shall ensure a reasonable equalization between financially strong and financially weak *Länder,* due account being taken of the financial capacity and financial requirements of communes and associations of communes. Such legislation shall specify the conditions governing equalization claims of *Länder* entitled to equalization payments and equalization liabilities of *Länder* owing equalization payments as well as the criteria for determining the amounts of equalization payments. Such legislation may also provide for grants to be made by the Federation from federal funds to financially weak *Länder* in order to complement the coverage of their general financial requirements (complemental grants).

Article 108 (Fiscal administration)

(1) Customs duties, fiscal monopolies, excise taxes subject to federal legislation, including the excise tax on imports, and charges imposed within the framework of the European Communities, shall be administered by federal revenue authorities. The organization of these authorities shall be regulated by federal legislation. The heads of authorities at the intermediate level shall be appointed in consultation with the respective *Land* governments.

(2) All other taxes shall be administered by *Land* revenue authorities. The organization of these authorities and the uniform training of their civil servants may be regulated by federal legislation requiring the consent of the Bundesrat. The heads of authorities at the intermediate level shall be appointed in agreement with the Federal Government.

(3) To the extent that taxes accruing wholly or in part to the Federation are administered by *Land* revenue authorities, those authorities shall act as agents of the Federation. Paragraphs (3) and (4) of Article 85 shall apply, the Federal Minister of Finance being, however, substituted for the Federal Government.

(4) In respect of the administration of taxes, federal legislation requiring the consent of the Bundesrat may provide for collaboration between federal and *Land* revenue authorities, or in the case of taxes under paragraph (1) of this Article for their administration by *Land* revenue authorities, or in the case of other taxes for their administration by federal revenue authorities, if and to the extent that the execution of tax laws is substantially improved or facilitated thereby. As regards taxes the revenue from which accrues exclusively to communes or associations of communes, their administration may wholly or in part be trans-

ferred by *Länder* from the appropriate *Land* revenue authorities to communes or associations of communes.
(5) The procedure to be applied by federal revenue authorities shall be laid down by federal legislation. The procedure to be applied by *Land* revenue authorities or, as envisaged in the second sentence of paragraph (4) of this Article, by communes or associations of communes, may be laid down by federal legislation requiring the consent of the Bundesrat.
(6) The jurisdiction of fiscal courts shall be uniformly regulated by federal legislation.
(7) The Federal Government may issue pertinent general administrative rules which, to the extent that administration is incumbent upon *Land* revenue authorities or communes or associations of communes, shall require the consent of the Bundesrat.

Article 109 (Separate budgets for Federation and *Länder*)

(1) The Federation and the *Länder* shall be autonomous and independent of each other in their fiscal administration.
(2) The Federation and the *Länder* shall take due account in their fiscal administration of the requirements of overall economic equilibrium.
(3) By means of federal legislation requiring the consent of the Bundesrat, principles applicable to both the Federation and the *Länder* may be established governing budgetary law, responsiveness of the fiscal administration to economic trends, and financial planning to cover several years ahead.
(4) With a view to averting disturbances of the overall economic equilibrium, federal legislation requiring the consent of the Bundesrat may be enacted providing for:

1. maximum amounts, terms and timing of loans to be raised by public administrative entities, whether territorial *(Gebietskoerperschaften)* or functional *(Zweckverbaende),* and
2. an obligation on the part of the Federation and the *Länder* to maintain interest-free deposits in the German Federal Bank (reserves for counterbalancing economic trends).

Authorizations to enact pertinent ordinances having the force of law may be issued only to the Federal Government. Such ordinances shall require the consent of the Bundesrat. They shall be repealed in so far as the Bundestag may demand; details shall be regulated by federal legislation.

Article 110 (Budget of the Federation)

(1) All revenues and expenditures of the Federation shall be included in the budget; in respect of federal enterprises and special funds, only

allocations to or remittances from them need be included. The budget must be balanced as regards revenue and expenditure.
(2) The budget shall be established by means of a law covering one year or several fiscal years separately before the beginning of the first of those fiscal years. Provision may be made for parts of the budget to apply to periods of different duration, but divided into fiscal years.
(3) Bills within the meaning of the first sentence of paragraph (2) of this Article as well as bills to amend the budget law and the budget shall be submitted simultaneously to the Bundesrat and to the Bundestag; the Bundesrat shall be entitled to state its position on such bills within six weeks or, in the case of amending bills, within three weeks.
(4) The budget law may contain only such provisions as apply to revenues and expenditures of the Federation and to the period for which the budget law is being enacted. The budget law may stipulate that certain provisions shall cease to apply only upon the promulgation of the next budget law or, in the event of an authorization pursuant to Article 115, at a later date.

Article 111 (Payments before approval of the budget)

(1) If, by the end of a fiscal year, the budget for the following year has not been established by law, the Federal Government may, until such law comes into force, make all payments which are necessary:

- (a) to maintain institutions existing by law and to carry out measures authorized by law;
- (b) to meet the Federation's statutory, contractual, and treaty obligations;
- (c) to continue building projects, procurements, and other services, or to continue to grant subsidies for these purposes, provided that pertinent amounts have already been appropriated in the budget of a previous year.

(2) To the extent that revenues provided by specific legislation and derived from taxes or duties or any other charges or sources, or the working capital reserves, do not cover the expenditures referred to in paragraph (1) of this Article, the Federal Government may borrow the funds necessary for the conduct of current operations up to a maximum of one quarter of the total amount of the previous budget.

Article 112 (Expenditure in excess of budgetary estimates)

Expenditures in excess of budgetary appropriations and extrabudgetary expenditures shall require the consent of the Federal Minister of Finance. Such consent may be given only in the case of an unforeseen and compelling necessity. Details may be regulated by federal legislation.

Article 113 (Increases in expenditure)

(1) Laws increasing the budget expenditures proposed by the Federal Government or involving, or likely in future to cause, new expenditures shall require the consent of the Federal Government. This shall also apply to laws involving, or likely in future to cause, decreases in revenue. The Federal Government may require the Bundestag to postpone its vote on such bills. In this case the Federal Government shall state its position to the Bundestag within six weeks.
(2) Within four weeks after the Bundestag has adopted such a bill, the Federal Government may require it to vote on that bill again.
(3) If the bill has become a law pursuant to Article 78, the Federal Government may withhold its consent only within six weeks and only after having initiated the procedure provided for in the third and fourth sentences of paragraph (1) or in paragraph (2) of the present Article. Upon the expiry of this period such consent shall be deemed to have been given.

Article 114 (Rendering of accounts, Audit Office)

(1) The Federal Minister of Finance shall, on behalf of the Federal Government, submit annually to the Bundestag and to the Bundesrat for their approval an account, covering the preceding fiscal year, of all revenues and expenditures as well as of property and debt.
(2) The Federal Audit Office, the members of which shall enjoy judicial independence, shall audit the account and examine the management of the budget and the conduct of business as to economy and correctness. The Federal Audit Office shall submit an annual report directly to the Federal Government as well as to the Bundestag and to the Bundesrat. In all other respects the powers of the Federal Audit Office shall be regulated by federal legislation.

Article 115 (Procurement of credit)

(1) The borrowing of funds and the assumption of pledges, guarantees or other commitments, as a result of which expenditure may be incurred in future fiscal years, shall require federal legislative authorization indicating, or permitting computation of, the maximum amounts involved. Revenue obtained by borrowing shall not exceed the total of expenditures for investments provided for in the budget; exceptions shall be permissible only to avert a disturbance of the overall economic equilibrium. Details shall be regulated by federal legislation.
(2) In respect of special funds of the Federation, exceptions from the provisions of paragraph (1) of this Article may be authorized by federal legislation.

Xa. STATE OF DEFENSE

Article 115a (Determination of a state of defense)

(1) The determination that the federal territory is being attacked by armed force or that such an attack is directly imminent (state of defense) shall be made by the Bundestag with the consent of the Bundesrat. Such determination shall be made at the request of the Federal Government and shall require a two-thirds majority of the votes cast, which shall include at least the majority of the members of the Bundestag.
(2) If the situation imperatively calls for immediate action and if insurmountable obstacles prevent the timely meeting of the Bundestag, or if there is no quorum in the Bundestag, the Joint Committee shall make this determination with a two-thirds majority of the votes cast, which shall include at least the majority of its members.
(3) The determination shall be promulgated in the Federal Law Gazette by the Federal President pursuant to Article 82. If this cannot be done in time, the promulgation shall be effected in another manner; it shall subsequently be printed in the Federal Law Gazette as soon as circumstances permit.
(4) If the Federal territory is being attacked by armed force and if the competent organs of the Federation are not in a position at once to make the determination provided for in the first sentence of paragraph (1) of this Article, such determination shall be deemed to have been made and promulgated at the time the attack began. The Federal President shall announce such time as soon as circumstances permit.
(5) When the determination of the existence of a state of defense has been promulgated and if the federal territory is being attacked by armed force, the Federal President may, with the consent of the Bundestag, issue internationally valid declarations regarding the existence of such state of defense. Subject to the conditions mentioned in paragraph (2) of this Article, the Joint Committee shall thereupon deputize for the Bundestag.

Article 115b (Power of command during state of defense)

Upon the promulgation of a state of defense, the power of command over the Armed Forces shall pass to the Federal Chancellor.

Article 115c (Legislative competence of the Federation during state of defense)

(1) The Federation shall have the right to exercise concurrent legislation even in matters belonging to the legislative competence of the *Länder*

by enacting laws to be applicable upon the occurrence of a state of defense. Such laws shall require the consent of the Bundesrat.
(2) Federal legislation to be applicable upon the occurrence of a state of defense to the extent required by conditions obtaining while such state of defense exists, may make provision for:

1. preliminary compensation to be made in the event of expropriations, thus diverging from the second sentence of paragraph (3) of Article 14;
2. deprivations of liberty for a period not exceeding four days, if no judge has been able to act within the period applying in normal times, thus diverging from the third sentence of paragraph (2) and the first sentence of paragraph (3) of Article 104.

(3) Federal legislation to be applicable upon the occurrence of a state of defense to the extent required for averting an existing or directly imminent attack, may, subject to the consent of the Bundesrat, regulate the administration and the fiscal system of the Federation and the *Länder* in divergence from Sections VIII, VIIIa and X, provided that the viability of the *Länder,* communes and associations of communes is safeguarded, particularly in fiscal matters.
(4) Federal laws enacted pursuant to paragraph (1) or subparagraph (1) of paragraph (2) of this Article may, for the purpose of preparing for their execution, be applied even prior to the occurrence of a state of defense.

Article 115d (Shortened procedure in the case of urgent bills during state of defense)

(1) While a state of defense exists, the provisions of paragraphs (2) and (3) of this Article shall apply in respect of federal legislation, notwithstanding the provisions of paragraph (2) of Article 76, the second sentence of paragraph (1) and paragraphs (2) to (4) of Article 77, Article 78, and paragraph (1) of Article 82.
(2) Bills submitted as urgent by the Federal Government shall be forwarded to the Bundesrat at the same time as they are submitted to the Bundestag. The Bundestag and the Bundesrat shall debate such bills in common without delay. In so far as the consent of the Bundesrat is necessary, the majority of its votes shall be required for any such bill to become a law. Details shall be regulated by rules of procedure adopted by the Bundestag and requiring the consent of the Bundesrat.
(3) The second sentence of paragraph (3) of Article 115a shall apply *mutatis mutandis* in respect of the promulgation of such laws.

Article 115e (Status and functions of the Joint Committee)

(1) If, while a state of defense exists, the Joint Committee determines with a two-thirds majority of the votes cast, which shall include at least the majority of its members, that insurmountable obstacles prevent the timely meeting of the Bundestag, or that there is no quorum in the Bundestag, the Joint Committee shall have the status of both the Bundestag and the Bundesrat and shall exercise their rights as one body.
(2) The Joint Committee may not enact any law to amend this Basic Law or to deprive it of effect or application either in whole or in part. The Joint Committee shall not be authorized to enact laws pursuant to paragraph (1) of Article 24 or to Article 29.

Article 115f (Extraordinary powers of the Federation during state of defense)

(1) While a state of defense exists, the Federal Government may to the extent necessitated by circumstances:

1. commit the Federal Border Guard throughout the federal territory;
2. issue instructions not only to federal administrative authorities but also to *Land* governments and, if it deems the matter urgent, to *Land* authorities, and may delegate this power to members of *Land* governments to be designated by it.

(2) The Bundestag, the Bundesrat, and the Joint Committee, shall be informed without delay of the measures taken in accordance with paragraph (1) of this Article.

Article 115g (Status and functions of the Federal Constitutional Court during state of defense)

The constitutional status and the exercise of the constitutional functions of the Federal Constitutional Court and its judges must not be impaired. The Law on the Federal Constitutional Court may not be amended by a law enacted by the Joint Committee except in so far as such amendment is required, also in the opinion of the Federal Constitutional Court, to maintain the capability of the Court to function. Pending the enactment of such a law, the Federal Constitutional Court may take such measures as are necessary to maintain the capability of the Court to carry out its work. Any decisions by the Federal Constitutional Court in pursuance of the second and third sentences of this Article shall require a two-thirds majority of the judges present.

Article 115h (Legislative terms and terms of office during state of defense)

(1) Any legislative terms of the Bundestag or of *Land* diets due to expire while a state of defense exists shall end six months after the termination of such state of defense. A term of office of the Federal President due to expire while a state of defense exists, and the exercise of his functions by the President of the Bundesrat in case of the premature vacancy of the Federal President's office, shall end nine months after the termination of such state of defense. The term of office of a member of the Federal Constitutional Court due to expire while a state of defense exists shall end six months after the termination of such state of defense.
(2) Should the necessity arise for the Joint Committee to elect a new Federal Chancellor, the Committee shall do so with the majority of its members; the Federal President shall propose a candidate to the Joint Committee. The Joint Committee can express its lack of confidence in the Federal Chancellor only by electing a successor with a two-thirds majority of its members.
(3) The Bundestag shall not be dissolved while a state of defense exists.

Article 115i (Extraordinary power of the *Land* governments)

(1) If the competent federal organs are incapable of taking the measures necessary to avert the danger, and if the situation imperatively calls for immediate independent action in individual parts of the federal territory, the *Land* governments or the authorities or commissioners designated by them shall be authorized to take, within their respective spheres of competence, the measures provided for in paragraph (1) of Article 115f.
(2) Any measures taken in accordance with paragraph (1) of the present Article may be revoked at any time by the Federal Government, or in the case of *Land* authorities and subordinate federal authorities, by *Land* Prime Ministers.

Article 115k (Grade and duration of validity of extraordinary laws and ordinances having the force of law)

(1) Laws enacted in accordance with Articles 115c, 115e, and 115g, as well as ordinances having the force of law issued by virtue of such laws, shall, for the duration of their applicability, suspend legislation contrary to such laws or ordinances. This shall not apply to earlier legislation enacted by virtue of Articles 115c, 115e, or 115g.
(2) Laws adopted by the Joint Committee, and ordinances having the force of law issued by virtue of such laws, shall cease to have effect not later than six months after the termination of a state of defense.

(3) Laws containing provisions that diverge from Articles 91a, 91b, 104a, 106 and 107, shall apply no longer than the end of the second fiscal year following upon the termination of the state of defense. After such termination they may, with the consent of the Bundesrat, be amended by federal legislation so as to lead up to the settlement provided for in Sections VIIIa and X.

Article 1151 (Repealing of extraordinary laws, Termination of state of defense, Conclusion of peace)

(1) The Bundestag, with the consent of the Bundesrat, may at any time repeal laws enacted by the Joint Committee. The Bundesrat may request the Bundestag to make a decision in any such matter. Any measures taken by the Joint Committee or the Federal Government to avert a danger shall be revoked if the Bundestag and the Bundesrat so decide.
(2) The Bundestag, with the consent of the Bundesrat, may at any time declare the state of defense terminated by a decision to be promulgated by the Federal President. The Bundesrat may request the Bundestag to make a decision in any such matter. The state of defense must be declared terminated without delay when the prerequisites for the determination thereof no longer exist.
(3) The conclusion of peace shall be the subject of a federal law.

XI. TRANSITIONAL AND CONCLUDING PROVISIONS

Article 116 (Definition of "German," Regranting of citizenship)

(1) Unless otherwise provided by law, a German within the meaning of this Basic Law is a person who possesses German citizenship or who has been admitted to the territory of the German Reich within the frontiers of 31 December 1937 as a refugee or expellee of German stock *(Volkszugehoerigkeit)* or as the spouse or descendant of such person.
(2) Former German citizens who, between 30 January 1933 and 8 May 1945, were deprived of their citizenship on political, racial, or religious grounds, and their descendants, shall be regranted German citizenship on application. They shall be considered as not having been deprived of their German citizenship if they have established their domicile *(Wohnsitz)* in Germany after 8 May 1945 and have not expressed a contrary intention.

Article 117 (Temporary ruling for Article 3 and Article 11)

(1) Law which conflicts with paragraph (2) of Article 3 shall remain in force until adapted to that provision of this Basic Law, but not beyond 31 March 1953.

(2) Laws which restrict the right of freedom of movement in view of the present housing shortage shall remain in force until repealed by federal legislation.

Article 118 (Reorganization of the *Länder* of Baden, Wuerttemberg-Baden, and Wuerttemberg-Hohenzollern)

The reorganization of the territory comprising the *Länder* of Baden, Wuerttemberg-Baden, and Wuerttemberg-Hohenzollern may be effected notwithstanding the provisions of Article 29, by agreement between the *Länder* concerned. If no agreement is reached, the reorganization shall be effected by federal legislation which must provide for a referendum.

Article 119 (Refugees and expellees)

In matters relating to refugees and expellees, in particular as regards their distribution among the *Länder,* the Federal Government may, with the consent of the Bundesrat, issue regulations having the force of law, pending the settlement of the matter by federal legislation. The Federal Government may in this matter be authorized to issue individual instructions for particular cases. Except where there is danger in delay, such instructions shall be addressed to the highest *Land* authorities.

Article 120 (Occupation costs and burdens as consequence of the war)

(1) The Federation shall meet the expenditure for occupation costs and the other internal and external burdens caused as a consequence of the war, as provided for in detail by federal legislation. To the extent that these costs and other burdens have been provided for by federal legislation on or before 1 October 1969, the Federation and the *Länder* shall meet such expenditure between them in accordance with such federal legislation. In so far as expenditures for such of these costs and burdens as neither have been nor will be provided for by federal legislation have been met on or before 1 October 1965 by *Länder,* communes, associations of communes or other entities performing functions of *Länder* or communes, the Federation shall not be obliged to meet expenditure of that nature even if arising after that date. The Federation shall pay the subsidies towards the burdens of social insurance institutions, including unemployment insurance and public assistance to the unemployed. The distribution between the Federation and the *Länder* of costs and other burdens caused as a consequence of the war, as provided for in this paragraph, shall not affect any legislative settlement of claims for indemnification in respect of consequences of the war.
(2) The corresponding revenue shall pass to the Federation at the same

time as the latter assumes responsibility for the expenditure referred to in this Article.

Article 120a (Implementation of equalization of burdens legislation)

(1) Laws concerning the implementation of the equalization of burdens legislation may, with the consent of the Bundesrat, stipulate that they shall be executed, as regards equalization benefits, partly by the Federation and partly by the *Länder* acting as agents of the Federation, and that the relevant powers vested in the Federal Government and the competent highest federal authorities by virtue of Article 85, shall be wholly or partly delegated to the Federal Equalization Office. In exercising these powers, the Federal Equalization Office shall not require the consent of the Bundesrat; with the exception of urgent cases, its instructions shall be given to the highest *Land* authorities (*Land* Equalization Offices).
(2) The provisions of the second sentence of paragraph (3) of Article 87 shall not be affected hereby.

Article 121 (Definition of "majority")

Within the meaning of this Basic Law, a majority of the members of the Bundestag and a majority of the members of the Federal Convention (Bundesversammlung) shall be the majority of the respective statutory number of their members.

Article 122 (Legislative competencies hitherto existing)

(1) From the date of the first meeting of the Bundestag, laws shall be enacted exclusively by the legislative organs recognized in this Basic Law.
(2) Legislative bodies and bodies participating in legislation in an advisory capacity, whose competence ends by virtue of paragraph (1) of this Article, are herewith dissolved with effect from that date.

Article 123 (Continued validity of old law and old treaties)

(1) Law in force before the first meeting of the Bundestag shall remain in force in so far as it does not conflict with this Basic Law.
(2) Subject to all rights and objections of the interested parties, the treaties concluded by the German Reich concerning matters which, under this Basic Law, shall be within the competence of *Land* legislation, shall remain in force, if they are and continue to be valid in accordance with general principles of law, until new treaties are concluded by the agencies competent under this Basic Law, or until they are in any other way terminated pursuant to their provisions.

Article 124 (Old law affecting matters subject to exclusive legislation)

Law, wherever applicable, affecting matters subject to the exclusive legislative power of the Federation, shall become federal law.

Article 125 (Old law affecting matters subject to concurrent legislation)

Law, wherever applicable, affecting matters subject to the concurrent legislative power of the Federation, shall become federal law:

1. in so far as it applies uniformly within one or more zones of occupation;
2. in so far as it is law by which former Reich law has been amended after 8 May 1945.

Article 126 (Disputes regarding continued validity of old law)

Disputes regarding the continuance of law as federal law shall be decided by the Federal Constitutional Court.

Article 127 (Legislation of the Bizonal Economic Administration)

Within one year of the promulgation of this Basic Law the Federal Government may, with the consent of the governments of the *Länder* concerned, extend to the *Länder* of Baden, Greater Berlin, Rhineland-Palatinate and Wuerttemberg-Hohenzollern any legislation of the Bizonal Economic Administration, in so far as it continues to be in force as federal law under Article 124 or 125.

Article 128 (Continuance of powers to give instructions)

In so far as law continuing in force provides for powers to give instructions within the meaning of paragraph (5) of Article 84, these powers shall remain in existence until otherwise provided by law.

Article 129 (Continued validity of authorizations)

(1) In so far as legal provisions which continue in force as federal law contain authorizations to issue ordinances having the force of law or to issue general administrative rules or to perform administrative acts, such authorizations shall pass to the agencies henceforth competent in the matter. In cases of doubt, the Federal Government shall decide in agreement with the Bundesrat; such decisions must be published.

(2) In so far as legal provisions which continue in force as *Land* law contain such authorizations, they shall be exercised by the agencies competent under *Land* law.

(3) In so far as legal provisions within the meaning of paragraphs (1) and (2) of this Article authorize their amendment or supplementation or the issue of legal provisions instead of laws, such authorizations have expired.
(4) The provisions of paragraphs (1) and (2) of this Article shall apply *mutatis mutandis* where legal provisions refer to regulations no longer valid or to institutions no longer in existence.

Article 130 (Corporate bodies under public law)

(1) Administrative agencies and other institutions which serve the public administration or the administration of justice and are not based on *Land* law or treaties between *Länder,* as well as the Association of Management of South West German Railroads and the Administrative Council for the Postal Services and Telecommunications of the French Zone of Occupation, shall be placed under the Federal Government. The Federal Government shall provide, with the consent of the Bundesrat, for their transfer, dissolution, or liquidation.
(2) The highest disciplinary superior of the personnel of these administrations and institutions shall be the appropriate Federal Minister.
(3) Corporate bodies and institutions under public law not directly under a *Land* nor based on treaties between *Länder* shall be under the supervision of the appropriate highest federal authority.

Article 131 (Persons formerly employed in the public service)

Federal legislation shall regulate the legal position of persons, including refugees and expellees, who, on 8 May 1945, were employed in the public service, have left the service for reasons other than those arising from civil service regulations or collective agreement rules, and have not until now been reinstated or are employed in a position not corresponding to their former one. The same shall apply *mutatis mutandis* to persons, including refugees and expellees, who, on 8 May 1945, were entitled to a pension and who no longer receive any such pension or any commensurate pension for reasons other than those arising from civil service regulations or collective agreement rules. Until the pertinent federal law comes into force, no legal claims can be made, unless otherwise provided by *Land* legislation.

Article 132 (Temporary revocation of rights of civil servants)

(1) Civil servants and judges who, when this Basic Law comes into force, are appointed for life, may, within six months after the first meeting of the Bundestag, be placed on the retired list or waiting list or be given a different function with lower remuneration if they lack

the personal or professional aptitude for their present function. This provision shall apply *mutatis mutandis* also to salaried public employees, other than civil servants or judges, whose service cannot be terminated by notice. If, however, such service can be terminated by notice, periods of notice in excess of the periods fixed by collective agreement rules may be cancelled within the six months referred to above.

(2) The preceding provision shall not apply to members of the public service who are not affected by the provisions regarding the Liberation from National Socialism and Militarism or who are recognized victims of National Socialism, except on important grounds in respect of their personality.

(3) Those affected may have recourse to the courts in accordance with paragraph (4) of Article 19.

(4) Details shall be specified by a regulation of the Federal Government requiring the consent of the Bundesrat.

Article 133 (Bizonal Economic Administration, succession to rights)

The Federation shall succeed to the rights and obligations of the Bizonal Economic Administration.

Article 134 (Reich property to become federal property)

(1) Reich property shall on principle become federal property.

(2) In so far as such property was originally intended to be used predominantly for administrative tasks which, under this Basic Law, are not administrative tasks of the Federation, it shall be transferred without compensation to the agencies now charged with such tasks, and to the *Länder* in so far as it is being used at present, and not merely temporarily, for administrative tasks which under this Basic Law are now within the administrative competence of the *Länder*. The Federation may also transfer other property to the *Länder*.

(3) Property which was placed at the disposal of the Reich by *Länder* or communes or associations of communes without compensation, shall again become the property of such *Länder* or communes or associations of communes, in so far as it is not required by the Federation for its own administrative tasks.

(4) Details shall be regulated by a federal law requiring the consent of the Bundesrat.

Article 135 (Property in the event of territorial changes)

(1) If after 8 May 1945 and before the coming into force of this Basic Law an area has passed from one *Land* to another, the *Land* to which

the area now belongs shall be entitled to the property located therein of the *Land* to which it belonged.
(2) Property of *Länder* or corporate bodies or institutions under public law which no longer exist shall pass, in so far as it was originally intended to be used predominantly for administrative tasks or is being used at present, and not merely temporarily, predominantly for administrative tasks, to the *Land* or the corporate body or institution under public law which now discharges these tasks.
(3) Real estate of *Länder* which no longer exist, including appurtenances, shall pass to the *Land* within which it is located, in so far as it is not included among property within the meaning of paragraph (1) of this Article.
(4) If an overriding interest of the Federation or the particular interest of an area so requires, a settlement in divergence from paragraphs (1) to (3) of this Article may be effected by federal legislation.
(5) In all other respects, the succession in title and the settlement of the property, in so far as it has not been effected before 1 January 1952 by agreement between the *Länder* or corporate bodies or institutions under public law concerned, shall be regulated by federal legislation requiring the consent of the Bundesrat.
(6) Interests of the former *Land* of Prussia in enterprises under private law shall pass to the Federation. A federal law, which may also be in divergence from this provision, shall regulate details.
(7) In so far as property which on the coming into force of this Basic Law would devolve upon a *Land* or a corporate body or institution under public law pursuant to paragraphs (1) to (3) of this Article, has been disposed of through or by virtue of a *Land* law or in any other manner by the party thus entitled, the transfer of the property shall be deemed to have taken place before such disposition.

Article 135a (Discharging, wholly or partially, of certain liabilities of, *inter alia,* the Reich and the former *Land* of Prussia)

The legislation reserved to the Federation in paragraph (4) of Article 134 and in paragraph (5) of Article 135 may also stipulate that the following liabilities shall not be discharged, or not to their full extent:

1. liabilities of the Reich or liabilities of the former *Land* of Prussia or liabilities of such corporate bodies and institutions under public law as no longer exist;
2. such liabilities of the Federation or corporate bodies and institutions under public law as are connected with the transfer of properties pursuant to Article 89, 90, 134 or 135, and such liabilities of these entities as arise from measures taken by the entities mentioned under item 1;

3. such liabilities of *Länder* or communes or associations of communes as have arisen from measures taken by these entities before 1 August 1945 within the framework of administrative functions incumbent upon, or delegated by, the Reich to comply with regulations of occupying Powers or to remove a state of emergency due to the war.

Article 136 (First assembly of the Bundesrat)

(1) The Bundesrat shall assemble for the first time on the day of the first meeting of the Bundestag.
(2) Until the election of the first Federal President his powers shall be exercised by the President of the Bundesrat. He shall not have the right to dissolve the Bundestag.

Article 137 (Right of civil servants to stand for election)

(1) The right of civil servants, of other salaried public employees, of professional soldiers, of temporary volunteer soldiers, or of judges, to stand for election in the Federation, in the *Länder,* or in the communes, may be restricted by legislation.
(2) The electoral law to be adopted by the Parliamentary Council shall apply to the election of the first Bundestag, of the first Federal Convention, and of the first Federal President of the Federal Republic.
(3) The function of the Federal Constitutional Court pursuant to paragraph (2) of Article 41 shall, pending its establishment, be exercised by the German High Court for the Combined Economic Area, which shall decide in accordance with its rules of procedure.

Article 138 (Notaries)

Changes in the rules relating to notaries as they now exist in the *Länder* of Baden, Bavaria, Wuerttemberg-Baden, and Wuerttemberg-Hohenzollern, shall require the consent of the governments of these *Länder.*

Article 139 (Liberation Law)

The legislation enacted for the Liberation of the German People from National Socialism and Militarism shall not be affected by the provisions of this Basic Law.

Article 140 (Validity of Articles of the Weimar Constitution)

The provisions of Articles 136, 137, 138, 139, and 141 of the German Constitution of 11 August 1919 shall be an integral part of this Basic Law.

Article 141 ("Bremen Clause")

The first sentence of paragraph (3) of Article 7 shall not be applied in any *Land* in which different provisions of *Land* law were in force on 1 January 1949.

Article 142 (Basic rights in *Land* constitutions)

Notwithstanding the provision of Article 31, such provisions of *Land* constitutions shall also remain in force as guarantee basic rights in conformity with Articles 1 to 18 of this Basic Law.

Article 143 (Repealed)

Article 144 (Ratification of the Basic Law—Berlin representatives in the Bundestag and Bundesrat)

(1) This Basic Law shall require ratification by the representative assemblies of two thirds of the German *Länder* in which it is for the time being to apply.
(2) In so far as the application of this Basic Law is subject to restrictions in any *Land* listed in Article 23 or in any part thereof, such *Land* or part thereof shall have the right to send representatives to the Bundestag in accordance with Article 38 and to the Bundesrat in accordance with Article 50.

Article 145 (Promulgation of the Basic Law)

(1) The Parliamentary Council shall confirm in public session, with the participation of the deputies of Greater Berlin, the fact of ratification of this Basic Law and shall sign and promulgate it.
(2) This Basic Law shall come into force at the end of the day of promulgation.
(3) It shall be published in the Federal Law Gazette.

Article 146 (Duration of validity of the Basic Law)

This Basic Law shall cease to be in force on the day on which a constitution adopted by a free decision of the German people comes into force.

APPENDIX TO THE BASIC LAW

Article 136 (Weimar Constitution of 11 August 1919)

(1) Civil and political rights and duties shall be neither dependent on nor restricted by the exercise of the freedom of religion.

(2) The enjoyment of civil and political rights and eligibility for public office shall be independent of religious creed.
(3) No one shall be bound to disclose his religious convictions. The authorities shall not have the right to inquire into a person's membership of a religious body except to the extent that rights or duties depend thereon or that a statistical survey ordered by law makes it necessary.
(4) No one may be compelled to perform any religious act or ceremony or to participate in religious exercises or to use a religious form of oath.

Article 137 (Weimar Constitution)

(1) There shall be no state church.
(2) Freedom of association to form religious bodies is guaranteed. The union of religious bodies within the territory of the Reich shall not be subject to any restrictions.
(3) Every religious body shall regulate and administer its affairs independently within the limits of the law valid for all. It shall confer its offices without the participation of the state or the civil community.
(4) Religious bodies shall acquire legal capacity according to the general provisions of civil law.
(5) Religious bodies shall remain corporate bodies under public law in so far as they have been such heretofore. The other religious bodies shall be granted like rights upon application, if their constitution and the number of their members offer an assurance of their permanency. If several such religious bodies under public law unite in one organization, such organization shall also be a corporate body under public law.
(6) Religious bodies that are corporate bodies under public law shall be entitled to levy taxes in accordance with *Land* law on the basis of the civil taxation lists.
(7) Associations whose purpose is the cultivation of a philosophical ideology shall have the same status as religious bodies.
(8) Such further regulation as may be required for the implementation of these provisions shall be incumbent on *Land* legislation.

Article 138 (Weimar Constitution)

(1) State contributions to religious bodies, based on law or contract or special legal title, shall be redeemed by means of *Land* legislation. The principles for such redemption shall be established by the Reich.
(2) The right to own property and other rights of religious bodies or associations in respect of their institutions, foundations and other assets destined for purposes of worship, education, or charity, are guaranteed.

*Appendix to the Basic Law concludes on page 218.

GERMANY (within the boundaries of 1937)

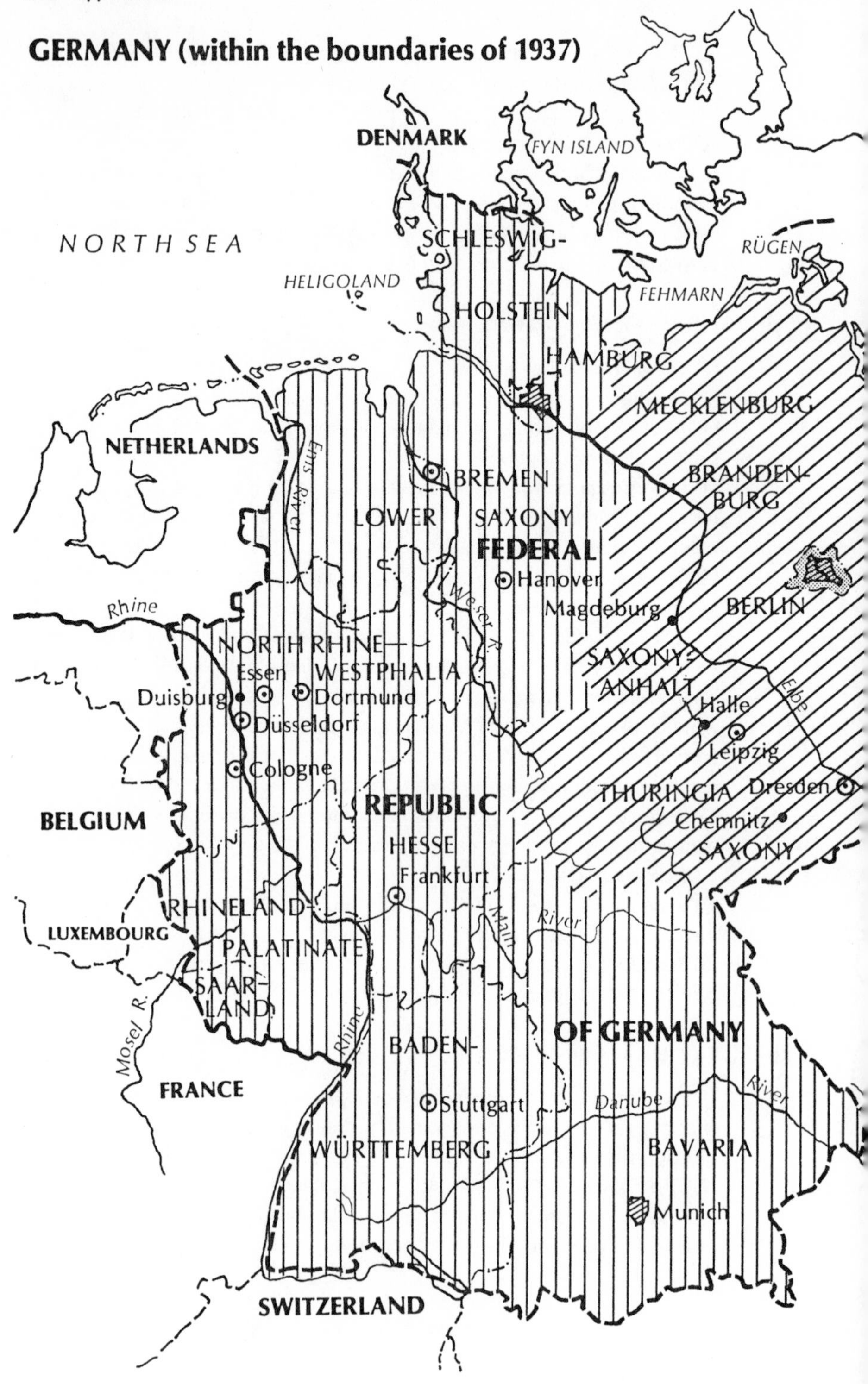

SWEDEN
GOTLAND
BALTIC SEA
SOVIET UNION
(LITHUANIA)
EAST PRUSSIA
Vistula
POMERANIA
Oder
Neisse River
Breslau
Oder River
SILESIA
POLAND
CZECHOSLOVAKIA
AUSTRIA
Federal Republic of Germany
Occupied by the Soviet Union in 1945
Placed under Polish or, as the case may be, Soviet administration in 1945
Berlin, under special Four-Power status
GERMANY within the boundaries of 1937
City of more than 1,000,000 inhabitants
City of more than 500,000 inhabitants
City of more than 100,000 inhabitants
Frontiers of Germany as in 1937
Boundaries of the Federal German States (Länder)
Line of demarcation in East Prussia
SCALE
0
50
100
MILES

Article 139 (Weimar Constitution)

Sunday and the public holidays recognized by the state shall remain under legal protection as days of rest from work and of spiritual edification.

Article 141 (Weimar Constitution)

To the extent that there exists a need for religious services and spiritual care in the army, in hospitals, prisons, or other public institutions, the religious bodies shall be permitted to perform religious acts; in this connection there shall be no compulsion of any kind.

Select Bibliography

The Period Before 1945

Bracher, Karl Dietrich. *The German Dictatorship.* New York: Praeger, 1970.

Bullock, Allan. *Hitler—A Study in Tyranny.* New York: Harper & Row, 1964.

Eyck, Erich. *A History of the Weimar Republic.* 2 vols. Cambridge, Mass.: Harvard University Press, 1962.

Feldman, Gerald D. *Army, Industry, and Labor in Germany 1914–1918.* Princeton, N.J.: Princeton University Press, 1966.

Fischer, Fritz. *Germany's Aims in the First World War.* New York: W. W. Norton, 1967.

Gay, Peter. *Weimar Culture.* New York: Harper & Row, 1968.

Gerschenkron, Alexander. *Bread and Democracy in Germany.* New York: Howard Fertig, 1966.

Heberle, Rudolf. *From Democracy to Nazism.* New York: Howard Fertig, 1967.

Krieger, Leonard. *The German Idea of Freedom.* Boston: Beacon Press, 1957.

Mann, Golo. *The History of Germany Since 1789.* New York: Praeger, 1968.

Moore, Barrington, Jr. *Social Origins of Dictatorship and Democracy.* Boston: Beacon Press, 1967.

Neumann, Franz. *Behemoth.* New York: Harper & Row, 1966.

Peterson, Edward N. *The Limits of Hitler's Power.* Princeton, N. J.: Princeton University Press, 1969.

Rosenberg, Arthur. *Imperial Germany: The Birth of the German Republic 1871–1918.* Boston: Beacon Press, 1964.

Rosenberg, Hans. *Bureaucracy, Aristocracy and Autocracy: The Prussian Experience 1660–1815.* Cambridge, Mass.: Harvard University Press, 1958.

Ryder, A. J. *The German Revolution of 1918.* Cambridge, England: Cambridge University Press, 1967.

Schoenbaum, David. *Hitler's Social Revolution.* New York: Doubleday, 1966.

Schorske, Carl. *German Social Democracy 1905–1917.* Cambridge, Mass.: Harvard University Press, 1955.

Stern, Fritz. *The Politics of Cultural Despair.* Garden City, N.Y.: Anchor Books, 1965.

Taylor, A. J. P. *The Course of German History.* New York: Capricorn Books, 1962.

Turner, Henry Ashby, Jr. *Stresemann and the Politics of the Weimar Republic.* Princeton, N.J.: Princeton University Press, 1963.

The Period from 1945 to 1949

Conze, Werner. *Jakob Kaiser: Politiker zwischen Ost und West 1945–1949.* Stuttgart: W. Kohlhammer Verlag, 1969.

Gimbel, John. *A German Community Under American Occupation.* Stanford, Calif.: Stanford University Press, 1961.

———. *The American Occupation of Germany: Politics and the Military 1945–1949.* Stanford, Calif.: Stanford University Press, 1968.

Golay, John Ford. *The Founding of the Federal Republic of Germany.* Chicago: University of Chicago Press, 1958.

Merkl, Peter H. *The Origin of the West German Republic.* New York: Oxford University Press, 1963.

Schwarz, Hans-Peter. *Vom Reich zur Bundesrepublik.* Neuwied, West Germany: Luchterhand Verlag, 1967.

Willis, F. Roy. *The French in Germany 1945–1949.* Stanford, Calif.: Stanford University Press, 1962.

Government and Political Institutions

Braunthal, Gerhard. *The West German Legislative Process.* Ithaca, N.Y.: Cornell University Press, 1972.

Ellwein, Thomas. *Das Regierungssystem der Bundesrepublik Deutschland.* Cologne: Westdeutscher Verlag, 1965.

Fromme, Friedrich Karl. *Von der Weimarer Verfassung zum Bonner Grundgesetz.* Tübingen, West Germany: J. C. B. Mohr (Paul Siebeck) Verlag, 1960.

Grosser, Alfred. *Die Bonner Demokratie.* Düsseldorf: Karl Rauch Verlag, 1960.

———. *Germany in Our Time.* New York: Praeger, 1971.

Heidenheimer, Arnold J. *The Governments of Germany.* New York: Crowell, 1961.

Holborn, L., G. Caster, and J. Herz. *German Constitutional Documents Since 1871.* New York: Praeger, 1970.

Loewenberg, Gerhard. *Parliament in the German Political System.* Ithaca, N.Y.: Cornell University Press, 1966.

Pinney, Edward L. *Federalism, Bureaucracy and Party Politics in West Germany: The Role of the Bundesrat.* Chapel Hill, N.C.: University of North Carolina Press, 1963.

Sontheimer, Kurt. *The Government and Politics of West Germany.* New York: Praeger, 1972.

Political Parties

Chalmers, Douglas A. *The Social Democratic Party of Germany.* New Haven, Conn.: Yale University Press, 1964.

Edinger, Lewis J. *Kurt Schumacher: A Study in Personality and Political Behavior.* Stanford, Calif.: Stanford University Press, 1965.

Heidenheimer, Arnold J. *Adenauer and the C.D.U.* The Hague: Martinus Nijhoff, 1960.

Kaack, Heino. *Geschichte und Struktur des deutschen Parteiensystems.* Cologne: Westdeutscher Verlag, 1971.

Schellenger, Harold Kent. *The S.P.D. in the Bonn Republic: A Socialist Party Modernizes.* The Hague: Martinus Nijhoff, 1968.

Social and Economic Forces

Arndt, Hans-Joachim. *West Germany: Politics of Non-Planning.* Syracuse, N.Y.: Syracuse University Press, 1966.

Beyme, Klaus von. *Die Politische Elite in der Bundesrepublik Deutschland.* Munich: R. Piper Verlag, 1971.

Boarman, Patrick. *Germany's Economic Dilemma: Inflation and the Balance of Payments.* New Haven, Conn.: Yale University Press, 1964.

Dahrendorf, Ralf. *Society and Democracy in Germany.* New York: Doubleday, 1967.

Edinger, Lewis J. *Politics in Germany: Attitudes and Processes.* Boston: Little, Brown, 1968.

MacLennan, Malcolm, Murray Forsyth, and Geoffrey Denton. *Economic Planning and Policies in Britain, France and Germany.* New York: Praeger, 1968.

Roskamp, Karl W. *Capital Formation in West Germany.* Detroit: Wayne State University Press, 1965.

Stolper, Gustav, Karl Häuser, and Knut Borchardt. *The German Economy: 1870 to the Present.* New York: Harcourt, Brace & World, 1967.

Wallich, Henry C. *Mainsprings of the German Revival.* New Haven, Conn.: Yale University Press, 1955.

Zapf, Wolfgang. *Wandlungen der deutschen Elite 1919–1961.* Munich: R. Piper Verlag, 1965.

Foreign Policy

Baring, Arnulf. *Aussenpolitik in Adenauers Kanzlerdemokratie.* Munich: R. Oldenbourg Verlag, 1969.

Besson, Waldemar. *Die Aussenpolitik der Bundesrepublik.* Munich: R. Piper Verlag, 1970.

Deutsch, Karl W., Lewis J. Edinger, Roy C. Macridis, and Richard L. Merritt. *France, Germany and the Western Alliance.* New York: Scribner, 1967.

Hanrieder, Wolfram. *German Foreign Policy 1949–1963.* Stanford, Calif.: Stanford University Press, 1967.

______. *The Stable Crisis: Two Decades of German Foreign Policy.* New York: Harper & Row, 1970.

Kaiser, Karl. *German Foreign Policy in Transition.* New York: Oxford University Press, 1968.

Richardson, James. *Germany and the Atlantic Alliance.* Cambridge, Mass.: Harvard University Press, 1966.

Willis, F. Roy. *France, Germany and the New Europe.* Stanford, Calif.: Stanford University Press, 1964.

Windsor, Philip. *Germany and the Management of Détente.* New York: Praeger, 1971.

Index

Guido Goldman received his B.A., M.A., and Ph.D. from Harvard University. In addition, he has studied at the University of Munich. He is a Lecturer in the Government Department, Executive Director of West European Studies, and Advisor to the German Kennedy Memorial Fellows, all at Harvard University. During 1972–1973 he was on leave from the University in order to serve as the Acting President of the new German Marshall Fund of the United States, which Chancellor Willy Brandt announced at Harvard on June 5, 1972, the twenty-fifth anniversary of the Marshall Plan. Dr. Goldman played a central role in negotiating and planning the establishment of the new fund.